Intranet Business Strategies

Intranet Business Strategies

MELLANIE HILLS

Wiley Computer Publishing

John Wiley & Sons, Inc.

New York • Chichester • Brisbane • Toronto • Singapore • Weinheim

Publisher: Katherine Schowalter
Editor: Theresa Hudson
Managing Editor: Frank Grazioli
Text Design & Composition: North Market Street Graphics, Lancaster, PA

This text is printed on acid-free paper.

Library of Congress Cataloging-in-Publication Data:
Hills, Mellanie.
    Intranet business strategies / Mellanie Hills.
       p.   cm.
    Includes index.
    ISBN 0-471-16374-0 (paper : alk. paper)
    1. Intranets (Computer networks)   I. Title.
HD30.385.H55   1996
004.6'8—dc20   96-30417
                         CIP

Printed in the United States of America

10 9 8 7 6 5 4 3 2 1

To my husband, Dave, and my son, Jason—thank you for your endless patience and support through these long months while I wrote both books

about the author

Mellanie Hills is the founder of Knowledgies, a consulting firm that focuses on helping Fortune 500 companies develop knowledge strategies with intranet and groupware technologies. She also consults with companies on using the Internet for competitive advantage and is a frequent speaker about the Internet and intranets.

Mellanie has more than twenty years of business experience. Prior to founding Knowledgies, she led J.C. Penney's cross-functional Internet/Intranet Team. Mellanie has always led organizational improvement and change, and is an experienced facilitator, trainer, and coach. She facilitated business process improvement teams at J.C. Penney, and also worked on the development of J.C. Penney's data warehouse. Her previous experience included managing end-user computing, financial accounting, and cost accounting, and she has a great depth of knowledge in the manufacturing, distribution, and retail industries.

She is also the author of *Intranet As Groupware,* published by Wiley.

mhills@knowledgies.com

http://www.knowledgies.com/knowledgies/

acknowledgments

Any book requires the efforts of more than just the author, but this book relied upon the efforts of so many for so much. I wish to thank the following people:

- My father, Howard True, for your assistance researching and proofing this book, and my mother, Celesta True, for your faith and encouragement
- My second set of parents, Dave and Joyce Hills, for always being there when we need you
- Jim Sterne, for inspiring me to write this book, and pushing me forward with it
- Terri Hudson, my editor, for pushing and pulling me along through this process
- My colleagues on the Internet Team at JCPenney, for all you taught me and for your support
- The following people who shared and contributed so much to this book—I am especially indebted to you:

  - Amgen—Peter Armerding
  - AT&T—Ron Ponder and Andy Daudelin
  - Bell Atlantic—Ralph Szygenda, Susan Gayle, Richard Austin, Eric Vaughn, Brenda Mason, and Eric Robinson
  - Booz Allen & Hamilton—Ed Vaccaro and Aron Dutta
  - EDS—Todd Carlson, Greg Mitchell, and Cathy Meister
  - JCPenney—Cathy Mills, Steve Wolff, and Lloyd Grover

- ◆ Rockwell International—Jim Sutter, Harry Meyer, and Dana Abrams
- ◆ SAS Institute—Lauren Bednarcyk
- ◆ Texas Instruments—Jodie Ray and Gene Phifer
- ◆ Turner Broadcasting—Jimi Stricklin, Susan Huffman, and Melissa Hoberg
- ◆ United Parcel Service—Marc Dodge
- ◆ Those who asked to remain anonymous and yet provided so much input

◆ Gale Duff-Bloom, of JCPenney, for helping me recognize the ability to explain complicated things in a non-complicated way

◆ Dave Evans, of JCPenney, for your guidance and support

◆ Dave Cahall, of JCPenney, for your technical assistance with this book

◆ Many friends and relatives, for passing along valuable information to me

My greatest thanks to all of you.

contents

Introduction xiii

Background xiii
Who Is This Book For? xv

Part 1   What Is an Intranet and How Will It Affect Your Organization?   1

Chapter 1   What Is an Intranet?   3

History of Intranets   4
Growth of Intranets   7
What Are the Uses of Intranets?   8
What Are the Pieces of Intranets?   9
The Future of Intranets   20

Chapter 2   Why Have Organizations Created Intranets and What Are the Advantages and Disadvantages?   23

Why Have Organizations Created Intranets?   23
Advantages of Intranets   28
Advantages of Intranets over Client/Server   42
Advantages of Intranets over Proprietary Groupware   44
Disadvantages and Risks of Intranets   46
What Size Company Does It Take to Need an Intranet?   49

Chapter 3   How Will Intranets Change You and Your Organization?   51

What Is Happening to Cause the Changes?   51
What Changes Will Occur?   54
Other Ways Intranets Will Impact Organizations   64

**Part 2   How Do You Use an Intranet and
Who Is Using Them?   69**

Chapter 4   How Do You Use an Intranet?   71

Introduction   71
Corporate Internal Home Page   72
Communications Processes   95
Support Processes   105
Product Development Processes   120
Operational Processes   122
Marketing and Sales Processes   128
Customer Support Processes   131

**Chapter 5   Who Is Using Intranets and How Are They
Using Them?   135**

Introduction   135
Amgen Incorporated   136
AT&T Corp.   136
Bell Atlantic Corporation   139
Booz Allen & Hamilton Inc.   141
EDS   145
JCPenney Company, Inc.   154
Rockwell International Corporation   154
SAS Institute Inc.   157
Silicon Graphics, Inc. (SGI)   161
Texas Instruments Incorporated (TI)   163
Turner Broadcasting System, Inc.   166
United Parcel Service of America, Inc. (UPS)   169
An Anonymous Company   170

Part 3   How Do You Create Your Intranet?   175

**Chapter 6   Two Different Ways to Sell the Intranet to Your
Organization   177**

Why and How Did Companies Create Their Intranets?   177
Two Different Ways You Can Get Started   180

Traditional Model   180
Internet Model   194
The Traditional Model or the Internet Model: To Bureaucratize
    or Not?   207
Checklist: Ways to Sell the Intranet to Your Organization   209

Chapter 7   Build Your Intranet   217

Determine and Develop Infrastructure Needs   217
Determine Security Needs and Implement Security   220
Evaluate and Select an Internet Service Provider   222
Select and Install Hardware and Software   226
Plan for Maintenance of Your Intranet   232
Checklist: Build Your Intranet   233

Chapter 8   Create Your Audience   237

Why Should You Create Your Audience?   237
What Tools Will Users Need?   237
How Will Your Users Get the Software?   240
How Will You Provide User Training and Support?   241
Checklist: Create Your Audience   242

Chapter 9   Promote Your Intranet   245

What Are Your Goals for Your Demo?   245
Build the Demo   246
Present the Demo   255
Other Ways to Promote Your Intranet   294
Checklist: Promote Your Intranet   297

Chapter 10   Create Widespread Enthusiasm and Capability: The Role of Your Intranet Team   303

Why Do You Need an Intranet Team?   303
How Does the Team Work?   309
What Are the Team's Objectives?   324
What Is the Impact of the Team?   339
Checklist: Create Widespread Enthusiasm and Capability   339

Chapter 11   Make Your Intranet Pervasive   347

How Do You Make the Intranet the Universal User Interface?   347
What Are the Critical Success Factors?   355
How Do You Measure the Results?   358
Checklist: Make Your Intranet Pervasive   361

Chapter 12   What Lessons Have We Learned and Where Do We Go from Here?   365

What Lessons Have We Learned?   365
What's Next and Where Do We Go from Here?   372
Checklist: What Lessons Have We Learned and Where Do We Go from Here?   376
Summary   379

Appendix   Intranet Resources   381

Netiquette—Chapter 1   381
Demands on Businesses Today—Chapter 2   381
Learning Organizations—Chapter 3   381
Uses of Intranets—Chapter 4   381
Companies That Contributed to This Book—Chapter 5   382
Building Your Intranet—Chapter 7   382
Designing and Authoring Documents—Chapter 9   386
WWW Sites in Sample Presentation—Chapter 9   386
Resources for the Intranet Team—Chapter 10   387
Usability Testing—Chapter 11   387

Index   389

introduction

Background

The media has started calling the intranet a real *no-brainer*. The only people who don't agree are those who don't get it! Guess what? That includes your CEO, and perhaps CIO. To you, it's obvious. Why doesn't everyone see it? It's not so obvious to them because they don't know anything about an intranet and don't understand what it can do.

How do you help your CEO and other executives see it as a true no-brainer? That's one of the things you'll learn from this book—how to sell them on the value an intranet can bring.

Intranets are one of the most exciting and important new technologies happening in organizations today. They involve using the tools developed for the Internet to create internets inside organizations.

Why is this so exciting, and what is happening in business that makes it so important? Today's organizations, in order to stay competitive, must do things cheaper, faster, and better. Intranets help businesses do just that by providing the information they need and helping them communicate more effectively. Intranets provide the tools for capturing and sharing corporate knowledge. This sharing of knowledge makes it possible for you to market new and better products faster than your competitors, and to meet or exceed the expectations of your customers.

With the right corporate culture, intranets can become living, growing, organic ecosystems. They promote learning and spawn the innovation that allows organizations to do things cheaper, faster, and better. They help organizations become or remain competitive, and can give them an edge over their competition.

I first became involved in all the exciting things you can do with intranets in 1994 when I worked for JCPenney, a Fortune 50 retailer. I had just finished facilitating a business process improvement team and was working on implementing the team's new process, which included use of the Internet. I frequently evangelized to anybody who would listen about the Internet and all the things we could do with it. Concurrently, our advanced technology group was building the infrastructure for accessing the Internet. They had created an internal version of the World Wide Web and called it jWeb. Our CIO asked me to create and lead a team to start developing jWeb and an external web site, and to market them to the entire company. It was very exciting for us to visualize the many ways we could use jWeb to benefit the company and its employees.

The term *intranet* has come into common use in recent months to describe internal webs, but there are distinctions between the two. I will use *internal webs* to refer to the use of World Wide Web (WWW) technology, such as Web servers and browsers, inside the organization. I will use *intranets* to refer to the larger environment inside the organization, made up of the network, internal web, e-mail, newsgroups, mail lists, and other Internet tools and technologies.

This book also talks about knowledge systems. *Knowledge systems* are groupware tools that capture and store corporate knowledge, generally through discussion databases or newsgroups. They may also consist of sets of rules embedded in workflow to capture the process by which you do things.

Throughout this book, I will use the term *user.* I don't like the term, but will use it for the sake of clarity. The terms *internal customer* and *internal client* are much nicer terms, but are also confusing.

In researching this book, I spoke with many companies. Some of these companies were able to share lots of information and others couldn't share anything. One company was able to tell me about their experiences but was unable to have their name used here. In some industries, intranets are rare and considered a competitive advantage. Such companies don't want to give away their trade secrets. In other industries where many companies have intranets, they're not so highly confidential. The 13 companies that contributed their experiences and insights to this book are:

1. Amgen Incorporated
2. AT&T
3. Bell Atlantic Corporation
4. Booz Allen & Hamilton Inc.
5. EDS
6. JCPenney Company, Inc.
7. Rockwell International Corporation
8. SAS Institute Inc.
9. Silicon Graphics, Inc.
10. Texas Instruments Incorporated (TI)
11. Turner Broadcasting System, Inc.
12. United Parcel Service of America, Inc. (UPS)
13. One anonymous company

Who Is This Book For?

This book is for senior business managers with a technical background, IT managers, systems analysts, network administrators, webmasters, web developers, and others interested in developing an intranet for their company. It is also for those organizations who already have an intranet and are looking for ways to expand it or to find other appropriate ways to use it.

This book will talk about some of the technical issues involved in creating an intranet. Since creating an intranet requires the involvement of all parts of an organization, this book will go into great depth about the organizational and political issues that can influence the adoption and assimilation of your intranet.

This book is *not* about specific Internet tools. I will refer you to other resources to learn more about them.

When I started our intranet project, there were no road maps or checklists to help me develop it. My goal in writing this book is to make the process as easy and painless as possible for you. I hope to help you learn about the value of intranets, how companies have used them, and how to create one for your organization. I also want to help you prepare for and deal with the organizational issues you will face as you build your intranet.

Table I.1 shows the organization of this book.

TABLE I.1

Part 1: What Is an Intranet and How Will It Affect Your Organization?	
Chapter 1: What Is an Intranet?	Explains what intranets are, where they came from, how fast they're growing, how they're used, and what components make them up.
Chapter 2: Why Have Organizations Created Intranets and What Are the Advantages and Disadvantages?	Discusses why organizations are creating intranets, the advantages and disadvantages of them, and what size company it takes to need one.
Chapter 3: How Will Intranets Change You and Your Organization?	Describes what's happening to cause changes in your organization and what changes your intranet will cause.
Part 2: How Do You Use an Intranet and Who Is Using Them?	
Chapter 4: How Do You Use an Intranet?	Provides examples of how to use intranets in specific business processes and shows screen shots from some companies' intranets.
Chapter 5: Who Is Using Intranets and How Are They Using Them?	Discusses the companies that participated in this book and talks about how they created their intranets, how they're using them, and what they see as the future for them.
Part 3: How Do You Create Your Intranet?	
Chapter 6: Two Different Ways to Sell the Intranet to Your Organization	Explains how companies have created their intranets and the two ways you can create yours.
Chapter 7: Build Your Intranet	Describes how to build your intranet, including how to determine your infrastructure needs and your security needs, evaluate and select your internet service provider, select and install your hardware and software,

	and plan for maintenance of your intranet.
Chapter 8: Create Your Audience	Discusses how you create an audience for your intranet, including identifying and selecting the tools they need, determining how to deploy these tools, and developing a plan for training and supporting your users.
Chapter 9: Promote Your Intranet	Explores the reasons you should create a demo to sell your intranet, and how to build and present this demo.
Chapter 10: Create Widespread Enthusiasm and Capability: The Role of Your Intranet Team	Details why you need an intranet team, who should be on that team, how the team works, the team's objectives, and the impact the team will have.
Chapter 11: Make Your Intranet Pervasive	Explains how to make your intranet the universal user interface for all applications, discusses the critical success factors for your intranet, and talks about measuring the results.
Chapter 12: What Lessons Have We Learned and Where Do We Go from Here?	Discusses the lessons that companies have learned in building their intranets and explores what kind of applications you should do next.
Appendix: Intranet Resources	

All Internet locations and URLs cited in this book were accurate at the time of this writing. Because of the very fluid and evolving nature of the Internet, some may have changed. The various search engines can be helpful in finding current locations for that information.

I believe that the benefits of an intranet to enhance communication and collaboration are far greater than the effort of getting one up and running. I wish you success with your project and would love to hear from you about your results. My e-mail address is mhills@knowledgies.com. Please let me know if you have learned lessons that you would like to share with others in future editions of this work. Good luck!

PART ONE

What Is an Intranet and How Will It Affect Your Organization?

chapter one

What Is an Intranet?

Imagine for a moment that you are the CIO of a company that has locations spanning the globe. The director of communications comes to you with a problem. She has to communicate company news and corporate policy changes to employees in 2,000 locations in 50 countries around the world. She also has to help these employees feel like they are part of the *company family.* She needs a better way to do this.

Right now, none of her options are ideal. They are:

1. Mail—much too slow.
2. E-mail—time-consuming to keep up with the changing names and e-mail addresses at all these locations.
3. Telephone—expensive and time-consuming. Besides, who can keep up with the constantly changing contact names and phone numbers?
4. Fax—expensive and time-consuming. Same problems as telephone when it comes to keeping up with changing contacts.
5. Overnight letters and packages—too expensive for 2,000 locations.
6. Videoconference—much too expensive.

How can you help her? You already made her job much easier in communicating with people outside the company by putting the earnings' reports and press releases on your Web site. Now the media and analysts can come get information from the Web site whenever they need it. Can you do the same kind of thing for her in order to reach employees?

The answer is yes, you can, with an *intranet*. An intranet allows you to post information that everyone should see on an *internal* web site. In fact, the intranet is all about communications *inside* your organization.

So what's this intranet thing anyway? By now you are probably familiar with, and may have used, the Internet. An intranet is simply a small-scale version of the Internet inside your organization. A firewall keeps out intruders from the outside. The intranet typically is a network based on the Internet's TCP/IP protocol. It also uses World Wide Web (WWW or Web) tools, such as Hypertext Markup Language (HTML), Common Gateway Interface (CGI) programming, and Java. You can get all the functionality of an Internet on your own private intranet inside your company.

The Web tools, which primarily make up the intranet, make any information just a few mouse clicks away. On the Internet, you can click on WWW links that connect you to almost anyplace in the world. That's much like a telephone, where you enter a *phone number* to connect you to almost anyplace in the world. The big difference is that the Web is probably easier to use. You don't even have to remember a phone number, you simply point and click.

Not only are intranets easy for your users, they are easy for you as well. An intranet may be just the solution you need. With an intranet, you can bridge your islands of information and provide that information to everyone to make it easier for them to make decisions and to serve customers.

Does this sound great? Of course it does! So what's the catch? It must be expensive—anything that comes along to help solve your problems is always expensive. The good news is, it's not! In fact, it's pretty cheap. The components of an intranet range from relatively inexpensive to free. If you want, you can do it *on the cheap.*

History of Intranets

This sounds great, but you have some questions, right? Where did intranets come from? To answer this question, we first have to talk about the Internet itself and where *it* came from. If you already know all about the Internet and the Web, just skip the next two sections in this chapter. These sections are for those who are new to the Internet.

First, the Internet

These days, it's hard to pick up any magazine or newspaper without seeing a reference to the Internet. It has captured our imaginations. Until recently, the Internet was the province of the U.S. government and universities. It originated in the 1970s to provide the U.S. military with communications in case of nuclear attack. The destruction of one computer on the network would not shut down the entire network.

In the 1980s, the National Science Foundation (NSF) used Internet tools to create a communications network, or backbone, for linking scientists with expensive supercomputers. This network was for use by government and universities, and was only for research purposes.

By the early 1990s, the NSF started pulling back from its funding of the Internet backbone and allowed commercial interests to take over. Since then, commerce has flourished on the Internet, and it has grown into a global network of millions of people.

Enter the Web

In 1989, Tim Berners-Lee, at the European Laboratory for Particle Physics (CERN), created the World Wide Web. The Web uses hypertext to link information. Hypertext allows you to use your mouse to click on a highlighted word or phrase and link to that information regardless of where it resides. It really doesn't matter whether the information is located in a computer in your building or one on the other side of the world.

Home pages form the basis of the Web. Home pages are simply starting points for locating information, and employ hypertext links to provide access to information in the form of text, pictures, sound, and video.

In 1993, Marc Andreessen created *Mosaic* with the help of fellow students at the University of Illinois' National Center for Supercomputing Applications. Mosaic was a graphical user interface that made the Web easy to use. Mosaic was available for downloading from the Internet for free, and the Web started to take off. Even businesses took notice, and the great land rush for the Internet began.

The Intranet

Some of the earliest organizations to adopt the use of intranets were Lockheed, Hughes, and SAS Institute. Each of these organizations had someone on board from an academic environment who was familiar with Internet tools. They already knew about gopher, FTP, the Web, and lots of others. They were aware of what these tools could do, and they decided to try a pilot program to see if there was any value in using these tools in a commercial environment. Sure enough, they found the tools to be useful. Word of their experiences started leaking out just as companies were starting to take an interest in the Internet itself.

Based on these successes, many companies started experimenting with the Internet. Most probably began by putting up an Internet gateway to hook their e-mail systems to the rest of the world. They soon added Web servers and Web browsers for accessing the Internet itself. It became obvious that they could use those same browsers to access internal information, such as policy manuals and documentation. Soon they added access to Internet newsgroups, and realized they could create their own internal newsgroups as well. It all just kind of happened.

We started calling the internal use of Internet technology by many different names. Some companies called them internal webs, while others called them internet clones, corporate webs, or private webs. Sometime in 1995, someone in the media called them *intranets* and the name stuck. There are lots of differing stories about the source of the term *intranet.* One version I have heard more times than any other is that Amdahl started using the term in 1994, and the media picked it up from them. I have also heard others say they were using the term even earlier. I tend to believe that it was one of those good ideas that pops up simultaneously in different places. Once the media picked up on it, everyone started using the term.

Growth of Intranets

Every book or article about the Internet shows graphs of its growth because that growth has been so spectacular. As books about intranets start appearing, they, too, will show graphs of intranet growth. Since graphs help make the numbers more meaningful, I won't deviate from that norm.

Most graphs show the growth in the number of hosts, the number of domains, the number of users, the number of access providers, and anything else related to the Internet. They all look alike, only some have steeper slopes than others.

Figure 1.1 is my single graph for everything related to the Internet or intranet. The x-axis shows the years from 1990 to 1995 and estimates for 1996 to 1998. You can fill in the y-axis with anything you like related to the Internet or intranet. It can be the number of Internet hosts, domains, servers, or users, or the number of intranet servers or users. You name it and, if it's related to the Internet or intranet, it will work in this graph!

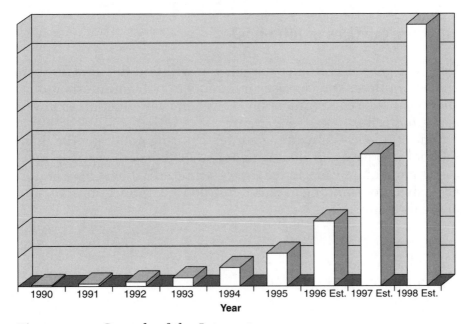

Figure 1.1   Growth of the Internet.

How many intranets are there? How fast are they growing? We really don't know the answers. Since intranets exist inside organizations, and very few organizations are willing to talk about them, we really don't know exactly how many there are or how fast they are growing. We do know that some of the Web server and browser vendors are claiming that most of their sales are for intranet use.

Ian Campbell, Director of Collaborative Technologies for International Data Corporation (IDC), estimates that there were 100,000 *intranet* web servers in 1995, and that this number will grow to 4.7 million by the year 2000. He also said that there were approximately 10 million Web browsers in use in 1995, and he estimates that number will be 40 million in 1996 and 180 million in the year 2000. By any yardstick, that is phenomenal growth.

This book talks about 13 companies that have built intranets. These companies have anywhere from 1 to over 2,000 internal web servers. It appears that we will see more and more internal web servers within each organization as people become more and more willing to share their information with others.

What Are the Uses of Intranets?

Once you get your intranet started, you will find the uses for it are almost limitless. You can use an intranet to publish information and to enhance communication. They can even function as low-cost groupware.

Some of the uses are quite simple, requiring nothing more than internal web pages created using HTML. Others are very sophisticated and require links to databases, while still others may require extensive programming to create full-fledged applications. Some of the uses are:

♦ E-mail
♦ Directories
♦ Organization charts
♦ Memos
♦ Personnel manuals

- Benefits information
- Newsletters and publications
- Systems user documentation
- Training
- Newsgroups
- News extracts
- Job postings
- Sales reports
- Financial reports
- Customer information
- Quality statistics
- Vendor information
- Product information
- Marketing brochures, videos, and presentations
- Product development information and drawings
- Supply and component catalogs
- Inventory information
- Network management
- Asset management

Chapter 4 talks about these applications in greater detail.

What Are the Pieces of Intranets?

An intranet consists of many different pieces which vary from company to company. Some companies think of the internal web and related tools as the intranet. Others consider the entire network, including the internal web and related tools, as the intranet. I will use the broader definition in this book. Here are some of the most common components of an intranet.

- Network
- E-mail

- ◆ Internal web
- ◆ Mail lists and Listservs
- ◆ Newsgroups
- ◆ Chat
- ◆ FTP
- ◆ Gopher
- ◆ Telnet

Network

The first, and most complicated, part of any intranet is the network. The Internet is the network of many networks. In large organizations, the intranet may also be a network of networks. In smaller organizations, it may be just a single network. At any rate, the network is at the heart of the intranet. The intranet can't exist without it.

There can be a wide variety of networks. They can be simple, like a local area network (LAN), which serves only a single building or portion of a building, such as a workgroup or department. LANs can be Ethernet, Token Ring, or Fiber Distributed Data Interface (FDDI).

- ◆ *Ethernet.* Ethernet LANs consist of coaxial cables or twisted-pair (standard telephone) wire hooked to a device called a *hub.* The hub is the traffic cop that directs traffic along the network.
- ◆ *Token Ring.* Token Ring LANs consist of coaxial cables or twisted-pair wires attached into a Media Attachment Unit (MAU). The MAU simulates all devices being connected into a ring. Computers on the ring take turns transmitting. A token passes sequentially to each device on the ring to indicate when it is their turn to transmit.
- ◆ *FDDI.* FDDI networks are similar to Token Ring Networks in that they also pass a token. However, they use fiber-optic cable instead of twisted-pair wires.

In addition, wireless LANs, based on infrared and radio frequencies, are an emerging technology. Since they are slow and expensive, their primary use is for niche applications where wired networks aren't feasible.

Transmission Control Protocol/Internet Protocol (TCP/IP)

The Transmission Control Protocol/Internet Protocol (TCP/IP) is the foundation of the Internet. It is the mechanism that transmits information across the networks of the Internet. The purpose of TCP/IP is to move data from place to place.

It is possible to create an intranet without TCP/IP if you have no interest in connecting to the Internet itself. Generally, your intranet must have TCP/IP.

E-Mail

Electronic mail allows you to very easily compose a message and send it electronically to the person in the office next door or to someone on the other side of the world. The receiver can just as easily reply. E-mail is no longer just text. You can send formatted documents, presentations, sound files, and video clips just as easily as you send a text message.

Organizations generally had e-mail long before they became cognizant of the Internet. E-mail was probably the first Internet application at most companies. When they decided the Internet might be of use, they stuck a toe in the water by creating an e-mail gateway. That way, they could send e-mail to other companies across the Internet and receive mail back from them. To do so requires an e-mail server and e-mail software that can accommodate the longer Internet e-mail addresses.

By default, e-mail is generally an organization's first intranet application. It provides the opportunity to communicate from one person to another person or to many people. E-mail is an important component of mail lists, which I will talk about later in this chapter.

Internal Web

After an organization gets Internet e-mail up and running, then comes the Web. When people think about intranets, they are usually thinking about internal webs. The internal web is not synonymous with intranet. It is only a part of it, albeit a very important part.

The combination of the World Wide Web and Mosaic caused the Internet to really explode. They have done the same for intranets.

The internal web is simply using Web tools inside your organization. It makes your corporate information easy to access. All users have to know is how to use a mouse to point and click. If they can do that, then any information they need can be available at their fingertips. With the addition of search tools to the internal web, if they can use a keyboard, the possibilities become almost endless.

Imagine this scenario, which probably occurs more times in businesses than most would admit. A potential customer calls and says he wants to buy your product, but he has some questions. You know you can get his business if you can just answer his questions. However, you can't locate the information you need. It's probably in a file somewhere on the LAN. If only you knew where to look. That information belongs to marketing, but alas, if you found it, would you be able to access it? They probably created it with that program they use that isn't even available for your computer, so it wouldn't help even if you could find it. You know you saw something with the answers you need, but you can't find it in your e-mail or in your files. It will be in the new literature, which is at the printer right now. Surely you can find someone who knows. You put the customer on hold and try to track down someone who can help. You get their voice mail. The customer is ready to place an order and doesn't want to wait. You offer to call back with the answer, but you know that when you hang up the phone, he will be on the phone with your competitor. You've lost the sale, and it's not the first time.

If this happens in your organization, you can take hope. An internal web is an affordable solution that lets you bridge those islands of information so people have access to the information they need. This allows them to make better decisions and to better serve your customers.

Let's change our story a little bit and see what it is like after we create an internal web. Let's say that your customer has just called wanting to buy, but he needs answers to his questions first. You know that most applications are on the internal web. You merely move your mouse over to the Search icon and click on it. You type your customer's question into the search box and click the Submit button. Almost immediately you receive a page of the new marketing brochure that answers all his questions. That's just what the customer wanted to know, and he's ready to buy. With a few keystrokes and mouse clicks, you type in his order and submit it. It's on its way to shipping, and will soon be headed toward your customer. What a difference an internal web can make!

Your internal web will provide access to all the kinds of information that you want to give your users. That may include resources on the Internet itself. You can set it up so that the internal web provides users with hypertext links to relevant sites on the WWW. That access will be transparent to the user, except that external pages take longer to retrieve.

The internal web consists of two major components.

1. Server
2. Browser or client

Server

The first component is the Web server, which is the hub of any intranet. It is the computer that contains your web pages and uses a protocol called *hypertext transfer protocol* (HTTP).

Companies with intranets have anywhere from one to hundreds of internal web servers. One company I spoke with has over 2,000 of them.

Browser or Client

The second component of the internal web is the browser, which is often referred to as a *client*. This is the part that is on *your* computer. It's a graphical user interface (GUI) that sits between you and the web server.

The function of a browser is to request pages from the Web server and display these returned pages. These pages contain rich, multimedia information, consisting not only of text, but also graphics, sound, and video. You can use a mouse to point and click your way through information from all around the world.

Marc Andreessen and his fellow students developed the first browser, Mosaic. It now appears in several commercial products. Marc and some of his fellow developers went on to develop a commercial Web browser, Netscape. Currently, there are numerous Web browsers from Netscape, Microsoft, IBM, and a host of others. Browsers are available for virtually every platform.

The browser is the key to the intranet because it is the tool that connects people to the intranet. The browser is quickly becoming the universal user interface. Everyone will have one on their computer. Those without computers will have access to a browser at a kiosk or on an inexpensive Internet terminal. Most of the companies I worked with on this book said that they plan for browsers to be *the* interface for all future systems.

Web Browser Enhancement Tools

Web browser enhancements, such as built-in audio, video, and 3D, continue to come quickly. They give you a peek into why companies believe the browser will be the interface for future systems. Netscape is announcing browser enhancements as I write this section. Some of those enhancements, and where they fit into an intranet, include:

◆ *Live Audio.*   Embedded audio provides music and voice directly from Web pages. Great for training, corporate announcements, and executive speeches.

◆ *Live Video.*   Play embedded movies without a separate movie player. Great for training and marketing videos.

◆ *Live 3D.*   View interactive 3D worlds with a Virtual Reality Modeling Language (VRML) viewer. Use your imagination as to the many ways you could use this!

◆ *Cool Talk.*   Use phone, chat, and whiteboard to communicate and collaborate. Great for product development teams and other workgroups. This has the potential for enormous cost savings for large, global organizations.

- *LiveCache.* Enables CD-ROM content to be preloaded into cache for fast access and viewing. Great for leveraging your investment in CD-ROM training applications.

In addition to these built-in enhancements, there are lots of plug-ins that you can add to your browser to do specialized things. Some of these, and ways you could use them in an intranet, include:

- Remote-control software that allows you to control another PC over the Internet. Great tool for Help Desks.

- Collaborative software that allows you to review documents and watch editing on another user's screen. Good for collaboration among geographically dispersed workgroups and teams.

- Engineering-drawing viewers for viewing computer-aided designs using your browser. Great for engineers and designers.

- Chemical-structures viewer for viewing 2D and 3D structures within a Web page. Great for chemists and other scientists.

- Viewers of all kinds to allow you to view, copy, and print documents created in Acrobat, Word, Word Perfect, Excel, Power Point, and other software. Leverage your investment in existing documentation throughout the organization.

- Data-entry forms with validation checking in the client browser. Great for any area that needs to update databases; helpful for applications developers.

- Installation plug-in that allows software distribution and installation from a Web page in a single step. Great for electronic software distribution throughout the organization.

- News service that downloads news to the viewer's computer screen. Great for internal and external news delivery throughout the organization.

- ◆ Application development tools, with drag-and-drop features, Visual Basic scripting, and more. Ease the job of applications developers.
- ◆ Speech synthesis to convert text to speech or singing. Great for training applications.
- ◆ Viewer for delivering existing computer-based training (CBT) courses using a browser. Leverage your investment in existing CBT.

Mail Lists or Listservs

Mail lists are essentially like e-mailing your message to a long list of people who share a common interest with you. People can ask questions related to the topic or can maintain ongoing discussions. Unlike regular e-mail, you don't have to keep a long list of the members on your computer. The list owner is the one who maintains the list. All you do is send your e-mail to the list owner and it's automatically distributed to the entire list.

Obviously, the list owner must maintain a constantly changing list of members. New members join and some members leave. Fortunately, the two major mail list programs, Listserv and Majordomo, handle subscription changes automatically.

You will find Internet mail lists on almost any subject you can imagine. You will find mail lists on business topics and personal topics. Most have members from all over the world.

You can have mail lists inside your organization on your intranet. You might have some on business topics and some on hobbies and recreation. You may have members from all areas of the organization and all countries in which you have locations.

To use a mail list, all that a person needs is access to e-mail. Therefore, mail lists work well for those in your organization who have access only to e-mail. For those with access to web browsers, newsgroups may be a better choice.

Newsgroups

Newsgroups consist of threaded discussions and serve the same purpose as mail lists. Your web browser may act as a newsreader, or you may need a separate newsreader to provide access to the newsgroups.

To post a message to a newsgroup, or to reply to one, you can use e-mail or the reply feature in your newsreader. These messages then get posted on a bulletin board for anyone to access. Newsgroups, then, are a form of groupware.

One advantage of newsgroups over mail lists is that you can check newsgroups whenever you wish, rather than being pelted with e-mail messages whenever you check your mail. Newsgroups are more efficient with resources. On a mail list, every member receives a copy of every message. On newsgroups, there is only a single copy of each message, which everyone can access simultaneously. Newsgroup users also do not have to subscribe or unsubscribe to the discussion as they do in a mail list.

The uses for newsgroups are the same as the uses for mail lists. You can ask questions or discuss subjects of common interest. The Internet newsgroups, called Usenet, have a group for discussion of almost every topic you can imagine. These newsgroups number in the thousands. There are hundreds of them just for computer-related topics. For instance, if you have an interest in groupware, there are several newsgroups on that subject:

comp.groupware	Discussion of groupware software and hardware in general
comp.groupware.groupwise	Discussion of Novell's Groupwise product
comp.groupware.lotus-notes.admin	Discussion of Lotus Notes system administration
comp.groupware.lotus-notes.apps	Discussion of application software for Lotus Notes
comp.groupware.lotus-notes.misc	Discussion of miscellaneous topics related to Lotus Notes
comp.groupware.lotus-notes.programmer	Discussion of programming for Lotus Notes

On your intranet, you can have newsgroups for any topic you choose. Here are some examples of groups you might create a newsgroup to support:

- *New-product developers.* They can discuss the schedule and status, as well as problems and the solutions they have found.
- *Engineers.* Engineers who focus on a specific technology can share the resources they have found, such as on the Internet, and help each other address certain types of problems.
- *Computer techies.* They can share information related to specific computer applications.
- *Users.* This could be a moderated group that supports users who need assistance with specific applications.
- *Everyone.* Newsgroups for personal interests such as sports, hobbies, or volunteer opportunities.

On the Internet itself, certain rules of etiquette have developed. *Netiquette* is the name used for these rules. People expect certain manners and common courtesy in their interaction with others on the Net. These are very important to help prevent misunderstandings, especially between cultures. In spite of these rules, misunderstandings do happen frequently on the Internet and result in anger and hurt feelings. Many are the result of differences in cultural norms and expectations of others. Rules notwithstanding, some people will still be rude or use obnoxious language on the Internet. You can find out the rules of netiquette by checking out *The Net: User Guidelines and Netiquette* at http://www.fau.edu/rinaldi/net/index.htm.

Everyone should follow the rules of netiquette on the intranet as well. You can just imagine the impact of this kind of abuse happening inside your organization. What would happen if you used inappropriate language and the boss saw it, or the boss's boss? Users should not need reminding that the general rules of etiquette in use in the office apply to intranet newsgroups as well.

However, I can say from personal experience that you may need to gently remind some users that "flaming" colleagues on the intranet is not a good way to impress people! You may want to create and publish your own *intranetiquette* guidelines.

You can have moderated or unmoderated newsgroups and mail lists. In a moderated list or newsgroup, the moderator simply reviews all postings for appropriateness prior to posting or distributing them. The question will arise as to whether you should moderate your intranet newsgroups. One would expect that if normal business etiquette prevails, people will post only appropriate messages, and moderation will not be necessary.

Chat

Internet Relay Chat (IRC) facilitates conversations over the Internet in close to real time. On an intranet, chats can take the place of long-distance phone calls between locations. They allow you to communicate ideas more quickly than through e-mail. Chats facilitate brainstorming sessions for participants who can convene at the same time, but not at the same place. You can schedule a chat about any topic of common interest and anyone can participate. You can also use chat for impromptu conversations.

FTP

File transfer protocol (FTP) provides you a repository of information that is readily accessible. Anyone with FTP can log in to the repository and download what they need to their computer. FTP works well for transferring files that are too large to send by e-mail. Some web browsers, such as Netscape 2.0 and higher, let you upload to and download from FTP sites. There are also stand-alone FTP tools.

Here are some ways FTP can be useful on an intranet:

◆ Allow sophisticated users to access and download software and patches.

◆ Provide web publishers a way to upload their web pages to the server.

◆ Permit file transfer of very large files, such as technical drawings and specifications, or computer-aided design files.

Gopher

Like much of the Internet, gopher provides text-only information. Gopher is menu-driven, making it easy for you to drill down through levels of menus to get to the information you need. Before the advent of the Web, gopher servers provided the richest repositories of information on the Internet.

Today, you no longer need a gopher tool to access gopher servers, since many web browsers, such as Netscape, have gopher access built in. Though the Web has replaced gopher servers, there are still great collections of information available on the Internet from government and university gopher servers.

The Web has largely supplanted gopher, so unless you already have some gopher repositories of information, you probably do not need a gopher server on your intranet.

Telnet

Telnet allows you to log in to a remote computer. It typically provides access to resources that reside on remote mainframes. Telnet (TN) 3270 allows you to access a mainframe and emulate a 3270 host–based terminal. A major use for TN3270 is to provide access to university library card catalogs and databases. You can use it to open up your mainframe applications to your intranet; however, it's not as pretty as using the Web.

The Future of Intranets

With the Web browser becoming the universal user interface, this is where employees will spend most of their time in the future. They will use it to communicate with others, to publish and share information, and to find resources to help them with their jobs. In fact, many users will operate their own internal web sites to share information with the rest of the organization. The internal web will become the strategic computing platform for the future.

What will be the impact of intranets on proprietary client/server computing and groupware? It appears to be a case of *if you can't beat 'em, join 'em.* We will see virtually every kind of application becoming Web-enabled and being accessible from a browser. We already see examples of this among the groupware vendors as they rush to turn their products into Web applications. One of the first Web-enabled, integrated, groupware applications is Livelink from OpenText. This is a groupware application that very recently became a Web application. Netscape recently purchased Collabra and is incorporating its groupware environment into the Netscape Navigator browser. We will soon start to see intranets supporting all business processes. Intranets will become woven throughout the fabric of the business.

If you can access everything from your Web browser, then differences in operating systems will become inconsequential, and distinctions between operating systems may go away. People won't worry so much about which operating system they use, as their browser will provide most of the functionality they will need.

Finally, training will change. Since browsers are so easy to use, they require very little training. Once they are the universal front end, users will no longer need training in how to work applications. What they will need, in order for businesses to compete effectively, is training that focuses on the nuances of applications and how to get the most business benefit from them. There have been predictions for years that computer-based training (CBT) would replace traditional classroom training. This hasn't happened, and won't, because some training works best in a classroom. However, for training that doesn't require a classroom setting, there is a real advantage to delivering it just-in-time via the internal web. Users access the most up-to-date version of the training, and it's available when they need it.

These are only some of the ways that intranets will impact organizations. Now let's move on to take a look at why organizations are creating intranets.

chapter two

Why Have Organizations Created Intranets and What Are the Advantages and Disadvantages?

Why Have Organizations Created Intranets?

InfoWorld's *Corporate Intranets in the Enterprise* study determined that 54 percent of their 310,000 subscribers have an intranet in their corporations or plan to create one in the next 12 months. That is a mighty large percentage considering that a year earlier most corporations had never even heard of the concept of an intranet.

What is driving this explosion of intranets? The popularity of intranets comes from a combination of the demands on businesses today and the ability of intranets to help companies meet those demands. Let's look first at the demands on businesses today, and then we will take a detailed look at the advantages and disadvantages of intranets.

Demands on Businesses Today

Competition is fierce in all businesses today. Just to survive will require that you change virtually everything you do. Change occurs faster than ever and is now a fact of life in business. There are five major influences that drive the increasing pace of business change:

1. Customers want everything faster.
2. Customers want everything cheaper.
3. Customers want better-quality products and services.
4. Business has gone global.
5. All the rules have changed.

Customers Want Everything Faster

Customers want things faster and faster. In an effort to meet customers' needs, companies have reengineered and streamlined their processes. These companies can now operate faster. This puts increasing pressure on their competitors, who have to keep up or get ahead by speeding things up even further. Customers are starting to expect instant service and delivery of products overnight. The Internet is pushing the norm even further by delivering products, such as software, instantly as well.

A by-product of things getting faster and faster is that your products will have shorter and shorter lives. Your competitors are out to render your products obsolete and gain control of the market. Speed to market is a major competitive advantage. The first product out there, even if it is only ahead by a few weeks, will gain control of the market and ultimately become the most profitable. This is because cumulative experience in producing a product enables improvements in the process. You incrementally decrease the cost per unit with each cumulative increase in the quantity you produce. In other words, if you're the first to market, your costs will come down sooner than those of your competitors. That is because you have more cumulative experience in producing that product than they do. As your costs come down, you can start to shave your prices to a level that your competitors can't meet. Their costs have not come down far enough to compete. Your best solution then is to always try to be the one to render your products obsolete—don't allow your competitors to do it. Microsoft is one of the best examples of a company that uses this strategy.

To create products faster and faster, companies are turning to techniques such as concurrent development and shared development. *Concurrent development* enables different areas to work on a product simultaneously through the use of computer-aided design and collaborative tools. *Shared development* is having multiple shifts work on the same product. An example of this is used in the software development business where a company has a site in the United States, another in Europe, and another in India. As each shift goes home, they upload their work for the next shift to work on. Intranets provide tools for concurrent development and shared development.

Doing things faster doesn't happen just in product businesses. It also happens in service businesses, where companies have also been very active in reengineering and streamlining to produce their services faster. Customers today expect immediate service, and those companies that deliver instant service have a competitive advantage. One has only to think of how fast Federal Express has grown to see that providing fast service can be very profitable. Thanks to Federal Express, when you order something today you now expect it tomorrow instead of next week.

Companies that have reengineered have found that one way to do things faster is to allow their customers to perform services for themselves. This is effectively what we are now seeing with intranets. Information Technology (IT) groups in several companies have done that by creating intranets. They let their internal customers provide the level of services they need by creating and maintaining their own publications and information on the intranet.

Another example of this is what AT&T has done with its Internet. AT&T currently allows customers to access their bills, and plans to eventually allow customers to connect to its intranet to do things such as setting up their own 800-number trees.

Customers Want Everything Cheaper

Oh, yes, and by the way, not only do customers want things faster, they also want them cheaper at the same time. This is putting increased pressure on companies to cut costs everywhere they can.

Reengineering has allowed your competitors to cut their costs because they have taken unnecessary steps out of their processes. They may also have downsized along the way, so they have fewer people doing the same amount of work. Which means that they can probably sell their products and services for less.

Intranets have come along and helped the remaining employees do the work that several people used to do. Intranets are relatively inexpensive, too. That's one of the reasons they have become so popular so fast.

Intranets can help you decrease your costs, too, by improving productivity and shortening product development time. People can do things faster and get more done because they have quick and easy access to information they need. Intranets can dramatically improve the productivity of knowledge workers. Intranets improve internal communications while cutting communications costs. They can also help you cut costs by eliminating printing and publishing costs for many things that exist in paper form today.

Customers Want Better-Quality Products and Services

Oh, and one other thing, customers want things faster and cheaper, and they want improved quality, too.

The Total Quality movement has spread through businesses as customers have demanded higher-quality products and services. Customers will just not settle for less, so if you don't provide it, your competitors surely will. To meet that challenge, companies improve their processes and incorporate quality statistics and customer feedback. Intranets have become feedback mechanisms for the quality processes by making quality statistics available to all. As companies capture customer feedback, they put it on the intranet to share with everyone as well.

AT&T uses its intranet to provide better-quality service to its customers. When a customer calls in, customer care representatives use their Knowledge Management System to help them quickly and efficiently solve that customer's problem.

Business Has Gone Global

Your competition used to be down the street. Now it's on the other side of the world, and, in fact, so are your customers.

Technology has made all this possible. The Internet and intranets facilitate communication with customers in other parts of the world or just down the street.

All the Rules Have Changed

The people who work for you used to be located in your office. Increasingly now, they may work from home, as telecommuters, or from some other part of the world. They may not even be your employees, but instead be part of your virtual corporation. You may never even have met them.

With technology, you can now develop close partnerships with your customers and suppliers. Even competitors are becoming business partners with each other.

Marketing has changed as well. Today, marketing focuses on niches, with advertising tailored to the specific niche you're targeting. More and more, you use personalized messages to communicate with your target market. This is what Don Peppers and Martha Rogers talk about in their book, *The One to One Future— Building Relationships One Customer at a Time:*

> *The 1:1 future will be characterized by customized production, individually addressable media, and 1:1 marketing, totally changing the rules of business competition and growth. Instead of market share, the goal of most business competition will be share of customer—one customer at a time.*

How Do Intranets Help Meet These Demands?

The common link among these five drivers is the need to use technology to enable communications within the organization, between partners, and into the marketplace. Some of the ways intranets help meet those demands include:

- Provide operational efficiencies that save time and money.
- Allow access to up-to-date information.
- Improve communications.

- ◆ Enable better coordination.
- ◆ Allow sharing of expertise.
- ◆ Tap the creativity and innovation of your people.

Most companies I spoke with feel that the benefits of an intranet greatly outweigh the risks. Gene Phifer, Senior IT Manager at Texas Instruments, said that TI's use of the intranet is exploding, causing reevaluation of how information is shared within the company. Todd Carlson, CIO at EDS, said that his company's intranet has been a real competitive enabler. It's helping them reach their ambition of *Any⁵*, which states that *EDS will provide untethered, pervasive communications that will make any information available in any form, to anyone, anywhere at any time.*

After seeing the advantages and disadvantages, don't even bother to justify it, just go do it! Besides, your competition is doing it. Can you afford for them to do it and you not to?

Advantages of Intranets

Now let's talk about the advantages of intranets. The Web has become popular in organizations because it's so easy to set up and to use. Rich information, with graphics, sound, and even video, is only a mouse click away. Everyone can have access regardless of the type of computer they're using. It's relatively easy and inexpensive to add in access to existing legacy data and applications. New programming tools bring the capability of adding applications with incredible richness. While other tools do a better job of many of the things you do with the Web, nothing else brings it all together so well. You can add to the Web tools that allow you to send and receive electronic mail and promote discussions among colleagues for more full-featured intranets. To make it even better, all of this comes at a price that will not give you sticker shock! It is easy to see why organizations are creating internal webs and intranets at such an explosive rate.

Let's look at these advantages in more detail. Since there are so many, I have characterized them as two different types of benefits.

In the first group are *tangible benefits,* which are those that you usually can measure or quantify. In the second group are *intangible benefits,* which are those that are hard to measure but have a definite impact nonetheless. In fact, intangible benefits may have an even greater impact on profitability than tangible ones because they often spur the growth of the business.

1. Tangible benefits of intranets

   - Fast and easy to implement
   - Cheap to implement
   - Easy to use
   - Save time
   - Provide operational efficiency
   - Save cost
   - Based on open standards
   - Connect and communicate among disparate platforms
   - Put users in control of their data
   - Secure
   - Scalable
   - Flexible
   - Provide the richness of multimedia
   - Leverage your infrastructure and applications investment

2. Intangible benefits of intranets

   - Provide better communication
   - Provide access to accurate information
   - Capture and share knowledge and expertise
   - Provide better coordination and collaboration
   - Provide for creativity and innovation
   - Provide new business opportunities

◆ Provide new business partnerships through access by suppliers and customers

Tangible Benefits of Intranets

Tangible benefits are those you can measure or quantify. For instance, they can cause you to save a certain amount of money or a certain amount of time.

Fast and Easy to Implement

Intranets are easy to implement and you can set them up quickly. You can start with just a simple pilot program (see Chapter 7 for more detail) to learn about the technology and develop the skills required to use it. Many of the companies I spoke with started just this way. In only a short time, their intranets grew into full-scale information systems that have become critical to the operation of the business.

There are three areas to address:

1. *Server.* A Web server is fast and easy to configure and manage. After your initial server is up and running, other areas of the organization will probably want to set up their own servers. With sufficient technical skills, this is not very hard to do. You can make it even easier by creating a server installation kit. This kit should have all the necessary software, plus instructions about how to install it and the appropriate settings to use in your environment.

2. *Client or browser.* Browsers are also easy to install. You can create a client installation kit to make it even easier for users to install browsers themselves. The kit should contain the browser software, plus instructions and any helper applications and plug-ins that you want your users to have. You can set up the browser in advance to recognize these included applications.

   A lot will depend upon how technical your users are. In many of the early adopter organizations, the users have been quite capable of doing the installations themselves.

Once your users have a browser, you don't have to provide them with an additional user interface with each new application you develop. This makes it fast and easy to roll out new applications.

3. *Publishing and development.*   HTML is the language used to develop Web content. It is mostly a set of tags that you add to a document to tell the browser how to display that document. HTML is very easy to learn, and unlike client/server, you don't have to be a programmer to understand it. You can develop a kit for your Web publishers, which should contain authoring software, graphics tools, templates, and instructions and software for loading files on the server.

Development tools are coming along that allow you to hook your databases to the Web. These also seem fairly easy to use, especially for programmers who are knowledgeable of databases. Since you can develop things quickly, you can pilot applications and make refinements as you go along. This enables your users to get value from your application while you continue to tweak on it. You have only to change a single copy, the one on the server, when you make a change. You don't have to redeploy the application to all users' desktops. This makes the development cycle much faster and easier.

In all three areas, I mentioned creating an installation kit. The companies I spoke with frequently created installation kits to make installation smooth and easy for users. These installation kits were easily accessible by users. For example, EDS put its installation kits on FTP servers and on its desktop computing product catalog. EDS employees could install the software simply by selecting it from a menu of options.

The ease of setup was one of the factors that caused intranets to take off so rapidly in several of these companies.

Cheap to Implement

As I've indicated before, intranets are a very inexpensive and cost-effective client/server solution. They are fairly cheap to set up and to run.

- *Servers.*   Web servers and the other required servers are relatively inexpensive. You can start with a spare computer and download free server software directly from the Internet. You often hear the claim that much of the freeware on the Internet is more stable and better tested than a lot of commercial software. So many people download the free software from the Net that bugs are quickly reported and fixed.

  Not only is it inexpensive to set up a server, it is also inexpensive to run one. For instance, Booz Allen reports that they have only a single administrator running their intranet.

- *Client or browser.*   Browsers typically run less than $40 per user, and some of them are free. Some companies have found that browsers such as Netscape work so well that they have deployed them to the entire company to replace their own proprietary systems.

- *Publishing and development.*   With just a few hours of training in HTML, you can publish content on the Web. Many HTML publishers and web developers are self-taught from the free information available on the World Wide Web. It's hard to get much cheaper development training than that.

Easy to Use

What could be easier than to point and click with a mouse? Hypertext linking makes intranets very easy to use, so you can get users up and running very quickly. The browser provides a consistent user interface to a variety of applications and even allows you to access legacy applications and databases. In addition, you can use search engines to easily locate information and the forms to update information.

The ease of use comes not only through the point-and-click interface but also through ease of navigation. Users will find that Web applications are more flexible, as they can navigate through the data as they wish rather than having to follow a predefined path.

Training is minimal with an internal web. It is so easy to use and intuitive that most people figure it out in just a few minutes. Therefore, basic levels of training are virtually unnecessary and support is minimal. Setting it up on a user's machine is probably the hardest part. Since users use the browser for both internal and external applications, you are leveraging the skills they learn with one or the other. The need for very little training and support translates into cost and time savings for the organization.

Save Time

Since intranets provide fast access to information, they save time. As fast-paced as things are today in most businesses, nobody has time to waste. Therefore, you save time by having information at your fingertips rather than having to chase it down in your files or by phone. With access to an internal web full of current information, people also don't have to waste time validating that they have the most up-to-date information. In addition, you can work from wherever you are, which saves you from downtime. All of this means that you have more time to do the things that really matter in your business.

Provide Operational Efficiency

Intranets appear to be a welcome relief for overburdened IT administrators. Client/server systems have put a heavy load on IT to create and maintain them. Intranets not only put less of a load on IT, they even seem to take off some of the load. Users can take on the responsibilities of server setup and maintenance and content publishing for themselves. IT no longer has to build GUI screens because those come built into the browser. They also don't have to go out and configure lots of client PCs for every new application that comes along. You no longer need to do many of the administrative tasks of e-mail when using intranet e-mail.

The end result is that you need fewer people to maintain an intranet. For instance, Booz Allen has a single administrator for Knowledge On Line, and SGI has a staff of just five to handle Silicon Junction.

In addition to fewer human resources, an intranet may require fewer operational resources as well. For example, when you send e-mail, it sends a separate copy of each message to each addressee. With the Web, only a single copy exists and everyone can access it when they need it. On newsgroups, only a single copy of each message exists as well.

For proprietary groupware such as Notes, you have databases replicated all over the place. With the internal web, you need to maintain only a single database and you do not need replication and synchronization.

One of the best things about intranets seems to be that with your current budget you can do so much more.

Save Cost

The first reason that most companies create an intranet is to save money. With an intranet you no longer have to print and distribute information in paper form. It is expensive to prepare, print, and mail or distribute paper documents. Since businesses are moving so quickly today, most printed things are obsolete before the ink is dry. That means you either reprint those documents with ever increasing frequency, or you just live with outdated information. If you settle for the latter, then people spend a lot of time chasing around to determine if the information they have is accurate.

With an internal web server, it is pretty easy to keep information up-to-date, and people can be reasonably sure that if they get their information from the internal web, it is up-to-date and accurate. That can boost productivity, which saves money in the long run.

You can also save money by using the intranet for e-mail rather than sending faxes and memos. In addition, you can extend this to your suppliers and customers and save money by communicating with them electronically. The next step is to use the intranet and the Internet for electronic data interchange (EDI) with business partners. This is far less expensive than doing EDI through a proprietary value-added network (VAN). This use is just in its infancy, but we will see lots more of this over the next few years.

Another place you save cost with an intranet is from the tools used to access it. With many client/server applications, you have to develop a new set of GUI screens for each application, and you have to tailor them for each operating system platform. Then you have to roll them out to each desktop for every new application that comes along. With an intranet, you can simply put the browser on existing client/server computers. With a browser, the GUI already exists and you simply put new applications on the server. If users need a new plug-in, you can place it on the server as an icon. Clicking on the icon will download and install the appropriate version on your computer. All this costs far less than the tool and support costs for client/server applications.

Then you have the savings from training and support. Since the intranet tools are so easy to use, you will not need to provide much training. Support is minimal as well. Even developers and publishers require only minimal amounts of training. The cost savings from training and support are larger than the savings from the inexpensive cost of the tools. Finally, the internal web is a great way to deliver just-in-time training that is always up-to-date.

Based on Open Standards

One commonly cited advantage of intranets is that they are based on open standards such as TCP/IP, HTTP, HTML, CGI, MIME, and others. Today, open is much better than proprietary because of the flexibility it gives you.

Connect and Communicate among Disparate Platforms

To my knowledge, this is the first technology to come along that will connect all the different types of computers on the network, whether they are PCs, Macintoshes, or workstations. All can access and display a single version of a file without having to convert it, no matter which type of computer created it. This is an issue that almost all organizations have struggled with for years. It is such a relief to find a technology that will do this, and *not cost an arm and a leg*. It's almost more than most IT departments could have wished for.

Web browsers are available for all major platforms, and applications on the server don't care which platform the user is using. Developers can create and roll out applications so much faster when they don't have to worry about multiple versions for multiple platforms. Users have a single user interface, so the application looks the same and works the same for all users.

Put Users in Control of Their Data

This is a major advantage of intranets. Your users have wanted to control their own destiny, and now they can. Further, you can get out of the business of handling their data for them. You can then focus on the important ways to bring value to your organization.

The move away from centralized IT started with PCs, but one of the problems that created was islands of information. Something could reside on the marketing department server and be shared within marketing, but it was not available to the rest of the company. Now, marketing can control its own departmental web server, and if they wish to share information with the rest of the company, it is very easily available to everyone else.

If you set up a corporate web server, those who want to share their information with others can put it on the corporate server until they are ready to create their own. Either way, you can set up security so that individual departments can create, update, and delete their own information on the server. If you create a server and publishing kit to make it easy for them to start and to take responsibility, you will empower them to be more self-sufficient.

At JCPenney, when we first started talking about users being able to maintain their own information, there was a fear among some departments that they would have to hire programmers or train their people to program in order to set things up in HTML. What we discovered was that HTML coding was in many ways easier to learn than some of the nuances of sophisticated word processors and spreadsheets. Any user who can do sophisticated stuff with those tools can certainly handle HTML.

As you start converting existing documents to HTML, it is helpful to work with conversion tools. Most conversion tools that are available today are usable by nonprogrammers, but they expect a certain amount of discipline in applying style sheets to your documents. I suspect the use of style sheets is a big issue to address in most user departments. I hope that future tools will be much more lenient in that regard, as it is important for all departments to make their existing electronic documentation available to other departments. Perhaps that will be solved by the time you read this book.

Secure

There is a lot of concern over how secure your connection to the Internet is. Intranets have an advantage in that you do not generally connect them directly to the Internet, but instead employ firewalls and/or proxy servers to separate them from the Internet. Therefore, you can keep your intranet as secure as you wish and still provide your users with Internet access. This lets IT managers and other executives sleep at night!

Fortunately, you can enforce security at different levels on your intranet. For highly confidential information, such as that restricted to certain officers, you can restrict access to only those who need that information. For departmental information, such as accounting and finance, or confidential information, such as payroll or human resources, you can restrict access to only a certain department or certain users. You can also use security to allow suppliers or customers to access your intranet from across the Internet.

Scalable

Intranet applications easily scale up to a very large scale, just like those on the Internet. This can solve the problem of many client/server applications that *hit the wall* when you try to scale them upward. One of the most common complaints about client/server applications is that when they reach a certain number of users, they bog down and can't accommodate additional users. That isn't a problem for intranets because they use the technology that runs the very massive Internet.

Flexible

The real beauty of internal webs is their flexibility. Since you are working only with the application on the server and not on multiple desktops, you can create and revise as often as you wish. You can do enterprise-wide pilots where everyone can benefit from the application while you are still tweaking on it. This allows IT to rapidly develop and deploy an application to meet the dynamic needs of the business. You can both learn and reap the value at the same time as long as you and your users are willing to live with less than perfection while you are developing. This is what we have aimed for with rapid application development (RAD) and prototypes. Now, with the internal web, it is much easier to do and reap benefits at the same time.

Provide the Richness of Multimedia

Multimedia has been creeping its way into organizations for the past few years. The problem was that many users didn't have the fast computers and video cards, speakers and sound cards, and CD-ROM drives that were necessary for using multimedia. As some organizations upgraded their computers over the past few years, multimedia drove these features to become part of the standard configurations. Even so, they are not pervasive on the desktop or on the laptop.

With multimedia, you still have the problem of distribution of the applications. You can always re-press a CD-ROM with up-to-date information, but then you must redistribute it, which can be much more expensive than the cost of re-pressing the CD. When users finally get around to using your application, will it be out-of-date again?

With the internal web, multimedia can reside on the server and be distributed when you need it. You can be reasonably certain that it is up-to-date because you need only to change the one copy on the server, and you don't have to worry about distributing copies. You still need the fast computer and video card, and speakers and a sound card, but those have become much more common today. The ease of distributing up-to-date multimedia information via the internal web will continue to stimulate these features to become pervasive. The one critical issue related to multimedia is the requirement for higher bandwidth. If multimedia provides value, that will become a nonissue.

We have talked about the technical ease of using the internal web for multimedia, but the really important value from it is in its use as a communication and teaching tool. Roughly 35 percent of us are visual learners, who learn by seeing; 25 percent of us are auditory learners, who learn by hearing; and 40 percent of us are kinesthetic learners, who learn by doing. Multimedia more effectively fulfills the learning needs of all types of learners. With multimedia, you can see how something works, hear a description of it, and actually practice using it. This meets the needs of all types of learners. This multisensory approach can communicate in such a way that you can learn something in roughly half as much time, and retain it two to three times longer, than with conventional methods of learning. With the need to do everything faster and better, this certainly fills the bill. With the Web, it's less expensive, too.

In addition to the value of multimedia for teaching, it is a great communication tool. For instance, some companies use video and streaming audio on their internal webs to communicate messages from senior executives. Everyone gets a consistent message because it isn't garbled as it passes through various layers of management. If everyone understands the message and they are all working in the same direction, the effectiveness of the organization should increase dramatically.

Leverage Your Infrastructure and Applications Investment

Since Web solutions sit on top of your existing systems, you can leverage your investment in your existing hardware and software. You don't have to throw out what you already have and replace it. In addition, with Web-based applications, you can access your existing databases and legacy applications in a very user-friendly way.

Intangible Benefits of Intranets

While organizations can generally measure tangible benefits—for example, quantifying the amount of time or money saved—it is much harder to put a value on intangible benefits. However, the intangible benefits may be much more valuable than the tangible ones. That's because it's hard to put a monetary value on making the organization more competitive. If you have more knowledgeable and self-reliant employees, who are more productive, make better decisions, and do a better job of serving customers, how can you possibly put a value on that?

Provide Better Communication

Some companies start their intranets specifically to improve internal communications, while others discover that improved communication was a by-product of their intranets. An intranet offers a cost-effective and efficient way to improve those internal communications. Even with the push to save costs in most organizations, internal communication is not something you can cut back on. In fact, you need it more than ever in today's companies, where increased communication is essential.

Internal communications can take several forms:

◆ *Communications from executives, corporate communications departments, and other departments.* This can include announcements, bulletins, newsletters, and other communiqués published on the internal web. The intranet is the only easy and affordable way to get this information communicated simultaneously to all locations worldwide.

◆ *Communications among colleagues.* Intranet e-mail and newsgroups enhance the communication among individuals and can eliminate telephone tag among colleagues. Employees of far-flung companies can avoid getting up in the middle of the night to call a colleague on the other side of the world.

Information is valuable, and things may happen slowly when the information to make a decision is not available. In this fast-paced world, not having that information can lead to lost opportunities. Intranets can provide critical information to all your employees throughout the world at the same time.

Provide Access to Accurate Information

Most of the companies I spoke with cited access to information and better internal communication as the reasons that they built their intranets. Intranets provide quick and easy access to information when and where needed. You don't even have to know where the data resides in order to be able to access it. You can just as easily access something created by the person in the next office as by a person on the other side of the globe. It really doesn't matter.

Before intranets, there were vast reserves of data hidden away on departmental servers, untapped by those outside the department. If you could get to it, what did you have to go through to know it was there and to know how to get access to it?

Intranets provide access to more up-to-date information, especially when employees can do their own updates. Before, it wasn't easy to find out if you had the most up-to-date information. It is so much easier now to point and click on the internal web than to waste time going through your files or manuals looking for the same information.

Access to information means that you can have employees who are more knowledgeable and self-reliant. We finally have the opportunity to use computers in ways that we've wished for.

Capture and Share Knowledge and Expertise

Intranets provide a way and place to capture and save information so that it is available to anyone who needs it when they need it. This can be through internal web publishing by different departments or through captured knowledge from newsgroup discussions. It is typically a one-to-many type of communication. You can capture the knowledge of the experts, lessons learned, or information about key technologies or procedures. The value comes in that it saves the proverbial reinventing of the wheel. It can also be the foundation to enable better communication and coordination among workgroups and project teams. Many of the companies I spoke with used newsgroups to support impromptu special-interest groups around a specific issue and to share status and project information across the company.

Provide Better Coordination and Collaboration

Another advantage of intranets is that they enable better coordination and collaboration of workgroups and teams. This relates closely to using them to capture and share knowledge and expertise. The intranet can also be used to support workgroup conferencing.

Provide for Creativity and Innovation

Intranets facilitate creative processes. An example is to use news-groups or chat tools for group brainstorming. For example, a product development engineer dealing with a problem could put a description of the problem on an engineering newsgroup and ask for ideas and suggestions. By putting together several of the forth-coming suggestions, the engineer is able to solve the problem and keep the project on schedule. In another example, the same engineer monitors the newsgroup the company maintains for its customers. From this interaction, the engineer gets ideas for new features for the product being developed.

Provide New Business Partnerships through
Access by Suppliers and Customers

Intranets provide the opportunity to cultivate valuable business relationships with your suppliers and customers. For instance, you can provide them with access directly into your databases, as Federal Express did when it opened up its internal package-tracking application to its customers via the Internet.

As I mentioned earlier, EDI between trading partners one day will mostly take place over the Internet or by your customers putting the information directly into your intranet.

Provide New Business Opportunities

Some companies, such as SGI and Booz Allen, have realized that one of the advantages of an intranet is the new business opportunities that it provides. What new business opportunities could you cultivate because you have an intranet? What new products or services could you provide? Does a current product or service fit well in an intranet? Could other organizations benefit from it? What could this potential new business be worth to you?

Advantages of Intranets over Client/Server

Client/server is a really simple concept that came along to replace mainframe applications accessed from dumb terminals. With mainframes and terminals, all the intelligence and processing took place on the mainframe computer.

With client/server, you have a smart client, usually a PC, which provides the GUI and some local computing power. The client is tied into a LAN server, on which the database resides. The client dispatches a request to the server, which accesses the data in the database. The server returns the data to the client for display and final processing. The problem is that as applications have grown, the PC has required too much processing power, resulting in *fat clients.* This is two-tiered client/server. To solve the problem, three-tiered client/server environments were created, which involves putting a server in the middle to handle some of the local processing.

Interestingly, the internal web has come along at the same time. It is, in effect, a three-tiered architecture. Robert Bickel, in "Building Intranets: Internal Webs Give Companies a New Solution to an Old Problem" (*Internet World,* March, 1996, pp. 71–76), describes the web's three-tier architecture this way:

> *In the Web's architecture, the browser comprises the GUI tier; the Web server is the middle tier containing application logic with ties to back-end databases; and application servers are the third tier. Scalability is even greater when the idea of multiple Web servers is introduced. Even within a single application, one Web server can "hand off" a user to another less-used Web server without intervention.*

In earlier sections, I talked about the advantages intranets have over client/server. Just to recap, here are some of the key advantages of intranets, primarily internal webs, over client/server.

- ◆ Web browser software is typically very inexpensive compared to proprietary client/server systems.
- ◆ Intranets are easy to set up, easy to use, and easy to manage compared to client/server.
- ◆ The internal web already has the three-tier architecture that client/server is moving toward.

- The internal web is scalable far beyond the point where client/server hits the wall.
- Web browsers provide a common user interface for all applications, whereas the user interface varies from one client/server application to another.
- Web browsers exist for all the different operating systems, whereas you must build and roll out different applications for each platform with client/server.
- Client/server development requires lots of programming expertise, whereas developers need much less skill for internal web development. In many cases, nonprogrammers can do web publishing and development.
- Web applications can also be more flexible. With client/server applications, as well as mainframe applications, the flow of the program must be determined before coding, and users must follow a specific sequence of steps. Web applications are flexible and the user can follow any sequence desired.
- While mission-critical applications are not ready for intranets yet, the time will come.

Advantages of Intranets over Proprietary Groupware

Intranets also have advantages over proprietary workflow and groupware software. Let's first define workflow and groupware.

- *Workflow* is software that facilitates the movement of work through processes. It allows work products to flow among the various people who have responsibility for different parts of the process. Proprietary workflow tools include Lotus Notes, IBM FlowMark, and Action Technologies Action Workflow.
- *Groupware* is software that facilitates interaction among people working together. It allows work groups to communicate and collaborate through tools such as elec-

tronic mail, fax, scheduling, and discussion databases. Proprietary groupware tools include Lotus Notes, Microsoft Exchange, and Novell Groupwise.

Why would organizations choose an intranet over proprietary groupware tools?

◆ Web servers are based on open technology, which means that lots more tools and options are available than for the proprietary groupware products.

◆ Web browsers and servers are far less expensive than most proprietary tools. For instance, even though Notes prices are coming down as I write this, Notes clients are still at least twice as expensive as browsers. In addition, the cost of server hardware and software adds up very quickly. Plus, Notes requires an army of highly trained administrators and developers. There are reports that corporate investments in Lotus Notes implementation often run from one-quarter to one-half million dollars, and more. You can do a large portion of what Notes does with an intranet application for $10,000 to $20,000, or less.

◆ An internal web is very simple to manage and requires little training, unlike Notes, which requires highly trained programmers and administrators.

◆ Web tools are starting to incorporate many of the capabilities of proprietary groupware, such as electronic mail, discussion groups, scheduling, and videoconferencing, in a single, easy-to-use interface. The Web does not yet offer all the capabilities of proprietary groupware, but it will soon. For instance, Netscape has purchased Collabra and is incorporating the Collabra Share groupware product in the Netscape browser.

◆ Notes is a proprietary database that replicates data. You can access a Web server across the Internet from almost any location, and therefore it doesn't require replication.

◆ Web servers integrate easily into an existing environment to access ODBC-compliant databases. Lotus Notes

Release 4 has just started supporting ODBC-compliant databases.

Disadvantages and Risks of Intranets

After this litany of advantages and benefits, is it any wonder that organizations are building intranets? Well, there are, of course, some disadvantages and risks that we need to examine. They include:

◆ Potential for chaos
◆ Security risks
◆ Management fears
◆ Information overload
◆ Waste of productivity
◆ Not an integrated solution
◆ Hidden or unknown complexity and cost

Potential for Chaos

With all the hype around, everyone wants an intranet. Users can easily install this technology, so you should be aware that the situation can get out of control as it did in the early days of client/server. However, the costs of going back and changing things are not nearly so great with Web technology as they were with client/server.

To some IT managers, the thought of users setting up their own webs is frightening; others see it as an opportunity. It's the issue of control versus chaos that we will talk a lot more about in this book. My own personal view is that letting the intranet grow from a grass-roots effort is the best way to reach critical mass. You should involve all areas of your organization when building your intranet.

It may be easier for you in the long run if you take a leadership role. Get far enough out in front of your users that you can introduce this new technology to them. That way you can assist all areas in doing things cost-effectively. In addition, you can help bring together all areas to deploy an intranet that meets the needs of your business.

Security Risks

If you have been cautious in the design and setup of your security system, then the risks are more imaginary than real. If you have set up your firewall correctly, and isolated your intranet server from your Internet server, you should have very little worry. That way, people can't accidentally wander into your sensitive information.

The challenges are a little greater with remote users. You can use dial-back modems and challenge security/password systems to authenticate those who are trying to get into your intranet.

It is really much easier for critical information to get outside your organization via e-mail than for an intruder to come in and take that information from your intranet. It is important for people not to place proprietary information on your Internet server or your FTP server.

According to companies that have been there, the challenge wasn't in the security itself, it was in dispelling the fears of people who were concerned over the security of their data.

Management Fears: Fear of Sharing Information and the Loss of Control

The fear of sharing information is one of the most difficult disadvantages to deal with. Intranets scare those middle managers who have always hoarded information and refused to share it with their subordinates. These managers are afraid that their jobs are in jeopardy if everyone has information. That may be true. Intranets empower users and you don't have to manage them.

One of the companies spoke about an issue they dealt with. Some of their managers were afraid that giving employees too much information would make them harder to manage.

Information Overload

Another disadvantage of intranets is the potential for information overload. You have:

◆ Created an intranet and populated it with all the things people need to know

◆ Provided access to all your databases and legacy applications

◆ Brought in news feeds so people have the latest news on your competitors and marketplace

◆ Hooked up your intranet to the Internet and made all of that information available to your people

Then what do you do to help people deal with the information overload they will suffer? That is an issue that people are just starting to understand.

It appears that intelligent agents will be one of the answers to this question. We will probably see all kinds of innovative solutions emerge over time as intranets become pervasive in businesses of all sizes. When the advantage of access to information turns into a disadvantage, then you will want to have solutions ready to implement.

Waste of Productivity

Another disadvantage is the concern that once you open the company up and let people surf the Net, people will spend all their time surfing and not get their work done. That is a very common fear, but one that you may look back on one day and laugh at. Sure, people play with their new toy for the first few days. After that, they settle down and use the Web more appropriately. You can address this issue by creating a formal Internet Use Policy and making sure employees are aware of it. You can train them in how to use this new tool appropriately. Then the problem seems to go away.

Not an Integrated Solution

One problem with creating an intranet is that until recently you haven't been able to go to a vendor and ask to buy an intranet. You had to piece it all together from components from a lot of different sources and then make sure it all worked together smoothly. That wasn't always easy. However, vendors are starting to come out with integrated suites that fit together so you simply plug in all the pieces. This appears to be only a short-term disadvantage.

Hidden or Unknown Complexity and Cost

Though intranets are relatively inexpensive in comparison to client/server, they can still cost serious money for sophisticated applications linking internal Web servers with existing corporate applications. At this point, it is still too early to know what issues and complexity may lie ahead of us. Some things to consider are:

- *People.* Once you have trained your webmasters and publishers, how do you keep them?
- *Processes.* Can you use the intranet to improve your business processes? What data should you use to do that?
- *Technology.* How do you determine which applications are the right ones to link to your internal web? What tools will help you with that effort?

What Size Company Does It Take to Need an Intranet?

A commonly asked question is *What size company does it take to need an intranet?* I have seen this question posed on various discussion groups on the Net. The common answers seem to be that a company with 50 or 100 users or more can benefit from an intranet. Another frequent answer is to consider an intranet if you have widely dispersed locations. I have read about companies with as few as 10 or 12 who use intranets. I think that even smaller companies than that can benefit from them. I spoke with a friend just the other day who is considering putting together an intranet for her home-based business that works with six subcontractors spread around the city. I think the real question is *Do I have a need for an intranet?* If so, why not create one?

I won't be at all surprised to see them popping up in homes within a few years as families start to network their computers. I can see having the family address list, with birthdays, anniversaries, and other occasions, on a family intranet. The kids can check there to get the phone number for Grandma and Grandpa or their cousins. Think of all the possible ways you could use an intranet at home.

chapter three

How Will Intranets Change You and Your Organization?

What Is Happening to Cause the Changes?

Intranets will become pervasive in business. Why is that, and what is happening to cause these changes?

As we discussed in Chapter 2, the economy is changing, and demands on businesses are also rapidly changing. Customers want high quality, good service, low price, and they want it all now! If you don't give it to them, your competition surely will. In order to stay competitive, today's organizations must do things cheaper, faster, and better than ever before. Therefore, companies are forced to do whatever they can to compete. Companies are having to fundamentally rethink everything they do.

As companies work to do things cheaper, faster, and better, product life cycles shrink. You and your competitors race to get to market with new and better products. You feverishly try to replace your own products before your competitors do it to you. Innovation is the key to competitive advantage. Where does innovation come from? It comes from empowering your employees through learning, sharing knowledge, and collaboration.

Learning Organizations

We frequently hear that the only sustainable competitive advantage comes from an organization's ability to learn. The concept of the Learning Organization was first espoused by Peter Senge in *The Fifth Discipline: The Art and Practice of the Learning Organization. Learning Organizations* are those organizations that encourage learning, creativity, and innovation, and empower their people to solve problems. They do this as a way to get a jump on the competition and to learn quickly and incorporate that learning as part of the organization's history and culture. The Learning Organization is embraced by organizations that are moving ahead in the 1990s. By empowering people, they are tapping in to the best creativity and innovativeness of their people and allowing them the flexibility to make good judgments. Good judgments come from experience. To be able to share that experience throughout the organization is to give everybody a jump start on what is necessary to make those good decisions.

Intranets will be valuable to companies that are empowering their people. Why is this so important? Your very future is at stake—if your competitor does it before you do, you may be history! That sounds pretty strong and ominous, but in the crazy 1990s many companies have found that their strategic advantage evaporated overnight.

Shared Knowledge

We know that *communication* is people talking to each other, and *collaboration* is people working together. Just what is *knowledge?* How do you share it? A few years ago in business, we focused on getting data and reports. We transitioned from using just data, or raw numbers, to using tools to turn that data into information to help us make better decisions. With information, you could spot a trend and project its impact.

Now we have moved forward another step, toward capturing and using knowledge. That's where you capture not just numbers, but what people know. Knowledge can include what your experts know. It can include expertise you have learned in developing your products. Knowledge can include what you know about your competitors and their products. It's also what you know about your customers, their needs, their feelings about your products, and what they think about your competitor's products as well.

Once you have that knowledge, it's how you use it that determines whether it gives you a competitive advantage.

Since employees acquire knowledge and act upon it, those employees then become an organization's greatest asset. It's their ideas, inventions, and innovations that become the source of sales and profits. *Knowledge will be the currency of the future.*

Knowledge Systems

If knowledge is a key, then how do you collect and maintain that knowledge? This is what groupware does. Groupware facilitates communication, collaboration, and capturing the organization's knowledge. Groupware databases, known as *knowledge systems,* serve as the repository for recording people's learning and experiences. Lotus Notes was one of the first such programs, although there are now many others.

Many companies consider their knowledge systems to be a major competitive advantage. Since sharing knowledge has become critical for business survival in the 1990s, many organizations are investing millions of dollars in deploying groupware and knowledge systems. These systems make it easy to tap into the collective knowledge of the organization. By using search tools, it is easy to find the people with the knowledge you need. These systems can hold not only text, but also various types of multimedia. These knowledge bases can even extend beyond the boundaries of your organization and out to your business partners.

So why doesn't everyone have these knowledge systems? Well, for one, they have been very expensive, although that is changing. Companies are starting to see that they can get many of the benefits of these knowledge systems by creating intranets, and at very low cost. This is one of the reasons intranets took off. They provide a quick and easy way to capture and store knowledge. You can capture knowledge through threads of discussion groups and by publishing documents on the internal web. The tools are not yet as sophisticated as Lotus Notes and other groupware tools, but that will change. Because of the need for more sophisticated intranet tools, many companies are working fast and furiously on solutions, which we can expect to see soon.

The information captured through the intranet provides the foundation upon which to build a full-fledged knowledge base.

Collaboration

Collaboration is about working together and sharing together. Tapping into the collective wisdom and knowledge of your employees is a requirement to enable you to compete effectively today.

Teams

Organizations have created teams to tap into the collective knowledge and wisdom of their employees. Teams can accomplish far more than individuals alone. To support a team, you need groupware to provide for communication and collaboration.

Groupware

Groupware is a tool for collaborating and communicating. It promotes the free flow of information, enhances innovations, and supports and facilitates collective leadership. The end result will likely be an organization that is better able to meet the challenges in today's marketplace.

Groupware provides capabilities such as:

◆ E-mail
◆ Newsgroups and discussion databases
◆ Calendars and scheduling
◆ Whiteboards
◆ Videoconferencing

Lotus Notes is perhaps the most widely known groupware product.

What Changes Will Occur?

In Chapter 2, I talked about the reasons why companies created intranets. In this chapter, I will talk about the results from implementing them as well as other impacts that they have had. Let me emphasize that for most of the companies, intranets did indeed yield the results for which they were built. Therefore, some of the reasons for creating intranets that I cited in Chapter 2 appear in this chapter as results that the companies achieved. The results fit two major scenarios, with a lot of dimensions within each:

1. Improved competitiveness through operational efficiency and productivity, through

   ◆ Improved access to up-to-date information
   ◆ Cost savings
   ◆ Time savings
   ◆ Improved productivity
   ◆ Improved operational efficiency and effectiveness
   ◆ Improved decision making
   ◆ Improved ability to respond to customers and to be proactive
   ◆ Empowered users
   ◆ Leveraged intellectual capital
   ◆ Provided new business and revenue-generating opportunities
   ◆ Improved service to customers

2. Broke down walls and built a culture of sharing and collaboration, because they

   ◆ Improved communication
   ◆ Enabled sharing of knowledge and collaboration
   ◆ Empowered people
   ◆ Facilitated organizational learning
   ◆ Facilitated organizational bonding
   ◆ Improved the quality of life at work

Improved Competitiveness through Operational Efficiency and Productivity

When everyone can have an intranet, how does a company use an intranet for competitive advantage? It comes from integrating your databases and applications into the intranet. This allows your employees to leverage that information through improved decision making, productivity, and service to your customers. This also stimulates creativity and innovation. The value that your employees add becomes your competitive advantage. This is a natural by-product of the things you do with your intranet.

Improved Access to Up-to-Date Information

Almost every company I spoke with listed improved access to up-to-date information or timely delivery of information as major results from having an intranet. The types of information available were as varied as the companies. The intranet at SAS has become the de facto standard for publishing. People can now find information and documentation without having to search blindly through the file system or ask others for access locations. Amgen found that the most effective use of its intranet so far is to provide access to corporate library materials. AT&T believes that its information is now more accurate because people can update their own information. Even those without desktop computers at Turner Broadcasting can use freestanding kiosks to access human resource information.

Intranets are fast becoming the primary distribution and communications vehicles in many companies. Some are even extending the types of information available to users. For instance, the impact so far at EDS has been so great that it is committed to getting even more information delivered via the intranet. EDS has reached an agreement to add the PointCast I-Server to its intranet. By selecting from categories of information, employees will receive personalized news and other information directly on their computer screens. This includes not only outside information but also internal EDS news and announcements. This will allow EDS to immediately communicate bulletins to those who need that specific information.

Virtually every company I spoke with is adding Web interfaces to their legacy and client/server applications in addition to developing many new applications for their internal Web. The Web will become the universal interface for access to corporate information. So much so that SGI now makes several hundred thousand pages of operational data and ideas available through its intranet. EDS is now putting much of its information within the context of processes to convert that information into knowledge.

Cost Savings

Another frequently cited result is the cost savings. This is the one of most interest to executives. Most of the companies I spoke with replaced any paper that they could with an intranet to save money on printing, warehousing, and distributing documents. They also saved money by eliminating faxes and memos. Since the intranet includes the network, some companies found cost savings through eliminating redundancy in their networks. AT&T, for one, estimated that through consolidating its individual networks into a single global intranet it has saved about $30 million per year. This resulted from reducing duplication of people, equipment, and other costs. Bell Atlantic also reported that it has saved several hundred thousand dollars so far through consolidation and reduced printing. Bell Atlantic is now experimenting with moving EDI to the intranet, which should yield significant cost savings.

One other large area of cost savings relates to the cost of proprietary solutions. With browsers and servers cheap or free, nothing else competes on price for so much functionality.

Time Savings

Another often cited result was time savings. When the information they need is only a mouse click away, employees don't waste time trying to hunt things and verify their accuracy. This efficiency turns into greater productivity.

Improved Productivity

EDS reported improved efficiency and productivity because the intranet provides faster communication of information and a more intuitive user interface, which improves people's comprehension.

SGI is progressively implementing applications that increase organizational productivity. An example is its Electronic Requisition System, which it uses to manage purchase orders and the associated approval process. This workflow application reduces the time it takes to process and track requisitions.

Improved Operational Efficiency and Effectiveness

Intranets allow users to do things more efficiently, which allows them to use the time they save to do things more effectively. Turner Broadcasting feels that each employee who learns to use the intranet will be more effective. EDS even provides job aids through the intranet to assist employees in doing their work more efficiently. Workgroups at AT&T communicate electronically, which improves their efficiency.

The efficiency doesn't just apply to users. Intranets are a welcome relief to IT groups as well. They're easy to maintain, which requires fewer people. SGI, for instance, with over 2,000 servers, has a staff of only five to handle their intranet.

Many companies said that the Web is now their platform of choice for applications development and to modernize their legacy systems. The intranet even lets them reuse software components.

The end result of all of this for IT is that intranets stretch their budgets farther. You can now do more with the same budget.

Improved Decision Making

Intranets provide timely access to people and information in order to help you make better decisions. Often, when trying to get answers, you play telephone tag. It's even worse when employees and workgroups span time zones, especially on opposite sides of the globe. If employees don't have information available to them, they may make bad decisions. Even worse, they may make no decision at all because they can't get the information they need. Things happen slowly until the information becomes available, and in this fast-paced world, not having the right information can lead to lost opportunities.

With an intranet, the answers are at your fingertips and you can act quickly to make a decision. Decisions based on facts will inevitably be better than those made without facts.

Improved Ability to Respond to Competitors and to Be Proactive

The Net is particularly effective for situations where the competition has just come out with a new product. For instance, if Sun comes out with a new product, SGI can have a video on Silicon Junction in just 24 hours to enable salespeople to respond. By putting videos and sales information on the intranet, their selling can be more proactive.

Empowered Users

Intranets have provided a lot of good news for IT. Since they are inexpensive to deploy and maintain, companies have saved money over other solutions. Even better, users now take control of their own information. IT simply provides the infrastructure and services. At Texas Instruments, intranets empower the end users to provide their own information management solutions. This means that they have less dependence on the IT department. With absolutely no work other than to register their server, they can make the information available to anyone in the organization. As if this weren't good enough already, as better tools come along it will be even easier for end users to do almost everything themselves.

Leveraged Intellectual Capital

Booz Allen and EDS both said precisely the same thing: that their intranet allowed them to leverage their intellectual capital. It has changed the way they think about knowledge and information. EDS puts its customer profiles and project outlines on its internal web to capitalize on the intellectual capital available within the corporation.

Provided New Business and Revenue-Generating Opportunities

The intranet also opened up new business opportunities for several companies' products and services. Another interesting twist is that several companies are generating revenue from vendors who pay to advertise to employees on the internal web. These are ways these companies have tapped into the power of intranets. What could you do with your intranet?

Improved Service to Customers

The end result of all this should be improved service to customers. If intranets cause you to do things faster, cheaper, or better, then customers benefit. Happy customers translate into profits and happy shareholders.

Breaking Down Walls: Building a Culture of Sharing and Collaboration

While all the operational results are important, the most valuable results may come from the culture changes the intranet will cause. Intranets facilitate communication and collaboration among employees, flattening of the hierarchy, and organizational bonding.

Improved Communication

Improved communication was one of the two most often cited results from intranets. For example, Cathy Mills, Vice President and Director of Company Communications at JCPenney, believes that jWeb, JCPenney's intranet, is a critical tool for communicating with associates (employees) in 37 countries around the world. Without jWeb, communication requires phone calls, e-mail, and faxes, all of which are far more expensive and less effective than jWeb.

Some of the ways that intranets improved communications within these companies were:

- ◆ *Speed.* Communications took place much faster. EDS has an on-line news service to supplement its paper news. It allows for immediate distribution of information and provides more complete news than can be delivered on paper.

- ◆ *Comprehension.* The message was easier to understand because the interface was more intuitive.

- ◆ *Consistency.* The message is consistent to everyone. Leaders can communicate directly to all rather than going through layers of management. This avoids distorted messages with each subsequent delivery.

- *Free flow of information.* Intranets, by their very nature, stimulate free-flowing conversations with others whom you do not normally work with or contact. This helped break down barriers within organizations. SGI, for instance, found that its intranet facilitates its open culture.

- *Cross-organization.* The intranet facilitated communication and sharing between and among organizations. It helped to break down the barriers between different parts of an organization.

- *Universality.* Intranets make communications available to everyone at the same time. At SAS, as a worldwide company, getting news and communications out to all offices had been difficult. Now, widely distributed documents are published on the SWW so people in Cary, North Carolina, and in Japan can get the most current corporate information at the same time.

- *Availability.* Intranets make communications available when you need them. Universal access and availability are at the heart of the Any[5] vision at EDS. According to Todd Carlson, CIO, *Any[5]* means that *EDS will provide untethered, pervasive communications that will make any information available in any form, to anyone, anywhere at any time.* EDS*WEB will help accomplish this ambition.

Some companies have started to expand this communication beyond the corporate walls. They are giving suppliers and customers access to their intranet to facilitate communication and coordination.

Enabled Sharing of Knowledge and Collaboration

A large number of the companies I spoke with said that a major result is that the intranet enabled sharing of information across the enterprise. This became critical to company operations.

Several said that the intranet had facilitated collaboration among widely dispersed workgroups. At Texas Instruments, collaboration via newsgroups has allowed TI'ers worldwide to work as teams.

AT&T also has geographically dispersed teams that use the intranet as their virtual meeting place. Widely dispersed ad hoc interest groups also have formed to share knowledge on various technical issues. AT&T currently runs a corporate-wide project that impacts all 280,000 employees. Teams post their status on the internal web for the entire organization to view. The field deployment teams use the intranet to communicate about the project and coordinate their scheduling.

At JCPenney, we used the intranet to collaborate on development of Web-based training. Several members of our Internet Team developed a training program for one of our computer systems. They posted a request on the team's newsgroup asking us to review it and make suggestions. There were lots of ideas shared, which when incorporated made it an even better product. This kind of collaborative review by peers can be quite useful as long as you're willing to detach yourself from the product being reviewed. You can't take any comments personally.

Empowered People

Intranets make it easy for leaders to share their vision with everyone. When people have access to information and share the vision, they have a powerful yardstick on which to measure their decisions and to take action. This can be a potent force for change or for empowering the organization to meet the needs of customers.

Facilitates Organizational Learning

Intranets provide a variety of tools to enable people to learn. Some of the ways intranets enabled organizational learning included:

◆ *Career development.*   The intranet can serve as a repository of career development information to allow employees to be proactive in their development. EDS provides mentoring tools, such as their Career Library, to assist employees in their development process. Career path information can include moves that are available and the training that is available or necessary for them.

- *Training programs.* Web-based multimedia is perfect for just-in-time training, and is far more likely to be up-to-date. These programs usually combine the richness of sound, pictures, animations, and videos for maximum impact. Multimedia greatly increases learning speed and retention.

- *Scheduling of training.* For those classes that are best taught in a classroom setting, you can post training schedules on the intranet and let people sign up for them directly.

- *Documentation.* The internal Web is also a great repository for documentation and support materials for existing systems and for new applications.

- *Newsgroups.* Newsgroups, both internal and external, provide for access to knowledge and information.

Facilitates Organizational Change: Breaking Down Bureaucracy

The first step in organizational change is for the leader to share his or her vision with the troops. The intranet facilitates this communication directly to everyone so that it doesn't become garbled along the way. This helps develop the shared vision and commitment necessary to propel the organization forward.

The intranet also provides a forum upon which you can champion your risk takers and make them role models for the rest of the organization. They are the ones who will drive the organizational change.

Facilitates Organizational Bonding

One somewhat unexpected result from having an intranet is that it helps build what the folks at Rockwell call a *corporate consciousness.* The Turner Broadcasting intranet has made their employees in other locations around the world feel part of the team. Intranets promote bonding of employees and bonding to the organization. People feel a lot closer and know that they're part of a team. When the organization communicates its vision, goals, and strategies, people know and understand what is happening and why, and become part of making it happen.

Improves the Quality of Life at Work

Intranets have even gone so far as to improve the quality of life at work. The SAS intranet has made the atmosphere around the workplace more open. People are more satisfied because they can easily find what they need. At SGI, the intranet has changed the way people work and how they feel about their work. The intranet has helped to facilitate an open culture and communication.

Other Ways Intranets Will Impact Organizations

The foregoing results are just the early results, since most intranets are in their infancy. Intranets will cause more profound changes to the organization. Next, we will look at some of those changes:

- How will the role of information technology change?
- How will business processes change?
- How will the culture change?

How Will the Role of Information Technology Change?

As you probably guessed from some of the early results, the role of the IT organization will definitely change.

When employees have access to the information they need to do their jobs, IT will no longer have control. Users can take responsibility for creating and maintaining their own data, and the IT group focuses on providing the infrastructure and services to the rest of the organization.

This suggests changes in the skills that IT people need. Though legacy applications will be around for a long time, once you convert them to the internal web, you won't need as many of those kinds of programmers. With the move toward Web-enabled databases as the site for all future applications development, organizations will value Web and database skills.

The browser will be the universal user interface. You can deploy it by simply downloading directly to the user's machine.

There may not be as much need for technical support people, other than to support the network and the servers.

Since browser-based applications are so easy to learn and use, you won't need as many computer systems trainers, either.

The areas that will increase are those related to providing content and helping business users figure out how to use information to benefit the business. Opportunities exist for those who can help users to structure and to present their information in a way that has the most value to the business. IT people will need to be more business-focused than ever.

In this dynamic and constantly changing business environment, change will be the only constant for IT folks. They must be constantly learning and improving their skills. Good communication skills will be critical. They will be working on more and more cross-functional teams to develop Web-based applications. They must have the ability to understand the business and to communicate in words that their business partners understand.

One of the most exciting changes is in the role of IT relative to the business. IT is increasingly being viewed as a vital partner in the business, not just as a bunch of techies. An interesting theme is partnership at the executive level. Information systems or information technology executives were not the only ones driving the intranet projects. Several companies had a steering committee or team, either formally or informally. These teams typically consisted of the chief information officer, or equivalent, the director of corporate communications or public relations, and sometimes the director of human resources. In a few cases, some other executive, such as a director of engineering or director of research and development, was a member of the steering team. These partnerships help elevate the stature of IT executives and help the business partners to take ownership of the project. There will be more of these partnerships in future information technology projects.

How Will Business Processes Change?

Intranets will significantly impact business processes as new tools come along. For instance, intranet workflow tools will streamline business processes and reduce the time required to complete the process. Part of the problem with many current processes is that so many people have to check this or check that. With information accessible to all, including the workflow application, the application may one day handle many of the approvals and checks automatically. This will not only take time out of the process, but will take costs out as well.

As groupware tools evolve, they will allow cross-functional teams to share knowledge and ideas and to help them be more innovative. With groupware tools and empowered users, reengineering can eliminate layers of management. It can also put the information technology in place to support the reengineered processes. This should help reduce the cycle time of processes as well as overall costs.

The communication enabled by the intranet will support virtual offices. Your salespeople can spend more time with customers and still have the information they need. This should result in increased sales.

It will also enable more telecommuting because telecommuters can easily connect to all the information they need. This is another way to remove cost from processes.

One way some companies are speeding up business processes is to have multiple shifts involved in the development of products. With an intranet, you can have a 24-hour workday by moving work around the globe with each shift. When each new shift comes in, it picks up where the last one stopped. This cuts process cycle time.

You can also incorporate reengineering best practices and process-management tools into the intranet for sharing information about processes. Several companies are doing this.

How Will the Culture Change? A New Information Community

These changes will be some of the slowest in coming because cultures don't change overnight. Changing a culture, other than by brute force, takes a lot of time. Here are some of the ways I think intranets will cause cultures to change:

◆ Sharing and cooperation will become the norm. People will stop hoarding information.

- Managers will manage results, not people. Extra layers of management will go away, if they haven't already. The role of the new manager is to coach and empower the team. Some of the things managers will do include:

  - Help the team formulate their vision.
  - Acquire resources for them, including any necessary training.
  - Remove roadblocks.
  - Encourage, guide, and support the team.
  - Act as a sounding board for them.
  - Stay out of the team's way as they achieve their results.
  - Reward the team for their accomplishments.

- Empowered people aren't afraid to try new things. Most people are self-motivated. Empowerment, enabled by shared vision and access to knowledge, will help people feel more confident and self-sufficient. They will feel empowered to take care of customers and solve problems. This will make them feel more in control, which is very gratifying.

- Cross-functional teams will become the way of doing projects in the future. They already appear to be the norm for building intranets. This is not just a project for the techies. These teams have representation from several functional areas. Several companies commented that these cross-functional teams were so successful that they have become the prototype for future projects.

  These cross-functional teams start the communication between employees and areas that normally wouldn't come in contact with each other. The intranet provides the mechanism to support this communication. These evolving relationships start breaking down the functional walls and create more communication among areas. This free-flowing communication serves to further empower employees.

♦ Political power used to mean having information and knowledge. When everyone has information, the power structure changes. This access to information, coupled with a shared vision throughout the organization, will move the whole organization purposefully in a single direction. Different departments will no longer suboptimize the organization's results to produce good results for themselves. Shared power will propel organizations forward into the future.

In Part 1, we have explained the nature of an intranet and how it will affect your organization.

1. Chapter 1 discussed what an intranet is, the history and growth of intranets, uses of intranets, pieces of intranets, and the future of intranets.

2. Chapter 2 discussed why organizations have created intranets, the advantages and disadvantages, and what size company it takes to need an intranet.

3. Chapter 3 discussed how intranets will change you and your organization, what is causing the changes, what changes will occur, and other ways intranets will impact your organization.

In Part 2, we will look at how to use an intranet and who is using them.

1. Chapter 4 will give lots of uses for intranets and will show examples of intranets from five companies.

2. Chapter 5 will give profiles of each of the 13 companies discussed in this book.

PART TWO

How Do You Use an Intranet and Who Is Using Them?

chapter four

How Do You Use an Intranet?

Introduction

Let's look at how companies use intranets or potentially could use them. Chapter 2 dealt with the reasons why companies want an intranet, and Chapter 3 dealt with the impact from having one. Therefore, in most cases, I won't discuss the reasons or results in this chapter.

As we look at these uses for intranets, I'll use examples from some of the companies that worked with me to create this book. Five of the companies I worked with were able to share intranet pictures with me. All five companies are in vastly different businesses. The companies and their industries are:

1. *Bell Atlantic*—Telecommunications
2. *EDS*—Technology services
3. *JCPenney (JCP)*—Department store retailing
4. *Texas Instruments (TI)*—Electronics manufacturing
5. *Turner Broadcasting System (TBS)*—Entertainment

We will take somewhat of a different look at uses for intranets. Here are two approaches to discussing intranet uses:

1. *Technical.*   The technical approach looks at how the tools work and the capabilities they have, and matches those tools to specific uses.

2. *Process.*   The process approach looks at business processes. It determines the tools and uses that add value to the process, and the impact that they might have.

Because this is a strategy book, I have chosen to focus on the process approach for intranet uses.

Before we proceed, I would like to emphasize one important aspect of processes. Processes focus on adding value for the ultimate customer. All steps of a process go into fulfilling a customer need or request. Let's call any process a *support process* if it doesn't directly impact the customer. Human resources, information systems and technology, finance, and legal are all support processes. These processes support other processes, such as product development and customer support, that *do* produce results for customers.

Processes seem to radiate from the corporate intranet home page, so I'll use that as a starting point. I'll talk about the services that are part of the home page and the processes that radiate out from it. We'll look at the following:

- Corporate internal home page
- Communications processes
- Support processes
- Product development processes
- Operational processes
- Marketing and sales processes
- Customer support processes

One of the things I expected was that the intranet of each company would mirror its industry and its culture. I was not disappointed. I will talk about that as I unveil each company's home page.

Corporate Internal Home Page

It's only logical to start our discussion of intranet uses with the corporate home page, since it is the starting point for launching off in many directions. There are things we find on the corporate home page that are for all processes and really don't belong to a specific process. I'll discuss these things under the umbrella of the corporate home page.

What are some of the things we normally find on a corporate home page?

- Tools and resources

  - Search tools
  - Index or table of contents
  - Site map
  - Feedback or comments
  - Internet acceptable use policies
  - Internet resources
  - Starting points
  - Support
  - Tutorials and help
  - What's new
  - Other tools

- Directories, phone books, and organization charts
- History and mission
- Services
- Organizational home pages

Let's look at our first corporate home page. Figure 4.1 shows Bell Atlantic's new home page for the Corporate Wide Web (CWW). It is being installed as I finish this book, so it does not contain current information.

The appearance is very professional, as you would expect, but it has a little bit of a playful feel to it. Its look is traditional, but not its colors. Although you can't tell from a black-and-white picture, the buttons are olive green on a white background. The icons combine olive, apricot, grape, tan, and black for a striking, sophisticated look.

Figure 4.1   Bell Atlantic Corporate Wide Web home page. (*Used with permission. Bell Atlantic Corporation, copyright 1996.*)

The banner of graphical icons at the top is very intuitive and includes:

◆ Search

◆ Index

◆ Map

◆ Feedback

Yes, that really is a cow you see on the feedback icon! We will look at each of these in more detail.

The buttons allow you to choose:

What's Hot	Some of the things in What's Hot are the Webmaster Forum, What's Hot at Media Relations, and Quality and Diversity programs.
News & Information	This includes the Internal News, Industry and Technology News, Bell Atlantic Stock, and Weather.
Corporate Directory	The Corporate Directory.
Customer Services	This includes such things as Online Forms, Products and Services, Research and Technology, Corporate Wide Web Handbook, and Special Interest Groups.
Organizations	This includes various areas of the company.
Library	The Corporate Library.

Notice that there is also a space available near the top of the page for advertising by outsiders to the Bell Atlantic community. Ads run a month at a time.

Tools and Resources

The types of tools and resources available on corporate internal home pages are fairly standard and consistent. Let's take a look at some of these.

Search Tools

First is the search tool. If you click on the Search icon on Bell Atlantic's CWW home page, you see the Bell Atlantic Search page (Figure 4.2). It provides a search of the CWW or the LegalWeb using a simple, free-text, or Boolean search. Interestingly, while you are using this page, the border around the Search icon turns neon green. That helps users know where they are.

Figure 4.2 Bell Atlantic Search. (*Used with permission. Bell Atlantic Corporation, copyright 1996.*)

From this page, you can link to Internet search engines, such as Yahoo, WebCrawler, and Lycos. There is also a place to click if you want to know more about having the search tool index your server so your documents are available from the Search page.

Index or Table of Contents

Next, if you click on the Index icon, you see the CWW Index page (Figure 4.3). This is a listing of all the things available from each of the buttons. An index makes it easier for users to find what they need on your site. This time the index icon has the neon-green border.

Figure 4.3   Bell Atlantic Corporate Wide Web Index. (*Used with permission. Bell Atlantic Corporation, copyright 1996.*)

Site Map

If you click on the Map icon, you see the CWW site map (Figure 4.4). It is a graphical view of the same information found in the index. This type of visual tool may be more comfortable to some of your users. An important thing to keep in mind is that you should make the navigation of your internal web as user-friendly as possible, which may require accommodating different learning styles.

Figure 4.4 Bell Atlantic CWW Site Map. (*Used with permission. Bell Atlantic Corporation, copyright 1996.*)

Feedback or Comments

If you click on the Feedback icon, you see the CWW Feedback page (Figure 4.5). Users can send comments and questions about the CWW to the Internet Services Center of Excellence, which is the group that runs the CWW.

At this point, let's move on to take a look at the Texas Instruments internal web. TI's *Welcome to the WWW!* page (Figure 4.6) is really more of a launching pad than an official home page.

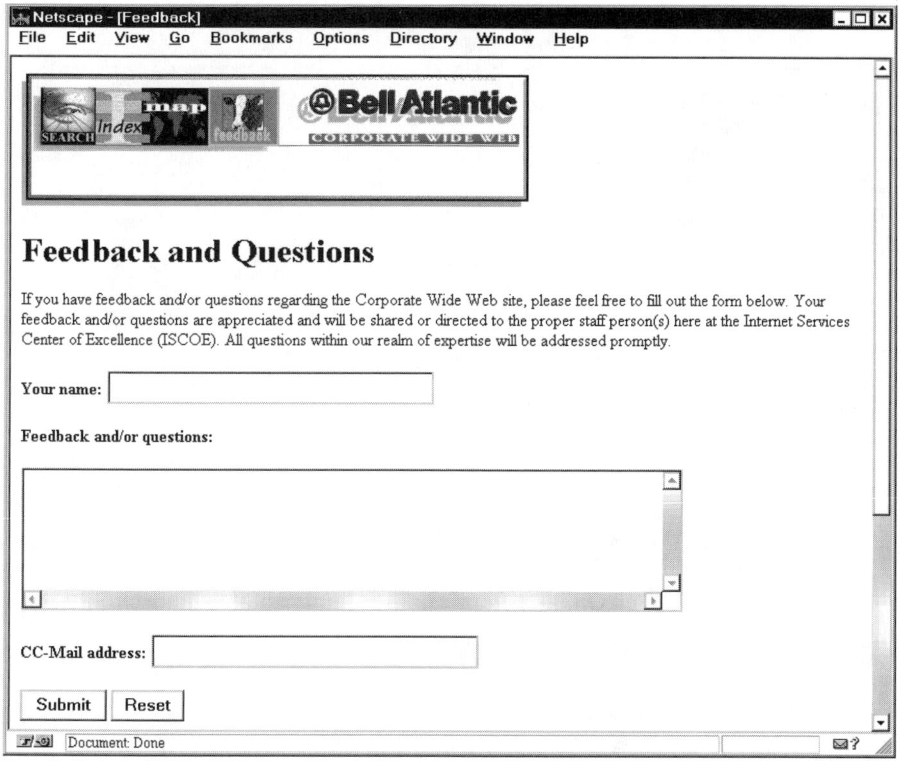

Figure 4.5 Bell Atlantic CWW Feedback. (*Used with permission. Bell Atlantic Corporation, copyright 1996.*)

Before we talk about that page, let me give you some clues as to what to expect to see on the TI internal web. TI is in the product development and manufacturing businesses, and has a software business as well. TI is a very engineer-oriented company, having been founded and run by engineers throughout most of its history. Engineers make up a very large percent of TI's population. As a generality, engineers tend to like things that are fast, efficient, and functional. They can be very fact-oriented, and don't like excessive words or descriptions. They often don't like, or trust, things that are flashy or glitzy. I know all this because I'm surrounded by engineers.

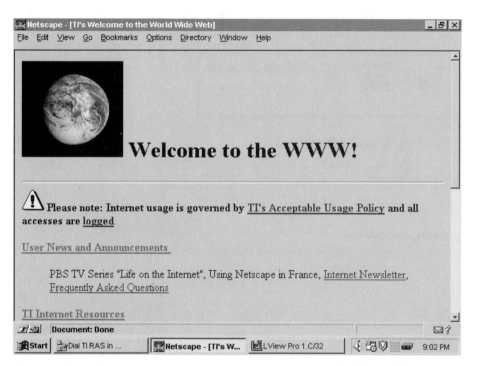

Figure 4.6   Texas Instruments' Welcome to the WWW! (*Used with permission. Texas Instruments Incorporated, copyright 1996.*)

You will notice that the TI internal web has a very utilitarian feel. There is minimal use of graphics. On the pages where you do find graphics, minimal use of colors allows faster loading. TI's intranet mirrors its culture.

Internet Acceptable Use Policies

The very first thing we see on the Welcome page is a link to TI's Acceptable Use Policy. TI makes this the first thing you see, so that before users venture onto the Internet they know how they should conduct themselves.

As we scan down the page (Figure 4.7), we see a list of topics you can link to:

◆ User News and Announcements
◆ TI Internet Resources

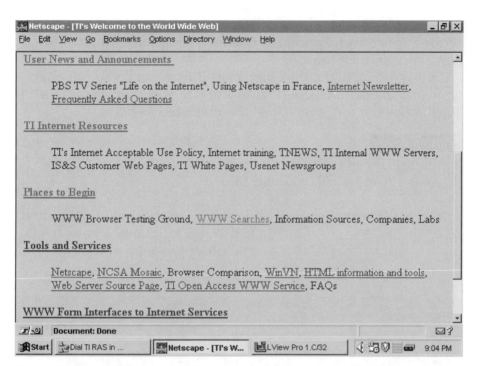

Figure 4.7 Texas Instruments' Welcome to the WWW! (continued). (*Used with permission. Texas Instruments Incorporated, copyright 1996.*)

- Places to Begin
- Tools and Services
- WWW Form Interfaces to Internet Services

Under each topic is a list of the information you'll find on a specific page if you link to it. This saves steps when you are looking for something specific.

Internet Resources

If you click on the TI Internet Resources link, you'll see a page (Figure 4.8) that also starts with a link to the Acceptable Use Policy. They are really serious about this! Here you find access to TI's external home page and FTP server, plus a list of internal web servers and Internet training. This is also the page to find TI's White Pages directory and the Usenet Newsgroups, though they don't appear in Figure 4.8.

If you go back to the Welcome page (Figure 4.7), you can click on Places to Begin, where (Figure 4.9) you will find access to a Testing Ground for users to test their web browsers.

Starting Points

If you page down the Places to Begin page to the Starting Sites (Figures 4.9 and 4.10), you will find:

Internet Information   Links to resources about the Internet, WWW, HTML, Web Servers, Unix, and other Net-related topics

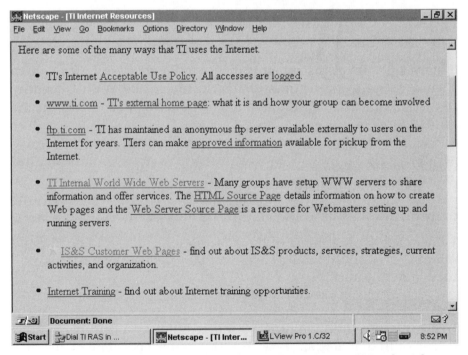

Figure 4.8   Texas Instruments Internet Resources. (*Used with permission. Texas Instruments Incorporated, copyright 1996.*)

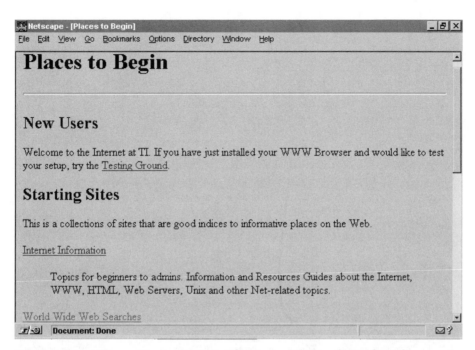

Figure 4.9   Texas Instruments Places to Begin. (*Used with permission. Texas Instruments Incorporated, copyright 1996.*)

WWW Searches	Links to search engines on the WWW
Index Sites	Links to collections of links about a variety of different topics
Companies on the Web	Links to locate companies on the WWW, plus general business resources on the WWW

Starting Sites or Starting Points lists provide a great way for new users to get out on the Web and quickly find the things they need. They are also great to help experienced users get to a desired location quickly without clogging their bookmark files. Most starting points pages have links to business and financial news, government sites, industry information, competitors, suppliers, and research sources, among others. If your culture per-

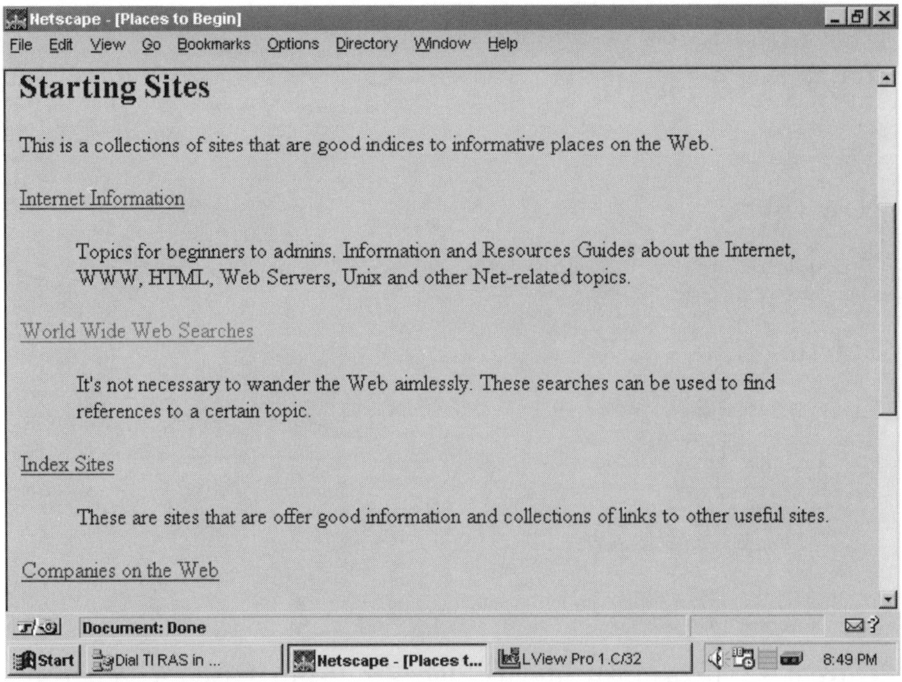

Figure 4.10   Texas Instruments Starting Sites. (*Used with permission. Texas Instruments Incorporated, copyright 1996.*)

mits, you can have links to fun sites such as the *Dilbert* comic strip page. A hearty laugh is a great way to start the day!

If you don't provide access to the Internet from your internal web, you might want to consider creating an internal site that mirrors your external WWW home page. You can use it as a staging server to test new content before you put it on the external Web site. You might also consider caching some of the Internet resources on your internal web server so people can have access to documents about things such as writing HTML.

TI currently has 115 internal web servers. The TI Web Registry (Figure 4.11) page has a place for registering your web server, plus a link to all registered internal web servers.

Let's continue our look at home pages with the JCPenney jWeb Home Page (Figure 4.12). At the top is a banner that says *JCPen-*

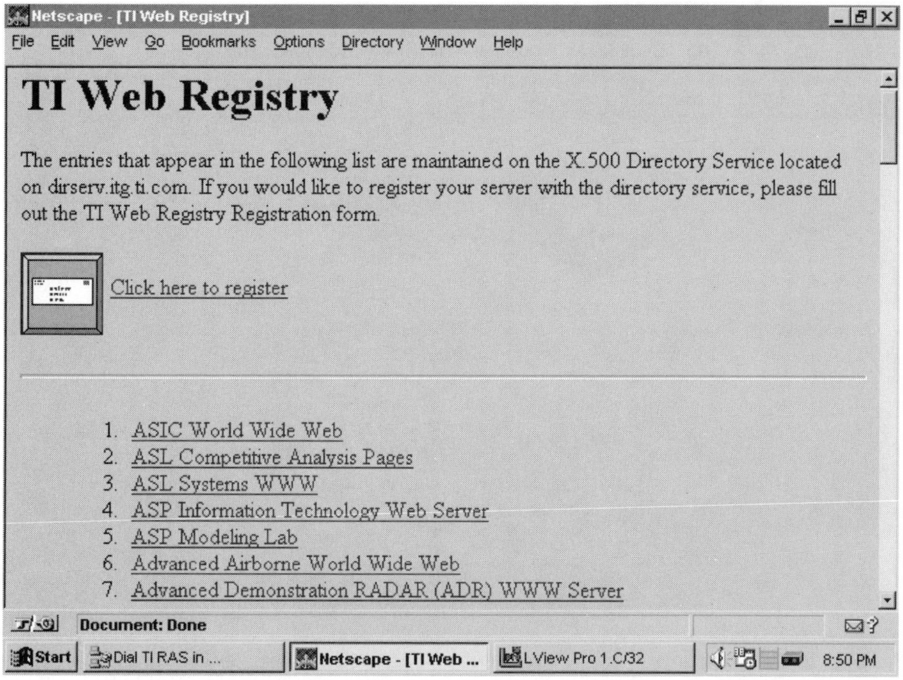

Figure 4.11 Texas Instruments Web Registry. (*Used with permission. Texas Instruments Incorporated, copyright 1996.*)

ney At The Speed of Change. This is a reminder to everyone of the need to do things faster and better.

The JCPenney Company is a retailer with a long and proud heritage. The company is looking forward to its one-hundredth anniversary. James Cash Penney started the company when he opened The Golden Rule store in 1902. He laid out the values that would guide his company in a statement called *The Penney Idea,* which includes:

1. *To serve the public as nearly as we can to its complete satisfaction.*
2. *To do all in our power to pack the customer's dollar full of value, quality and satisfaction.*

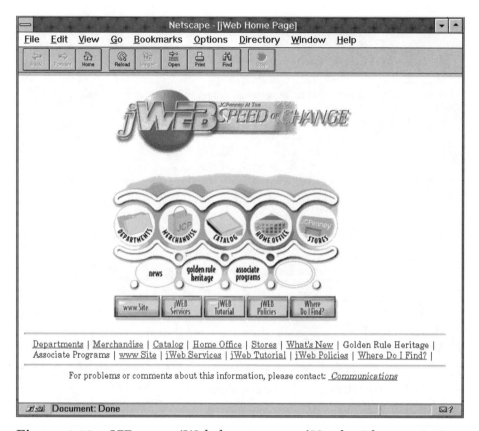

Figure 4.12   JCPenney jWeb home page. (*Used with permission. JCPenney Company, Inc., copyright 1996.*)

> 3. *To test our every policy, method and act in this wise: Does it square with what is right and just?*

These values guide the company today, just as they did in its early days. Though the company's values may seem old-fashioned to some, the company's merchandise certainly is not. It's a dynamic and progressive company focused on providing fashionable, high-quality merchandise at a good price.

The jWeb home page fits the company's heritage and direction. The colors are shades of gold metallic and bronze, accented by a pale-pink granite. It conveys a feeling of blending a stable and solid foundation with today's dynamic business environment.

On the home page, there are icons for each of the major business units and departments, such as:

Departments	Support organizations
Merchandise	The merchandise acquisition process
Catalog	The catalog business
Home Office	The corporate headquarters
Stores	The retail stores

In addition, there are ovals to click to see:

News	Newsletters, announcements, and special-purpose bulletins
Golden Rule Heritage	Company history and museum
Associate Programs	All kinds of things available to associates (employees)
News Flash	The blank oval on the right is filled in with "News Flash" if a hot news item is available

Support

On the JCPenney home page (Figure 4.12), there are buttons near the bottom. The first provides direct access to the JCPenney external Web site. The next button is for access to information about the jWeb Services group and the support they provide for users and developers of jWeb. There is a wealth of resources available there, including FAQs, information about tools, access to web publishing class schedules, and more.

Tutorials and Help

The next button is for the jWeb Tutorial. Though the browser is very easy to use, it never hurts to have information to help people get started. The tutorial tells about the capabilities of the browser and how to use them, as well as the features of jWeb and how to get around in it.

The last two buttons are for jWeb's Internet Policies and the "Where Do I Find?" tools, which help users locate what they need. "Where Do I Find?" includes a search engine, the corporate directory, and other similar tools. Finally, for feedback, there is a *MailTo* link to Communications, the owners of jWeb.

Before we move on to the next tool for corporate internal home pages, let's segue to the next home page, EDS. The EDS*WEB home page is infoCentre (Figure 4.13). It gives you the feeling of opening up a whole new universe of information. Its appearance is colorful, fun, and kind of far-out—they obviously designed it to grab your attention and draw you into it. The banner at the top is gold and the icons are bright primary blue and red. Colors of the universe graphic are blue, green, gold, yellow, orange, red, purple, and black.

The information available on infoCentre, the EDS Corporate Repository, includes:

Business	EDS Support Process Information, such as Financial, Purchasing, Accounting policies, Quality documentation, Customer contract information, Security, Staffing, and Product catalog
EDS Facts	Organizational Communications, such as Executive speeches, Leader profiles, Strategic intent, and Success stories
Employees	Human Resources information, such as Benefits, Career library, Job family matrices, Employee locator, Job postings, and Performance review tools
News	Organizational Communications, such as Corporate bulletins and announcements, Press releases, and Competitor information
Research	Marketing Research, such as Competitor profiles and Market research
Technology	Information Technology, such as Product evaluations, Standards, Communications, White

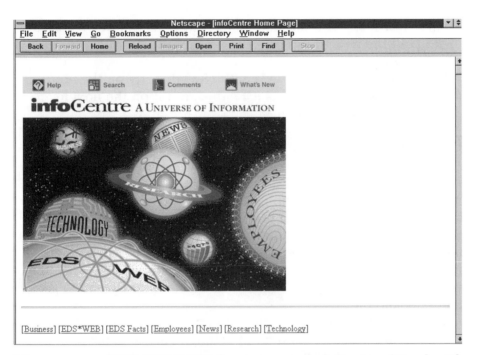

Figure 4.13 EDS EDS*WEB home page—infoCentre. (*Used with permission. EDS, copyright 1996.*)

	papers, Technology Architecture documents, Reusable code, Utilities, and Software distribution
Newsgroups	Interpersonal Communications, such as Internet newsgroups and EDS internal newsgroups

My perception of EDS is that it is a company known for its highly trained and highly professional people. They have mostly Fortune 200 clients. They project a very polished and precise image. While the infoCentre page is fun and inviting, most of the other pages I saw were very precise and polished. We will look at some of those as we continue our discussion of intranet uses.

What's New

You will note that infoCentre has the usual Help, Search, and Comments icons on the banner at the top. In addition, there's a

What's New icon. EDS has automated the What's New process to pick up all the new things on a daily basis and put them on the What's New page.

Some companies place the What's New directly on the home page, whereas others, such as JCPenney, put it on the next level down, under the News icon.

Other Tools

A company's stock price, updated throughout the day, is another feature that you sometimes see on corporate internal home pages. In other companies, you can find this feature on a resource page of some kind, perhaps with historical graphs of the stock price. Some companies have even implemented stock tickers across the bottom of the screen. Wherever you find it, this is one of those features that executives love. This can be a good way to encourage your executives to check the internal web frequently and to get them hooked on it.

There are other tools that are corporate in nature in that they cross over all processes and don't belong to any one process. EDS has just such a tool. EDS is a process-focused company, and it has a tool called the Process Sourcerer (Figure 4.14). The Process Sourcerer is a process management tool that assists users with the definition, customization, execution, and continuous improvement of business processes.

Directories, Phone Books, and Organization Charts

One of the most common uses of internal webs is to provide ways to communicate among people and organizations.

The EDS Organization Chart (Figure 4.15) is an employee locator where you can look up names, work addresses, organization charts, and electronic mail addresses. You can also do a search for an organization and see an organization explosion. This was an existing application that has been front-ended by the web.

Employee directories and organization charts come in many varieties and with different features. Most directories are simple searches that bring up the person's name, address, phone number, and e-mail address. Others branch to organization charts that

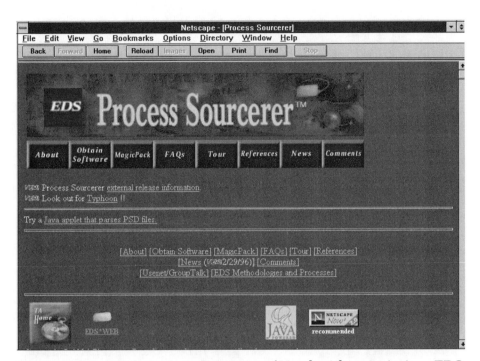

Figure 4.14   EDS Process Sourcerer. (*Used with permission. EDS, copyright 1996.*)

allow you to see visually the people who report to this person and to whom this person reports. Some organization charts even show pictures of people. Others provide links to personal home pages so you can get much more information. The features of these directories vary widely among organizations, and can even vary within organizations. For instance, at JCPenney each area is responsible for its own organization charts. Some areas choose to use pictures, and other areas choose not to.

Lauren Bednarcyk of SAS Institute talked about the use of organization charts and personal home pages on the SAS Wide Web (SWW).

> *Most divisions and departments at SAS Institute have estab-*
> *lished an online version of their organizational charts. These*
> *pages list the people that work in departments, divisions, and*

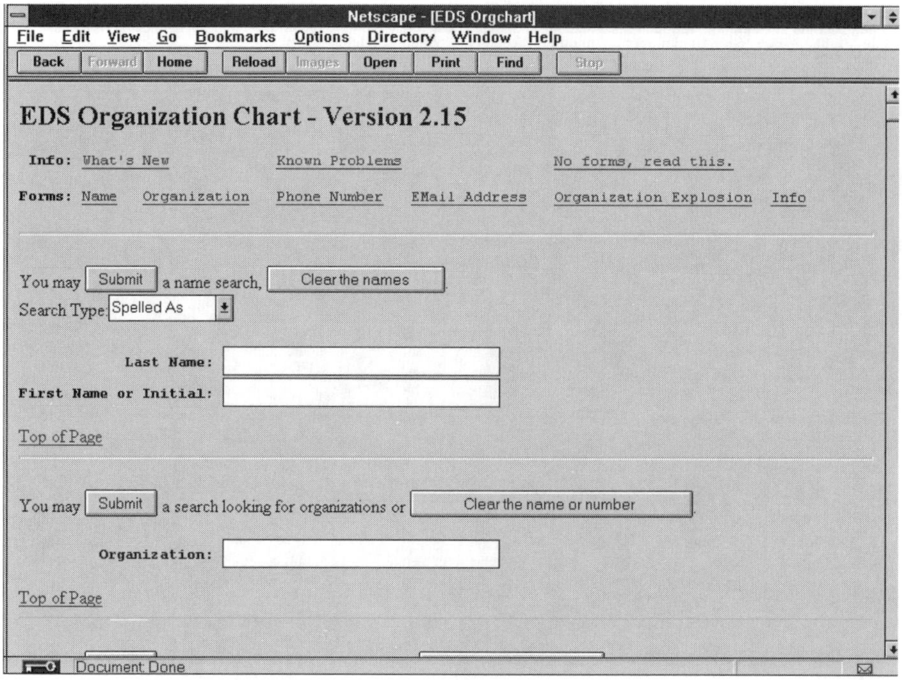

Figure 4.15   EDS Organization Chart. (*Used with permission. EDS, copyright 1996.*)

project teams, and often describe the responsibilities of the group. Generally structured in a hierarchy, they mirror the "reports-to" relationships between people, groups, departments, and divisions.

When an employee is new or begins to work on a new project with a different group of people, the person can easily get some background information about the unfamiliar organization. To fill in the detail behind organizations, individuals create personal home pages, where they usually list their office location, phone number, email address, and brief descriptions of their projects and responsibilities. Creativity, within practical limits, is also encouraged, and some personal home pages have become useful resources and reference points for many others.

*Building a personal home page is an excellent way for peo-
ple to enter the SWW; not only does it add to the pool of useful
organizational information, it also helps people learn HTML
and become familiar with authoring online documentation.
Furthermore, once they are given the chance to participate,
people get excited and enthusiastic about the SWW and often
go on to make new and innovative contributions to the SWW.
For these reasons, putting organizational information on the
SWW has been a worthwhile use of resources.*

While we're on the subject of personal home pages, companies
vary greatly as to whether they will allow them or encourage
them. Some see personal home pages as providing another information dimension within the organization. Others see them as a
waste of personal productivity.

Company History and Mission

Another thing you frequently find in conjunction with internal
home pages is information about the company history and its
mission.

If you look at the JCPenney jWeb home page in Figure 4.12, you
will see the Golden Rule Heritage icon. The company that J. C.
Penney founded almost 100 years ago has a strong sense of its history. This pride in the company's heritage comes through when
you see that company history and items from the JCPenney Historical Museum are accessible directly from the home page. You'll
find historical pictures, memorabilia, and information about past
leaders among the pages. There is also a copy of the company values statement, *The Penney Idea.*

You can also put your mission statement directly on your internal home page so that people always keep it in mind.

Services

Just as you need to locate people, you may also find it helpful to
have a way to locate company services and events. Some of the
services you may find links to include:

Facility and location information	Maps, contacts, conference room scheduling, and other administrative details.
Special events	Golf tournament, Blood Drive, United Way Fund Drive information, and other special events.
Cafeteria	Daily menus, hours of operation, and special events. Perhaps even pictures of things you can special order, such as birthday cakes or pizza, and instructions for ordering.
Credit union	Hours and services, newsletter, and maybe even loan applications. Perhaps you can check your account. The EDS Credit Union has its bulletin board on the internal web.
Fitness center	Sign-up information, hours, services, class schedules, newsletter, and special events.
Day care	Sign-up information, hours, rules, tour times, and special events for parents, such as Parent's Club. It may even have scanned-in artwork by the kids.
Health care center	Hours, services, information about doctors and nurses on staff, and schedules for special events such as health screenings, blood pressure checks, and flu shots.
Sports teams and hobbies	Baseball team, softball team, basketball team, golf team, bowling league, photography club, and other special interest groups.

Organizational Home Pages

In most of the companies I spoke with, all major departments and business units have their own departmental or business unit home pages. These organizations may be all around the world, but they're all accessible from a single point, such as the corporate internal home page or a server registry. These home pages usually contain the unit's mission, its responsibilities to the organization, the structure and organization charts, links to the home pages of subdivisions of the unit, projects that are under way, and the unit newsletter. There may also be links to unit-specific applications, such as purchasing's product catalog database.

Virtually every department or business unit has some kind of policies and procedures manuals, which you may find linked to its home page. Putting these on the internal web seems to be a high priority. This is especially true in the support-process parts of the organization, such as human resources, accounting and finance, information systems, and legal. Some areas even post their internal memos on the internal web rather than distributing them.

Communications Processes

The area known as corporate communications usually has the role of communicating with many different audiences. It must communicate with customers, shareholders, financial analysts, the general public, and employees. Often, public affairs is the area that communicates with those outside the company. Employee communications is the area that communicates with employees. These folks generally know what to say, and what language to use, to communicate with each different audience for their messages. Their biggest challenge is disseminating their messages, especially to audiences spread throughout the world. This is where the internal web comes in as a tool for the communications processes. I'll focus on two types of communications:

1. *Organizational communication.*   Official corporate, departmental, or business unit communications.

2. *Interpersonal and group communication.* Communications tools for use by individuals or workgroups.

Organizational Communication

Organizational communication is official company communication. It comes from management of the organization, a department, or a business unit. I'll talk about the following types of organizational communications:

- ◆ Corporate newsletters, bulletins, news, and magazines
- ◆ Business unit and departmental communications
- ◆ Repositories of corporate information

Corporate Newsletters, Bulletins, News, and Magazines

Companies want a single image conveyed to the world. Those responsible for establishing the corporate image should ideally determine the look and feel of a corporate external Web site. To reinforce that image, companies often use a similar format and feel throughout their internal webs. Corporate communications often decides this. The internal web usually has the same feel as existing internal corporate communications, such as newsletters, bulletins, and magazines.

Newsletters and magazines tend to reflect the personalities of the organizations they represent. They can be as individual as the companies. They may include the company vision, mission and goals, new company products and marketing programs, reprints of articles about the company from external sources, profiles of company personalities, new projects, and upcoming events.

EDSConnections on://line (Figure 4.16), is an electronic version of the EDS corporate newsletter. It features:

- ◆ Week in Review
- ◆ News Briefs
- ◆ New Business
- ◆ Trends

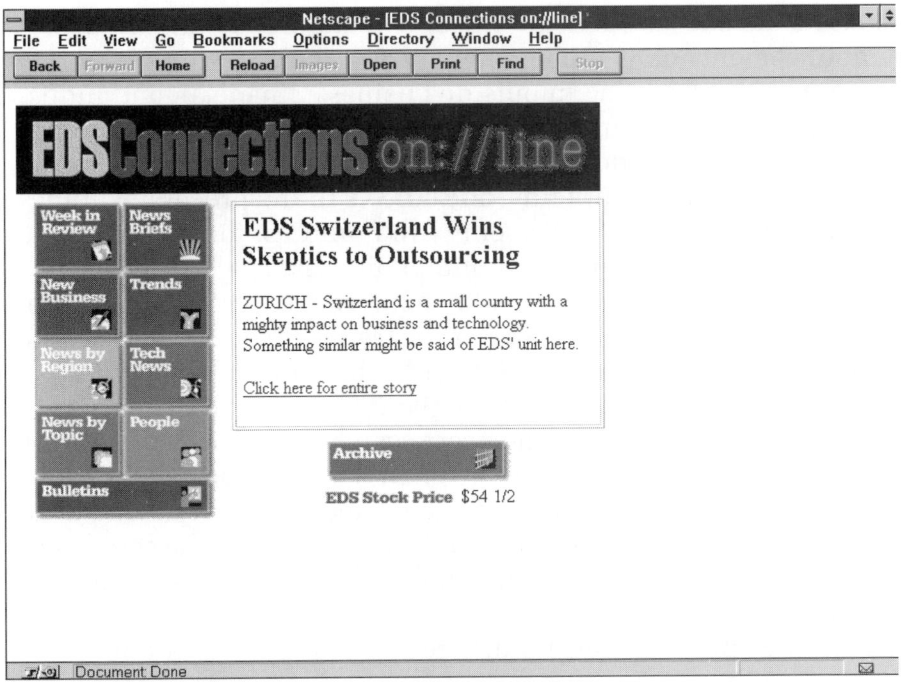

Figure 4.16 EDS newsletter—EDSConnections on://line. (*Used with permission. EDS, copyright 1996.*)

◆ News by Region
◆ Tech News
◆ News by Topic
◆ People
◆ Bulletins
◆ Archive
◆ EDS Stock Price

In addition to newsletters, companies are searching for better and better ways to distribute news flashes and bulletins to their employees. As you saw on the JCPenney jWeb home page (Figure 4.12), there was a News icon for regular news and bulletins, and an additional icon on the right, News Flash, which was blank at the time. Its purpose is to alert people to an urgent bulletin or announcement and get them to go read it.

Companies also bring in outside business, financial, and industry news for their employees through various news services. One of the latest ways to do this allows you to combine external news with your corporate bulletins, and EDS is in the process of doing this. It has reached an agreement with PointCast to use and support the PointCast network product. PointCast is a screen saver that you add to computers that have Internet access. It allows the user to specify what type news, industry information, sports, and weather information they wish to see. Then, PointCast regularly downloads that information throughout the day and displays it when the screen sits idle. The user receives broadcasts of personalized news (Figure 4.17, from http://www.pointcast.com) on a regular basis directly to the computer screen without having to go find the information. If a story headline appears on the screen and you want to read the story, you simply click on the headline and the entire story appears.

PointCast provides several different types of information:

◆ News—national, political, international, business, company, and industries
◆ Stock prices and graphs
◆ Weather
◆ Sports
◆ Lifestyle

When we talked about the corporate internal home page, we talked about putting the company's stock price there. Since Point-Cast delivers stock prices and graphs automatically (Figure 4.18, from http://www.pointcast.com), you may not want to bother setting up the stock price if you have plans to use PointCast.

The problem in a corporate environment is the drain on resources created when every computer goes outside the firewall to download this information for each individual user. EDS is now working with a PointCast server that brings the news inside the firewall so individual computers have only to go to the server to get their updates.

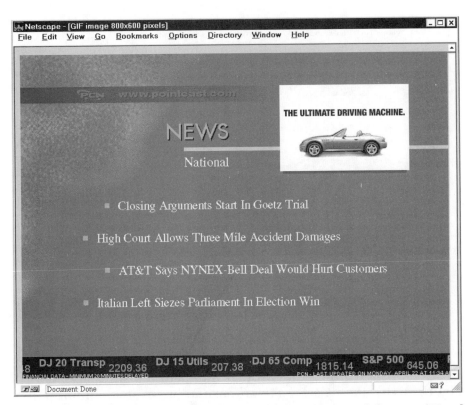

Figure 4.17   PointCast Network example of news delivery. (*Used with permission. PointCast Inc., copyright 1996.*)

One of the greatest benefits to corporations is the ability to incorporate their own bulletins and news stories in these broadcasts. The server broadcasts important news immediately throughout the organization. Further, more depth can be available on the internal web for conveying details. PointCast provides an example (Figure 4.19, from http://www.pointcast.com) of its network in use to broadcast news internally at EDS.

Business Unit and Departmental Communications

Not only do you find corporate newsletters on internal webs, you also find department and business unit newsletters, magazines, and other communications. For example, Connection (Figure

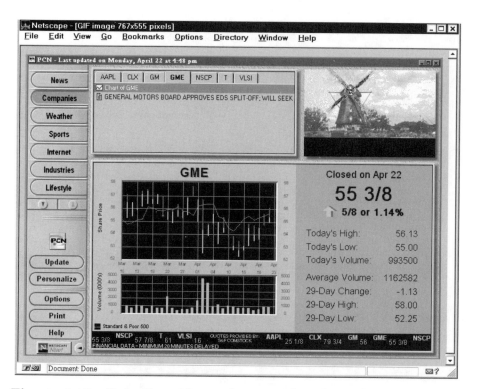

Figure 4.18 PointCast Network example of stock information delivery. (*Used with permission. PointCast Inc., copyright 1996.*)

4.20) is the newsletter for employees in JCPenney's Financial Services business unit. Regular features in this newsletter include:

◆ Events
◆ Career Moves
◆ New Hire
◆ Hot Topics
◆ Calendar
◆ Suggestions
◆ Penney Personals

This specific issue features information about management changes, guidelines for business casual day, team building steps,

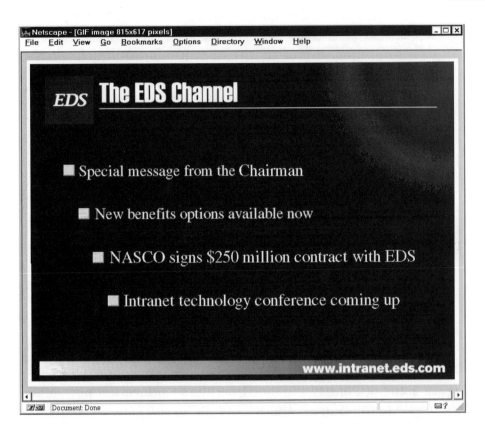

Figure 4.19   PointCast Network example of EDS broadcast. (*Used with permission. PointCast Inc., copyright 1996.*)

Health Fair information, Bring Your Child to Work Day information, and Coach's Corner: a chance to visit with the head coach.

Repositories of Corporate Information

In addition to newsletters, bulletins, and announcements, organizations often have a body of information that communicates to their employees what the company is all about and where it's heading. This information provides a context to the things that are happening in the business. Some of this information exists as press releases, executive speeches and presentations, profiles of leaders, success stories, information about competitors, and notes from company or industry forums or conferences. These items are

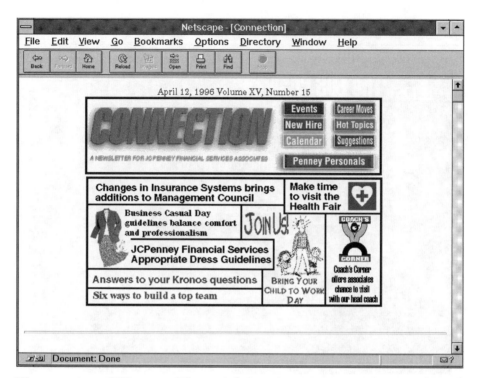

Figure 4.20 JCPenney Financial Services Connection newsletter. (*Used with permission. JCPenney Company, Inc., copyright 1996.*)

not just text, but are rich collections of multimedia, such as audio and video recordings.

Sun Microsystems, on their web site, talks about some of the ways they use their intranet for employee communications. This information comes from *How Sun saves money, improves service using Internet technologies* (http://www.Sun.com:80/960101/feature1/index.html/), which talks about ways that Employee Communications uses Sun's internal network.

> *Each quarter, Scott McNealy meets with all of Sun's vice presidents at an event dubbed "The Leadership Conference." Along with discussing Sun-related issues of the day, the attendees see demonstrations of new technologies.*

In a more rigid, hierarchical organization, attendees would be expected to share relevant proceedings of the event with their employees, which can be problematic. At Sun, notes and photos of the conference are posted on an internal Web page for all employees, around the world, to read and reference. Since notes of the meeting are taken as a matter of course, posting the proceedings costs little, yet yields untold dividends in keeping employees informed.

Sun appears to be blazing a trail in combining the richness of multimedia with its internal communications process. In the same article, Sun talks about a really innovative use of its internal web.

Perhaps the most innovative is WSUN Radio, a Web-based audio program employees can play on their workstations on demand. A representative program is The McNealy Report, *a monthly "radio talk show" hosted by Scott McNealy, Sun's CEO. In each program, Scott keeps employees up to date on Sun events, and conducts interviews with various Sun personalities, customers, and other notable people. As a talk show host, McNealy is humorous, personal, and occasionally serious.*

WSUN Radio is a hybrid application; it uses a home page as the primary user interface, and Sun's internal software distribution system to move the multi-megabyte audio files throughout Sun. WSUN Radio, and especially The McNealy Report, *is popular among employees, and is often used as technology demonstrations for customers.*

Sun is also using video to deliver communications to its employees on the internal web.

Interpersonal and Group Communication

Interpersonal and group communication tools allow people to communicate among themselves, keep current, and get answers to questions. The most widely used communication tool today is plain and simple e-mail. However, some additional intranet technologies are becoming popular as well.

- ◆ Newsgroups
- ◆ Chat
- ◆ Videoconferencing

Newsgroups

Many of the companies I spoke with provide their employees with access to Internet newsgroups to allow them to solicit information and to keep abreast of technology. In addition, many also make *internal* newsgroups available for employees. Since these tend to be somewhat proprietary in nature, I don't have pictures of internal newsgroups in use. However, they look just like and work just like Internet newsgroups, with the exception that they have participation only from inside the organization. In some cases, they are secure newsgroups that only certain users may access.

Some of the ways to use newsgroups include sharing expertise on a specific information technology or engineering area, sharing progress and notes about new product development and marketing strategies, and discussing changes to benefits.

Chat

Though chat groups aren't common inside companies at this time, they do appear to be growing. As companies expand beyond their internal webs, they seek other tools for knowledge sharing, communication, and collaboration. Chat is just such a tool.

EDS has a Global Communicators Network (Figure 4.21) that is a platform for sharing information, networking, and coordination of activities. The screen shot shows the area where you enter the chat rooms.

Chats typically are similar to conference calls in that they are prescheduled for a specific time. Instead of calling into the conference by phone, you call in by computer and participate from your keyboard. Chats may also be ongoing, similar to newsgroups, where you just join in with one that is already taking place.

Videoconferencing

While I don't have specific examples of companies using video-conferencing today on their intranets, it's inevitable that the day

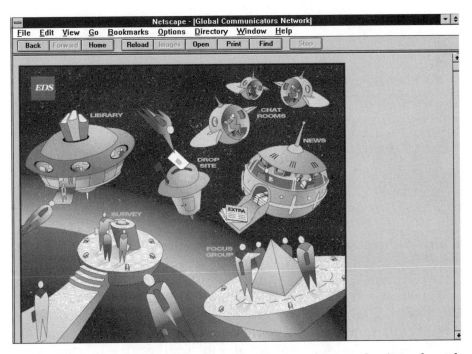

Figure 4.21 EDS Global Communicators Network. (*Used with permission. EDS, copyright 1996.*)

will come when it will be a commonly used tool for interpersonal and group communication. When bandwidth is more plentiful, many of the things that take place by chat today will take place by videoconferencing.

Support Processes

Let's move on to the support processes I mentioned earlier. This is really the area where much of the action has been so far.

If you recall, support processes are those that primarily benefit the company internally, and only indirectly benefit the end customer. Support processes include:

- ◆ Human resources (HR), or people processes
- ◆ Accounting and financial processes

- ◆ Information systems, or technology provisioning and support processes
- ◆ Legal Process
- ◆ Other processes, such as infrastructure or capacity development

Human Resources, or People Processes

To start our look at the ways companies use intranets for human resources, let's look at the intranet at Turner Broadcasting System. The Turner Broadcasting intranet started in an unusual way in that it was a project initiated by HR. The vice president of HR saw a need for treating employees as customers of the HR processes. It was his desire to find ways to better serve these customers. He commissioned a cross-functional team to look at the situation and recommend ways to accomplish this. This team recommended creating an internal web to provide employee services. The team created this web site by using focus groups of employees to identify the most important content and the goals for the internal web. A member of the team who led the project now has full time responsibility for an area called Employee Services Development.

Turner Broadcasting involved a creative agency in the development of the internal web content and kiosks for employees who don't have computers. Since Turner Broadcasting is in the broadcast and entertainment business, it decided to create its internal web as a network and treat it like its other networks. They called this network Turner Employee Services Network, or TESN (Figure 4.22). In keeping with the network theme, the company even employed an ad agency to help promote this network among employees.

Though Turner Broadcasting has been using an internal web to solicit reviews and comments on Web content before moving it to the external Web site, TESN is the first purely internal web application, and one that focuses totally on employees.

TESN is quite colorful—just what you would expect from a company in the entertainment business. The TESN logo is black and white and has that movie look to it. The banner is also black and white. The screen is very graphical and colorful in blue, pur-

Figure 4.22 Turner Broadcasting System—Turner Employee Services Network home page. (*Used with permission. Turner Broadcasting System, Inc., copyright 1996.*)

ple, yellow, red, tan, black, and white. There are six TV screens showing the six different programs on TESN, which are:

- ◆ Employee Information
- ◆ The Price You'll Like, with Bob Barter
- ◆ Inside Employee Benefits
- ◆ HR Review
- ◆ Purchasing Picks and Logistic Lineups
- ◆ Take One: Executive Message

At the bottom of the web page are icons for *What's Hot, Changing Channels,* and *Information by Location,* with maps and facility information for all Turner Broadcasting locations.

This internal web fits well with the entertainment-oriented Turner culture, which is very advertising and network savvy. It was very appropriate that the company rolled out TESN with an ad campaign featuring posters, mailings, and lots of hoopla, including kickoff meetings in most Turner Broadcasting locations.

Policies and Benefits

Some of the most fertile areas for using intranets are in HR, particularly policies and benefits. Manuals and benefits information have been among the first internal web applications at many companies. Turner Broadcasting employees, for instance, can use Inside Employee Benefits (Figure 4.23) for accessing:

♦ About Your Retirement Plan
♦ General Employee Benefits

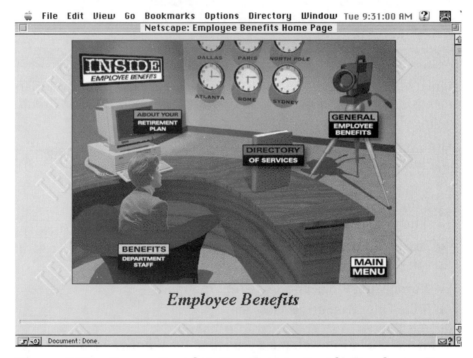

Figure 4.23 Turner Broadcasting System Inside Employee Benefits. (*Used with permission. Turner Broadcasting System, Inc., copyright 1996.*)

- Directory of Services
- Benefits Department Staff

Some of the uses for intranets in HR include:

- Publish policy manuals and benefits information.
- Scan benefits and enrollment forms for on-line access and printing.
- Use fill-in forms to query databases for status information, such as which medical and dental plan employees have, how many vacation days they have left, and which benefits options are available to them.
- Use on-line forms to enroll in benefits plans, make status changes, such as adding dependents, or to update other information.
- With security, provide your retirees with the same kinds of access that active employees have. They could use your Internet site to gain secured access to the intranet. They could easily access information about benefits, check their status, and make changes. Interestingly, access by retirees was an idea that some of our executives especially liked in my Internet and intranet presentations.

These are just a few applications to consider. There are lots more applications, which will vary from company to company. When you're ready to create HR applications for the intranet, take some time to talk with the people in HR who spend much of their time fielding questions.

- What are the most commonly asked questions, and what are the answers? What are the most common misconceptions? What clarifications are needed? Use this as a starting point for an on-line FAQ.
- Look at all the policies and procedures manuals. Which change the most frequently? Which are the most expen-

sive to print and distribute? These are good candidates for an internal web.

◆ Which forms are used most frequently? You can turn them into on-line forms that update the databases.

◆ Are there large groups of people with whom you need to communicate or who need updates (such as everyone enrolled in the retirement plan or a specific medical plan option)? Consider creating newsgroups where you can post changes and updates and seek feedback on changes needed in benefit plans.

Once you have done all this, you will have freed the HR staff from answering routine questions and handling forms and allowed them to handle difficult problems and facilitate improvements in benefits and procedures.

Let's just imagine for a moment the following application: Your child needs to see a certain kind of doctor. You first go to the medical plan information on your internal web to confirm coverage. After that, you look up the list of specialists in the medical plan, and even browse through their credentials to make it easier to identify the right specialist. After narrowing your list to a few specialists, you post a message to the medical plan newsgroup asking if anyone has experience with the doctors you've selected or if anyone can recommend a good specialist. Later, you get an answer that one of the specialists you chose is very abrasive and abrupt—not a good choice for treating a child. That message includes a recommendation for a specialist who has treated a similar problem.

Before the intranet, you would have had to track down the latest copy of the medical plan's list of doctors and hope that it was still current. With the intranet, there's much more information at your fingertips, and you can be quite confident that it's up-to-date. With an intranet, not only is the information available easily, but it allows you to make better-informed decisions.

Payroll

Payroll is another area of HR that can benefit from use of an internal web:

- ◆ Employees can submit forms to request automatic deposit of payroll checks.
- ◆ Employees can submit forms to change withholding and deductions.
- ◆ Employees can fill out on-line time sheets and submit them to payroll.
- ◆ Managers can submit pay-increase forms.

Job Postings

Another frequent use of intranets is for job postings. EDS uses an internal job-posting system, called E*TIPS (Figure 4.24), that allows employees to search for job openings. These openings are available throughout the corporation. You can search on a multitude of criteria, such as job category, job title, city, state, and country. This application already existed and has had a web front end added.

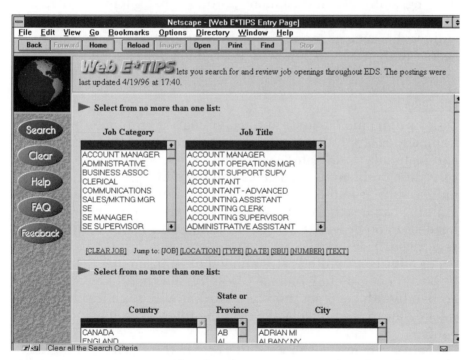

Figure 4.24   EDS E*TIPS job posting system. (*Used with permission. EDS, copyright 1996.*)

Turner Broadcasting also has a job-posting system. Turner Broadcasting is making TESN available on kiosks in central locations, since not everyone has a computer.

Career Development

EDS also has career development tools available on the internal web. Its Career Library is a repository of the corporate curriculum. It contains all the classes and other development activities required for each skill or behavior identified in the corporate framework. Both corporate-wide and job-family-specific skills have a variety of activities to support them.

With the knowledge of what skills and behaviors you need for a specific career path, you can then use the web to schedule classes or access on-line training.

Some organizations are allowing the use of personal home pages as a career development tool. You can list information about your training, skills, accomplishments, professional interests, outside activities, and interests. You might even post samples of your work and results, such as reports or plans. Through search tools, managers can then find people with the right skill sets for an unusual assignment, to tackle new projects, or to try out new technology.

Training

Today's dynamic business and technology environment puts a tremendous strain on training departments to keep courseware and materials up-to-date. An internal web is a convenient way to solve this problem. It even gives you the ability to use multimedia, such as audio and video, on your internal web for training. Training can be real time, always up-to-date, and accessed when needed. In other words, it's just-in-time training. It can also be self-paced.

For now, bandwidth is still enough of an issue that the internal web won't completely replace CD-ROM, but that time will come. As bandwidth becomes more plentiful, it will be common to conduct distance learning classes over the internal web using video-conferencing tools.

There's still an issue of when it's best to train in a classroom setting. There are some subjects you will always deliver by traditional classroom methods. For them, you can use the internal web to provide course catalogs and schedules, and to register people for training. You can also use it for training follow-up, such as course evaluations. You can do testing before and after training to determine the level of knowledge gained. Posttesting may occur immediately after the course and again several weeks or months later to determine the retention and application of the course materials.

The EDS Technical Consulting Continuum (Figure 4.25) provides ongoing education within EDS. Its internal web site provides curriculum, schedules, news, chats, and information about the training staff.

Other

There are other HR applications that are good uses for intranets. For instance, with the appropriate security, you can do perfor-

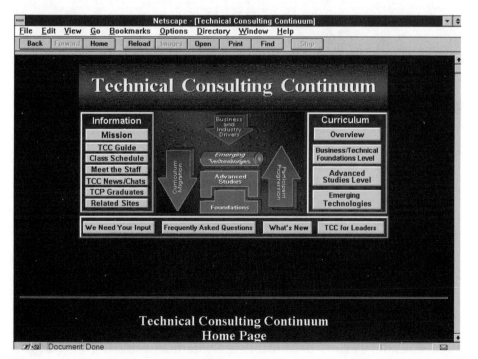

Figure 4.25 EDS Technical Consulting Continuum. (*Used with permission. EDS, copyright 1996.*)

mance reviews on the internal web. Turner Broadcasting has two other interesting applications under the umbrella of HR.

Since purchasing and logistics (Figure 4.26) are support activities at Turner Broadcasting, the company has incorporated them into TESN to give employees information on how to purchase the supplies, equipment, and services they need.

Turner Reciprocal Advertising Corporation (TRAC) (Figure 4.27) is an interesting employee benefit. The TRAC Barter Group is a clearinghouse for trips and other goods and services that Turner Broadcasting receives in exchange for advertising time. These goods and services are sold to Turner Broadcasting employees, and others, at a discount. This is the most frequently accessed site on TESN.

Figure 4.26 Turner Broadcasting System Purchasing and Logistics. (*Used with permission. Turner Broadcasting System, Inc., copyright 1996.*)

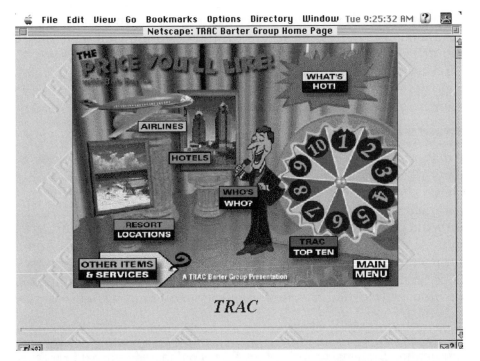

File Edit View Go Bookmarks Options Directory Window Tue 9:25:32 AM
Netscape: TRAC Barter Group Home Page

TRAC

Figure 4.27 Turner Broadcasting System TRAC—Turner Reciprocal Advertising Corporation. (*Used with permission. Turner Broadcasting System, Inc., copyright 1996.*)

Accounting and Financial Processes

There are many potential uses for intranets in accounting and
financial processes. Every accounting department has policies and
procedures that they can place on the intranet. This includes
accounts payable, accounts receivable, financial accounting, tax,
and auditing. In addition, you can put expense reports and requisitions on the internal web for filling out and routing to the appropriate area of accounting.

Financial Reports

Internal webs are good repositories for both publicly accessible
financial reports and confidential financial reports. Public companies release their financial reports to the press and analysts. If

these are openly available on the internal web, then everyone can see them. Companies can secure confidential financial reports by requiring a password or other security measures to access them. This keeps management up-to-date, with the latest information right at their fingertips. You can even add simple queries to allow managers to slice and dice the information in a variety of ways.

Asset Management

Another use for intranets is for asset management. Sun Microsystems talks about how it does this with its Asset Managers Workbench (*How Sun saves money, improves service using Internet technologies* at http://www.Sun.com:80/960101/feature1/index.html). By creating forms that query and update the corporate fixed-asset accounting system, managers can get information regarding their fixed assets. They can request that assets be transferred without ever having to contact the accounting department. Previously, they had to submit requests to accounting, a process that took several days.

Information Systems, or Technology Provisioning and Support Processes

Intranets are being used for all kinds of IS applications, some for internal use within the IS community and others for supporting the user community. I will talk about some selected uses, but this could probably be a whole book in itself.

TI's Information Systems & Services Home Page (Figure 4.28) shows its department mission and provides the following information:

- ◆ Products
- ◆ What's New
- ◆ Services
- ◆ Organization
- ◆ Futures

In addition, there are Search and Feedback icons, plus a Glossary, and my favorite, Acronyms. TI has made it easy for users to find their way around the division.

Figure 4.28   Texas Instruments' Information Systems and Services Division. (*Used with permission. Texas Instruments Incorporated, copyright 1996.*)

Software and Applications Development and Delivery

Here are just a few examples of using the intranet for software and applications development and delivery. EDS uses its internal web in software development and delivery with the following:

- ◆ Electronic software distribution
- ◆ Repository for software components
- ◆ Application development criteria and methodologies

An application for development and documentation at SAS uses CGI scripts to extract program structure dynamically, to show class, and to link to documentation about those classes on the fly. The structure of the software is being documented while it is still being developed.

SAS also provides downloaded resources for software developers on its internal web, such as papers from conferences brought in from the Web.

As software development starts to incorporate Java applets, this will allow the delivery of richer applications via the intranet.

And of course, the internal web and newsgroups can be used to provide progress reports and status of development projects, to share leading-edge technologies, and for problem solving.

User Documentation and Electronic Performance Support Systems

One thing an intranet does especially well is allow you to create user documentation and electronic performance support systems. You can easily embed pictures of screens and create an easy walk-through demonstration of how to use specific features of an application. You can even add sound and video to make it more effective.

Technical Support and Help Desks

IT departments are, like other departments, trying to do more with less. This puts a lot of strain on technical support and help desks. One solution is to use the intranet to let internal customers help themselves. Here are some ways to do that:

- ◆ Take the help desk's most frequently asked questions and put them into a FAQ.
- ◆ Create a form to allow users to search the help desk's own database.
- ◆ Create internal newsgroups for users to post questions and get help from other users.
- ◆ One day we will even use videoconferencing on the internal web to allow support staff to see what's happening on the user's machine so they can solve the problem more quickly.

If users can solve some of their problems themselves, that frees the support staff to deal with more difficult problems.

Network Management

The use of intranets for network management is just starting to emerge. Network managers can use the intranet to keep track of the resources in the network and to manage the environment itself.

Information and Knowledge Repositories

Some companies are adding information tools and repositories to their intranets. TI is creating a TI-wide information repository composed of Saros Mezzanine document repositories, web servers, and Lotus Notes servers, all front-ended by web browsers, and with search and retrieval across all of those server types. Booz Allen is planning to add decision support, engagement management, and EIS applications to their intranet.

EDS is working to convert much of their information into knowledge. This involves taking that information and putting it in the context of processes, and then making it available on the internal web.

Cache Internet Resources

Companies that choose not to provide Internet access can pull Internet resources in-house and keep a copy on the server for easy access. Companies that do provide Internet access may want to consider putting a copy of frequently accessed resources or URLs on their intranet. Make sure that when the resource changes, you download and cache a new copy.

Legal Process

Your legal organization probably has procedures manuals and documentation that are likely candidates for publishing and providing on an intranet. You can put legal library resources on the intranet. Draft contracts could be available on the intranet to speed up the process of writing and approving contracts.

Other Processes

The other support processes I talked about are fairly universal throughout most organizations. There may be other, more specialized, processes in your organization that can benefit from an intranet, too. These vary from company to company.

One supporting process that may be somewhat common is the infrastructure or capacity development process. This is the process that builds your factories, distribution centers, stores, or any other infrastructure required in your business. At JCPenney, Construction Services is responsible for the construction of new stores. This department posts progress reports on its internal web site, including pictures of stores during construction and after completion. For instance, few of us ever got the chance to visit the new stores being constructed in Chile and Mexico. On the web site, we could keep up with the progress and see what each new store looked like.

Product Development Processes

Now we are finally into the core business processes—those that produce a result for customers. It's much harder to show pictures of intranets used in core processes because these processes are proprietary in nature. In other words, core processes generate the competitive advantage of organizations and few companies are willing to share this kind of information.

Research and Development

There are several ways to use intranets in R&D, depending on the business of the organization.

Corporate research libraries may be heavy users of the Internet for research. They may access Securities and Exchange Commission filings, patents and trademarks, government economic and demographic data, industry data, and international trade information. This information is very useful for market research and product development research. You can even pay a fee to acquire information databases and put them on your internal web to share with all areas of your company. For instance, EDS has the Patent Information Services database, which provides full-text patentability and infringement searches of 1.7 million U.S. patents and weekly analysis of newly issued patents.

Amgen, a pharmaceutical company, has found that their corporate library is the most effective of their internal web applications.

In large research organizations that have researchers scattered around the globe, it can be quite helpful for researchers to publish their project descriptions and findings on the internal web. This keeps fellow researchers informed and encourages collaboration. In addition, researchers can also publish the proceedings from research conferences they have attended.

The R&D areas at SAS put their documentation on the SWW. This includes documentation for software developers, such as requirements and specifications, plus planning and direction documents.

Engineering

In the engineering part of the product development processes, there are many different applications that you can do with an intranet.

- ◆ Publish engineering reference information, such as design guides, engineering reference materials, and source pages, as they do at TI.
- ◆ Publish expertise on specific issues gained through the product development process.
- ◆ Publish customer needs and issues and customer feedback.
- ◆ Publish information about competitors' products and how well they meet customer needs.
- ◆ Create project newsgroups to promote and facilitate brainstorming and communications within product development teams.
- ◆ Publish research papers from colleagues and conferences.
- ◆ Publish information about engineering projects, including schedules, progress, plans, and team members.
- ◆ Publish product specifications, designs, and changes.

- ◆ Develop newsgroup communities of expertise where engineers ask questions and discuss topics related to their area of expertise. They may also request comments on their drawings or plans. These discussions form a knowledge base from which others can learn.
- ◆ Share design drawings and computer-aided design models with suppliers during planning and design by providing suppliers with access to the internal web. This can dramatically reduce product development time.
- ◆ In the future, use intranet-based computer-aided design tools to develop drawings and designs. Anyone with a browser could access the drawings and perhaps even attach comments to them.
- ◆ EDS has created an Engineers Affiliate Network to leverage engineering expertise by tying all EDS engineers into a virtual organization.

Your only limitation is your creativity and innovation when it comes to creating engineering applications.

Operational Processes

Operational processes are also core processes in that they produce results for customers. They may include:

- ◆ Purchasing
- ◆ Electronic data interchange
- ◆ Inventory
- ◆ Manufacturing
- ◆ Professional services development

Purchasing

Companies are moving toward providing their internal product catalogs on the intranet. They generally already have the application and have just added the web front end to it. The EDS product catalog (Figure 4.29) is an example of this. The application already existed—they just added the web front end. This product catalog provides the price, inventory status, average lead time, technical specifications, and more on over 25,000 systems, subsystems, peripherals, software products, and services from over 700 suppliers. A user can use the catalog by product or manufacturer, "hot products," availability, manufacturer partners, e-mail address index, search, and quick tour. This catalog hooks to an ordering system that allows them to order supplies or to order products from vendors.

To keep such a database updated, you could allow suppliers to sign on to your intranet to insert technical specifications and product descriptions into the database through forms or database uploads. The system could alert the purchasing department of

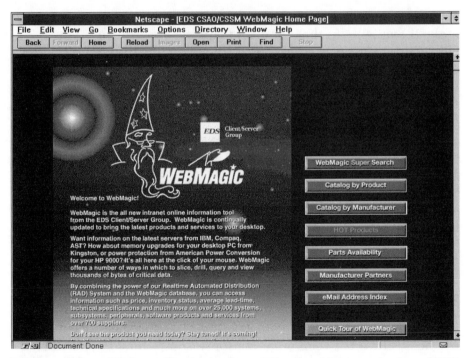

Figure 4.29   EDS product catalog. (*Used with permission. EDS, copyright 1996.*)

exactly what the supplier had submitted. You might even allow suppliers to advertise their products on your database, for a fee.

Some companies' products and processes don't lend themselves to product catalogs, such as those with seasonal and fashion products. They can publish preferred vendor lists and reviews from vendor site visits on their internal webs.

At JCPenney, merchandise purchasing is a core process required to stock over 1,200 stores and a catalog business. To do this, JCPenney has operations and employees in 37 countries. Buyers and product developers travel the United States and the world to locate just the right high-quality and fashionable merchandise. Therefore, Travel Procedures and Guidelines (Figure 4.30) is an important intranet application for purchasing. It provides all the expected travel information, plus contacts for assistance and specific travel information for any country to which a buyer may travel.

Once JCPenney buyers select which merchandise to carry, they make it available to the stores and catalog for ordering. The Direct Broadcast System (DBS) Buying Process (Figure 4.31) details the process involved in getting the merchandise selections to the stores for them to choose the merchandise they wish to carry. Any user can click on a picture in the process to see the details of that step.

Selecting and purchasing fashion merchandise is far more complicated than it might seem. A Glossary of Merchandising Terms (Figure 4.32) helps simplify the process for JCPenney store merchandisers and others who are selecting merchandise for customers. The glossary is just one of many pieces of merchandising information on the intranet, which includes merchandising procedures manuals and documentation for merchandising systems.

Electronic Data Interchange (EDI)

Large volumes of paper documents, such as purchase orders and invoices, move between organizations. Computers on one end generate many of these documents and then print them for mailing. Once received on the other end, someone has to enter them

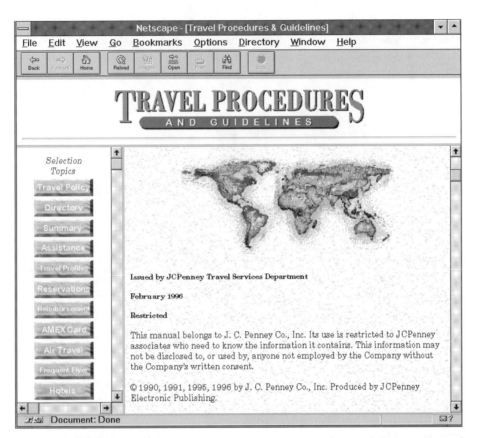

Figure 4.30 JCPenney Travel Procedures and Guidelines. (*Used with permission. JCPenney Company, Inc., copyright 1996.*)

into a computer for processing. This is extremely wasteful of paper, time, and people resources.

The solution to this has been electronic data interchange (EDI), which has been quite popular among businesses for the past decade. EDI transactions have a standardized format that allows them to flow from the computer at one business to a computer at the other. Recently, companies have started to experiment with using the Internet for EDI as a cheaper alternative to the value-added networks they have been using.

A trend in EDI is the use of intranets to facilitate the direct transfer of orders from one company to another. Bell Atlantic has

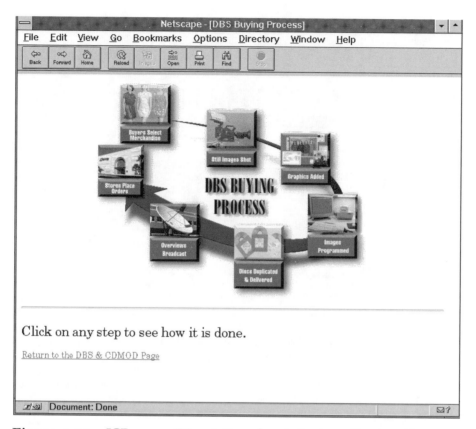

Figure 4.31   JCPenney Direct Broadcast System Buying Process. (*Used with permission. JCPenney Company, Inc., copyright 1996.*)

just recently begun to use the intranet for electronic commerce through its vendor/dealer order placement application.

Inventory

Companies can make inventory information available on the intranet. They can create forms that allow people to query inventory databases or they can use web front ends on existing inventory applications. Those companies that need inventory reports can publish them dynamically on the web by using HTML templates to convert the data to a report format.

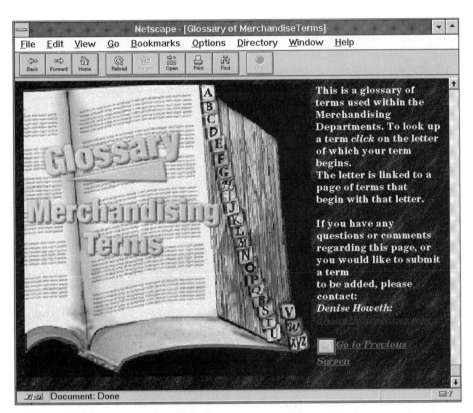

Figure 4.32 JCPenney Glossary of Merchandising Terms. (*Used with permission. JCPenney Company, Inc., copyright 1996.*)

Manufacturing

Manufacturing can use an intranet to post production schedules, procedures, bills of materials, and quality statistics. For global businesses with manufacturing units in various countries, intranets provide a way to share information about production processes. This shared information can help speed the production process and allow you to get your products to market faster. Intranets can be particularly useful for bridging time zone differences and language differences. The ability to use pictures and graphics aids communication and comprehension among those speaking different languages.

Professional Services Development

In consulting companies where the product is intellectual capital and the services it can provide, intranets can help in the collection and development of that intellectual capital. Booz Allen uses Knowledge On Line, its intranet, as a repository for reports, proposals, best practices, and collaboration conferences.

Marketing and Sales Processes

Marketing and sales processes are also core processes that benefit the customer. Again, since these are proprietary processes, companies are typically unable to share this information.

Marketing

In addition to some proprietary marketing information, TI's Semiconductor (sc) Marketing home page (Figure 4.33) provides access to TI internal semiconductor publications as well as TI semiconductor publications for customers. TI also references publications of interest to its internal web community.

Marketing provides support to sales by providing up-to-date information and materials on an internal web. Some of this may even be on your external Web site, depending on your sales process and who your customers are. This can vary depending on whether the customers are businesses or consumers, but the information generally includes:

- ◆ Sales and marketing strategies.
- ◆ Product direction.
- ◆ Market research information. Companies often put their market research on their internal webs. Sun has added a new twist to this. They acquire a competitive analysis package from an outside firm, and all of Sun's employees can link securely to this firm's Web site to access it (*How Sun saves money, improves service using Internet*

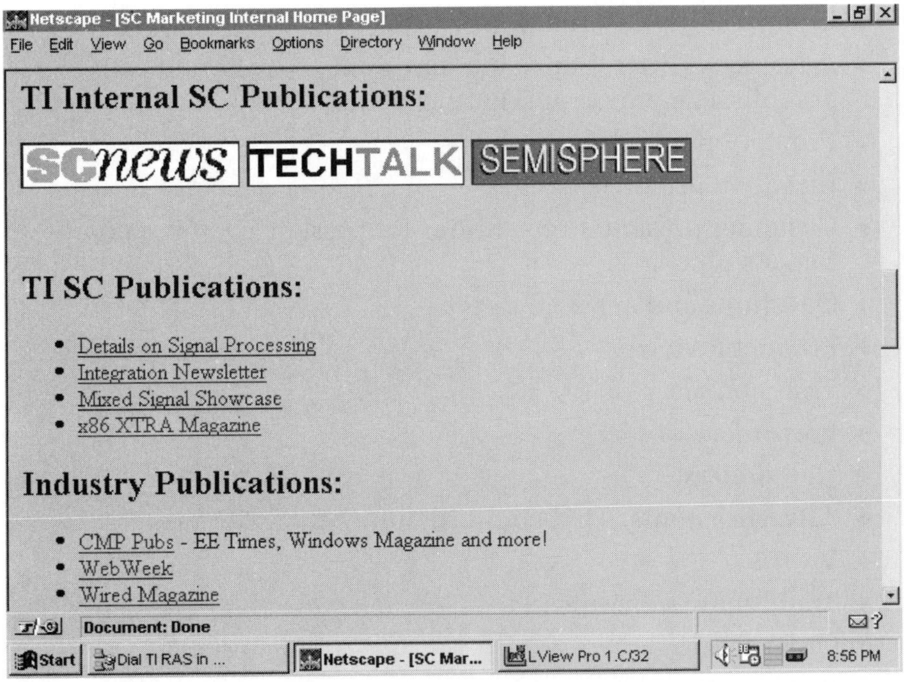

Figure 4.33 Texas Instruments Semiconductor Marketing Internal Home Page. (*Used with permission. Texas Instruments Incorporated, copyright 1996.*)

technologies at http://www.Sun.com:80/960101/feature1/index.html).

An internal Sun home page has a pointer to the Prolytix Web page in a secure manner that allows only Sun employees to view it. The Prolytix package has up-to-date industry analysis and colorful graphs that show Sun's competitive position on such key metrics as Gross Margin Percentage, Price-to-Earnings ratio, Revenue per Employee, and many others.

◆ Catalogs and brochures. These materials can go into as much detail as customers care to see.

◆ Technical specifications and requirements.

- Compatibility information.
- Price lists. Different pricing may apply to different geographic segments or market segments.
- Promotion schedules.
- Incentive pricing.
- Customer presentations. Slides for presenting at the customer's office.
- Questions and answers.
- Product reviews.
- Testimonials.
- Press releases.
- Newsletters.
- Advertisements. This could include actual TV ads.
- Videos.
- Trade show schedules.
- Order forms.
- Proposal templates.
- Dealer support materials.

Sales

With automation, your sales force can carry laptop computers to customer sites. These laptops can hook to your intranet and allow salespeople to show customers presentations and product brochures. They can also access price lists, ordering applications, and order-status inquiry applications. Other intranet applications for sales can provide:

- Customer leads.
- Customer information. Information about customers and their strategies.
- Competitor information. Information about competitors and their products, including how to sell against them.
- Sales forecasts.

- ◆ Promotion calendars.
- ◆ Sales reports.
- ◆ Training materials.
- ◆ Newsgroups. Discussions of accounts and competitors.
- ◆ Reseller or distributor applications. Provide resellers with sales and marketing information and product availability. There is an example of this on the SGI Web site (http://www.sgi.com), where you will find lots of pages for resellers that require a user name and password.

Order Fulfillment

In the order fulfillment process, if you happen to be in the software business, you can fulfill orders just by letting customers download the software themselves. This could be from a secured intranet site or from an open site on the Internet. I can't think of an easier order fulfillment process than that. You can also use the same facility for downloading demos and sample software.

Another similarly easy order fulfillment process is being used to deliver software manuals by printing them on demand. This requires absolutely no inventory other than paper and binding materials.

For those companies that can't fill customer orders instantly, they can provide intranet access for customers to check the status of their orders.

Customer Support Processes

The last processes are the customer support processes. That is only because I put the processes in an order similar to the steps required to take a customer need and fill it. The customer support processes are probably your most important processes, because without customers you don't have a business. Therefore, it is important to provide painless support to your customers. Most companies are unable to share much information about this process.

We already know many of the ways to do customer support over the Internet. These include:

- Provide customers with information on your Web site, such as:

    - Product brochures and detailed specifications
    - How to acquire your product, such as downloading it, ordering it on-line, or the location of the nearest store or dealer
    - How to get training and support

- Provide customers a way to ask questions or give you comments, feedback, and complaints. This can be by forms or *mailto* addresses on the Web site, e-mail addresses in your ads, or an Internet newsgroup for your products.
- Provide customers with access to product developers and technical resources for input into future products and to participate in on-line focus groups.
- Make your internal databases and applications available to customers on your Web site, as Federal Express did when it made its package-tracking database available on the Web.

What about using the intranet for customer support? Here are some ways:

- Put all customer information received over the Internet (as suggested in the preceding list) onto your intranet so that anyone—customer support, product development, sales, marketing, manufacturing, etc.—may access and use it. This information could include names and addresses, products they have acquired from you, problems they're having, things they want more information about, requests, comments, and suggestions. Anything that will improve customer service should be accessible on your intranet.

- ◆ Put Internet applications on the intranet for review and comment prior to putting them on the external Web site.
- ◆ AT&T created a Knowledge Management System that incorporates subject matter expertise on various customer-care issues and problems and makes all that knowledge available to customer-care representatives as they work to solve customer problems.
- ◆ Publish problem status updates for customer support people so they can better respond to customer calls.
- ◆ Provide customer support training on your internal web—use scenarios based on real customer support cases for trainees to resolve.
- ◆ Provide customers with order status when they call in, or let them access it themselves on your intranet.
- ◆ Let customers support themselves by downloading products and patches from an FTP server, accessing your intranet for placing orders, or accessing a support database to get bug reports, documentation, technical papers, and FAQs.
- ◆ Make sure that the people with answers and those who need customer feedback monitor your Internet newsgroups and share this information with others on the intranet.
- ◆ Alert salespeople right away to any special pricing or promotions for customers or changes about which they need to inform customers.
- ◆ Identify and publish sources of frequently recurring customer problems.
- ◆ Keep detailed repair records for analysis when building new products.

Intranets can be very effective in helping you support your customers. Remember, whatever you do, try to make it as personalized as possible.

chapter five

Who Is Using Intranets and How Are They Using Them?

Introduction

We can learn so much from companies that have been through the process of creating an intranet. In this chapter, I'll talk about the companies that participated in this book and the information they provided.

Though I've distilled some of this information and presented it in other chapters, there is much of value in this chapter. To avoid redundancy, however, I will leave out some of the things mentioned elsewhere in this book.

The 13 companies that participated in this book are:

1. Amgen Incorporated
2. AT&T Corp.
3. Bell Atlantic Corporation
4. Booz Allen & Hamilton Inc.
5. EDS
6. JCPenney Company, Inc.
7. Rockwell International Corporation
8. SAS Institute Inc.
9. Silicon Graphics, Inc. (SGI)
10. Texas Instruments Incorporated (TI)
11. Turner Broadcasting System, Inc.

12. United Parcel Service of America, Inc. (UPS)

13. An anonymous company

Amgen Incorporated

Amgen, based in Thousand Oaks, California, is one of the world's largest biotechnology companies. Its Web site is at http://www.bio.com/companies/amgen.html.

Peter Armerding provided the information about Amgen for this book.

Amgen's intranet, AmgenWeb, is available to 2,500 of its 4,000 employees. Amgen formed a cross-departmental team to plan its internal web. By analyzing the company's communications needs, the team determined that the company needed a way to store specific information and make it readily available to whomever needed it. Since many users already had the capability to browse the external Web, creating an internal web was a perfect fit. The company spent about eight months planning and piloting Amgen-Web.

Amgen's most effective application so far has involved integrating its corporate library materials into its internal web. As different organizations see the value of the intranet, they add other materials. They have HR information, such as forms, procedures, and position openings, and IS training classes and registration. Many departments initially posted their status and internal marketing information, but have found it hard to keep this information current.

AT&T Corp.

AT&T is based in New York and is one of the largest telecommunications companies. Its Web site is at http://www.att.com.

Ron Ponder, Executive Vice President of AT&T, provided the information about AT&T for this book.

AT&T defines an intranet as the IP network internal to the company. They started their intranet, called the Unified Global Network (UGN), in 1990. About 130,000 out of 280,000 employees at 750 locations are on the UGN. The UGN includes about 4,000 servers.

The intranet started as several private networks. AT&T built a private TCP/IP network between several major data centers and large locations to support a file transfer application with high-bandwidth requirements. Then it had Bell Laboratories design a backbone to support its needs.

Those involved were mostly from Bell Labs, the networking part of the business, and corporate IT. The champion was Bart Donohue, Director of Engineering and Product Management. Initially, there was no steering committee, but in 1994 Ron Ponder convened the Foundation Architecture Council to start working initiatives that crossed organizational boundaries. This group became the official steering committee for the intranet.

Uses

AT&T uses its intranet for organizational information, project information, and product information. Almost all groups are starting to have internal web pages. There are two main thrusts to the uses for the intranet:

1. *Top-down approach.* This is a one-way avenue to make information more widely available. Cost and lack of distribution capabilities had kept this information from being widely distributed. One example is the internal directory. Another example is the Knowledge Management System. It incorporates subject matter expertise on various customer-care issues and problems. It makes that knowledge available to AT&T's customer care representatives as they work to solve customer problems. This kind of expert system would have been very difficult to deploy previously.

2. *Local, bottom-up approach.* This includes geographically dispersed teams whose members need to work together for a time and use the intranet as their meeting place. This also includes impromptu special-interest

groups, whose members find they can now easily share information on a technical issue, and organizations that are testing their own home pages as a complement to paper newsletters.

AT&T is also running a corporation-wide project that impacts all 280,000 employees. It uses internal web pages to provide status and project information across the company. The field deployment teams use the web pages to communicate about projects and coordinate scheduling.

Results

The cost to start the intranet was about $50 million, and the total intranet cost so far has been about $100 million over the last five years. AT&T estimates that it has saved about $30 million per year as a result of the intranet. The primary source of the savings is in the reduction of duplication (people, equipment, network, and tariff costs) resulting from the consolidation of many individual networks into a global unified network. In addition, the intranet has provided greater communications capabilities.

The intranet has greatly improved communications and application performance. Among employees, the intranet has enabled much more mobility. The culture has become more of a virtual workgroup that communicates electronically rather than in person or by phone.

Lessons Learned

Among the issues and challenges were:

◆ Connecting many networks with gateways
◆ Rapid and unpredictable growth in requirements
◆ Conversion of legacy applications to utilize the IP network

Among the things that worked particularly well were:

- ◆ With the CIO as its champion, the project received support at the highest level of management.
- ◆ AT&T created a *Network Board of Directors,* made up of CIOs of each of the Business Units. This assured buy-in across the corporation and provided a forum to obtain network user requirements. This enabled AT&T to make decisions quickly. This management model was critical to successful integration of the 20-plus networks into one unified global intranet.

Future

According to Ponder,

> in the near future, the intranet will enable a significant degree of electronic bonding with our customers. We currently have WWW pages that our customers can access to see their bills, drill down somewhat to query data and, of course, get to a variety of marketing information. The long-term vision is to allow customers to connect to our intranet to do things like setting up their own 800-number tree.

Bell Atlantic Corporation

Bell Atlantic is Philadelphia-based and is one of the largest regional Bell operating companies. Its Web site is at http://www.bel-atl.com.

Richard Austin of Intranet Services Software Development provided Bell Atlantic's information for this book.

Bell Atlantic's intranet is the Corporate Wide Web (CWW) and/or BAinet (Bell Atlantic Intranet). About 11,000 out of approximately 65,000 employees use the CWW. This includes 20 major locations and hundreds of smaller ones. There are approximately 15 web servers on the CWW. Strategic applications also use the intranet, which increases the total use to a number much greater.

Bell Atlantic's internal network has been around for approximately 10 years, but the company made a major push toward Web technologies in the latter part of 1994. A group of interested and talented individuals initially created the intranet. Then the CIO created the Internet Services organization, which provides consulting and development support for Web-related technologies as well as gateway support and engineering. This fueled major growth and expansion of the intranet.

The champion was Ralph Szygenda, CIO. There was no steering committee.

Uses

The information on the CWW includes corporate documentation for HR, legal, internal systems, processes and procedures, and others. Applications include a Personnel Locator, Supply Catalog, Employment Opportunities, and many others. I mentioned some of these things in Chapter 4 when I discussed Bell Atlantic's screen shots. Every line of business, HR, legal, and IS has content on the intranet. This content comes from Internet Services, over 40 webmasters throughout the company, and end user/authors.

Bell Atlantic is starting to use its intranet to perform electronic commerce, such as vendor/dealer order placement and benefits enrollment. It's planning to add personalized news and personal home pages.

Results

Bell Atlantic estimated that through consolidation and reduced printing it has saved several hundred thousand dollars. The impact has been to make timely information available to a wide audience via a standard interface.

Lessons Learned

One of the issues Bell Atlantic faced was how to coordinate the cooperation of several groups. The following actions worked well.

- Establishing standards for content, look, and feel
- Treating the entire corporate intranet as a single information resource
- Developing standards that allow new servers brought into the web to fit properly in the information hierarchy

Future

Austin sees the future as including:

- *One year.* Increased employee access to current information.
- *Two years.* More applications front-ended by the Web, such as data analysis.
- *Three years.* Continued move into making the Web browser the user's heads-up display for access to timely corporate- and business-related information.

Booz Allen & Hamilton Inc.

Booz Allen & Hamilton is a management and technology consulting company based in McLean, Virginia. Its Web site is at http://www.bah.com.

Edward Vaccaro, CIO, provided the information about Booz Allen & Hamilton. Aron Dutta, Principal, Information Technology Group, provided additional information.

Booz Allen's intranet, Knowledge On Line (KOL), is available to approximately 2,000 users out of a total of 2,100 employees in its Worldwide Commercial Business (WCB). At the time of this writing, the company was making the system available to its Worldwide Technology Business (WTB), which has approximately 4,500 employees. Booz Allen has about three dozen offices worldwide. It has 10 servers, with more being added as it makes new applications available.

The company started developing its intranet in January, 1995, and made it available to users in several phases. In April, 1995,

Booz Allen implemented a proof-of-concept program to validate its ideas for navigation, content, and access. In June, 1995, it began development of the second-generation system, Knowledge On Line II. This system took advantage of lessons learned in the proof of concept. The system rollout to end users began in March, 1996.

According to Vaccaro,

> *Booz Allen & Hamilton's intranet came about as the result of the firm's effort to capture and make available our intellectual capital. Our original global network was implemented to support the activities of our professional staff. The main applications were electronic messaging, document exchange and document management. We also provided access to the Internet. Our global network supports both local and remote access for mobile users anywhere that Booz Allen & Hamilton conducts business in the world. We had deployed a web server on the Internet to provide information about us to any interested party. As it came time to choose the deployment architecture for our intellectual capital program, we realized the benefits that web technology offered to us.*

Creating Knowledge On Line involved the following steps:

1. Booz Allen determined how it was going to manage the content and what type of nontechnical initiatives it needed to develop the process of collecting and maintaining the information.
2. The company implemented a proof-of-concept program to validate its assumptions around content, access, navigation, and features.
3. It took the lessons learned and used them to design the functional capabilities and technology architecture for the target platform.
4. The firm then went into a development program to create the final product. In addition to the application development efforts, changes to the infrastructure were

required to ensure that all 6,500 users in the firm would have access. The majority of the user community is mobile, working at client sites as well as in the office. Supporting this mobile capability involved modifying the network to support dynamic TCP/IP addressing. That way, users could access the network anywhere in the world without the need to make changes to their machine configuration. They use both Macintosh and Wintel equipment.

The champion of KOL was Chuck Lucier, Chief Knowledge Officer, and the steering committee consisted of members from the following areas of the business:

◆ Worldwide Commercial Business—End-user representation
◆ Intellectual Capital Professional Community—Content management
◆ WCB Information technology group—Project management and coordination
◆ Corporate Systems—Development, implementation, and operations

Uses

Booz Allen uses KOL to capture the firm's body of intellectual capital, which includes reports, proposals, best practices, and collaboration conferences. It's planning to add decision support, engagement management, and EIS applications.

Users can search KOL for subject information related to work performed by consultants. The searches link the documents to the authors, client, and staff who participated on the engagement. They provide dynamic hot links to authors, clients, and staff such that they can retrieve résumés, determine the person's participation in the engagement, get a profile on the client, get a description of other engagements, and find experts. They also use the intranet to find staff for planning new projects. It allows free-text searches and creates a pick list as direct input into the Job Manager system.

An additional function of KOL is its collaboration. Users can conference on topics related to their specific business activities. Finally, KOL links to other Booz Allen internal web sites as well as external sites on the Internet.

Results

KOL has allowed Booz Allen to leverage a strategic asset: intellectual capital. It has changed the way employees think about knowledge and information and has opened up new business opportunities. In addition, the cultural impact has been very positive. KOL has provided information access across the firm, and has become an integral part of the way Booz Allen does business.

Lessons Learned

Some of the issues the company faced included the following:

◆ Booz Allen wanted its intranet to represent leading-edge application technology. This presented challenges, since not all of the technology was ready when needed.

◆ The firm had to train its people in skills that weren't readily available in the market at the time, and still aren't.

◆ Content management also proved to be a challenge. Booz Allen's intranet pulls information from various legacy application databases and matches it with original content.

Things that worked extremely well included:

◆ The integration of the team representing all facets of the business.

◆ The team focused on content, function, and use as opposed to the common pitfall of making the technology the primary focus. The technology was secondary.

Booz Allen & Hamilton recommendations were:

1. Focus on your business problem first.
2. Try to avoid bleeding-edge technologies as much as possible—tried-and-true products can produce very slick systems.
3. The business must lead the effort and take ownership.
4. Don't get too cute with the graphics—economy pays off here, especially if you have remote users who come in over dial-up services.
5. Avoid excessive hierarchy in your navigation. It gets in the way.

Future

Company plans for the future include continuing to expand the services of KOL and intranet-type applications across the business.

EDS

EDS, based in Plano, Texas, is one of the largest information and technology services companies in the United States. Its Web site is at http://www.eds.com.

Todd Carlson, CIO, provided the information about EDS for this book.

The EDS intranet, EDS*WEB, is accessible by 25,000 of the more than 95,000 employees in 42 countries. If you count dial-up, then all employees can reach EDS*WEB. It consists of more than 35 servers located throughout the world. EDS has multiple sites in more than 450 major cities around the world.

The EDS Technology Architecture group began researching Internet technologies in late 1993. In March, 1994, the group developed a business plan and prototype of how to use the technology. In April, 1994, the group presented it to Todd Carlson, the CIO. His approval started a project known as *Wildfire,* and EDS implemented the first intranet site within a month.

In the beginning, the project was basically technology-driven by the *rank and file* of EDS. They implemented the corporate repository, called infoCentre, in June of 1994 and the Wildfire project became EDS*WEB.

In the following months, more groups implemented servers on EDS*WEB and the corporate repository grew. They added more security, and communicated more and more about it throughout the corporation. By January, 1996, there were more than 35 internal web sites in EDS, in addition to infoCentre.

From a business standpoint, to start their intranet they sent out internal communications and gave presentations and demonstrations to each of the business units within EDS. They provided follow-up assistance to those groups that were anxious to become part of the project.

From a technical standpoint, they developed the initial prototype into a fully functioning web site and created installation kits for the client software. They added the kit to the FTP servers and to the *product catalog* for the desktop computing environment. Once in the product catalog, an EDS employee could install the software simply by selecting it from a menu of options.

The development and rollout of EDS*WEB involved the following organizations:

- Technology Architecture (TA) group members served as the initial experts on the technology, and assisted other groups.
- Corporate Information Systems (CIS) served in an early-adopter role, and gradually took over more and more of Technology Architecture's role as its experience grew.
- Corporate Communications served as the primary content provider, graphics provider, and worked on how to communicate information electronically.
- Infrastructure Services Communications Group (ISCG) was responsible for the internal network architecture, including the firewall, to enable the intranet.
- Client Server Technical Services (CSTS) has responsibility for the EDS employees desktop and LAN environ-

ment. This included making the necessary client software available on the product catalog.

The role of champion was a joint effort between Todd Carlson, the CIO, and Joe Holmes, the Chief Technologist.

The EDS*WEB Improvement team served as the steering committee for things that affected all of the intranet. There are representatives from all of the groups mentioned previously.

Uses

The list of what's on the intranet at EDS is quite extensive. I'll include it here to give you an idea of the many different types of information you can include in your intranet. I mentioned some of these things in Chapter 4 when I discussed the EDS screen shots.

The following is a list of some of the information available on infoCentre, the EDS Corporate Repository:

Business	Financial, Purchasing, Accounting policies, Quality documentation, Customer contract information, Security, Staffing, and Product catalog
EDS Facts	Executive speeches, Leader profiles, Strategic intent, and Success stories
Employee	Benefits information, Career library, Job family matrices, Employee locator, Job postings, and Performance review tools
News	Corporate bulletins and announcements, Press releases, and Competitor information
Research	Competitor profiles, SEI information, and Market research
Technology	Product evaluations, Standards, Communications, White papers, Technology Architecture documents, Reusable code, Utilities, and Software distribution

Newsgroups   Group Talk, Internet newsgroups, and EDS internal newsgroups

The following is a list of some of the information available on the intranet as a whole.

- Career Library.   An on-line library of the corporate curriculum. It contains all the development activities for each skill or behavior identified in the corporate framework. Both corporate-wide and job-family-specific skills have a variety of activities to support them.
- Corporate Shared Financial Services.   Accounts Payable, Accounts Receivable, Asset Management, General Accounting, and their support services.
- Comprehensive Tool Infrastructure Framework home page.   The detailed criteria for a comprehensive application development environment.
- Electronic Software Distribution System.   Offers electronic software distribution services over EDS*LINK.
- Engineers Affiliate Network.   An Engineering steering committee initiative to leverage expertise by tying all EDS engineers into a virtual organization.
- Global Communicators Network.   A platform for information sharing, networking, and coordination of activities.
- Fulcrum.   A repository for software components.
- Messaging Engineering Services.   Offers messaging-related topics
- Leadership Development Knowledge Network.
- Marketing Centers.   Client/Server Technology Center (CSTC), EDS Pavilion (INFOMART), Information Age (Smithsonian), Information Technology Center (ITC).
- Mobile Computing, Personal Digital Technology, Wireless Communications, and more.
- Organization Chart.   Provides an on-line phone book of EDS employees.

- Patent Information Services. Provides full-text patentability and infringement searches of 1.7 million U.S. patents and weekly analysis of newly issued patents.
- Credit Union Bulletin Board.
- Process Sourcerer. A process management tool that assists users with the definition, customization, execution, and continuous improvement of business processes.
- Project Management. Information about the EDS Project Management methodology.
- Project Management Consulting Services.
- Software License Compliance.
- Standards.
- Systems Life Cycle. Information about the EDS Systems Life Cycle methodology.
- Technical Products Division Catalog. System used for ordering products from vendors.
- Trillium. An Enterprise Reengineering Project.
- Virtual Reality Center. Offers a description of Virtual Reality technology and EDS' role.
- Web E*TIPS. EDS Job Posting System.

EDS has several applications that already existed and have had a web front end added to them. Some of these are:

- An employee locator application that allows the employee to look up phone numbers, work addresses, and organization charts
- An internal job-posting system that allows employees to search for job openings throughout the corporation based on a multitude of criteria
- A product catalog and ordering system that allows employees to order supplies or to order products from vendors

In addition to applications, there are several other areas that have been of great benefit. These include:

- ◆ Job aids that assist employees in doing their work
- ◆ Mentoring tools, such as the Career Library, that assist employees in their development process
- ◆ An on-line news service to supplement paper news, allowing immediate distribution and delivery of more complete news
- ◆ Customer profiles and project outlines, which enable EDS to capitalize on the intellectual capital of the corporation

The new things EDS is doing include:

- ◆ The firm has reached an agreement with PointCast to use and support its PointCast network product. This product allows the broadcast of personalized news and information directly to a user's computer screen. This adds more of a *push* capability to the Internet and to the EDS intranet. By selecting from categories of interest, each employee gets personalized information sent to his or her computer. This information comes from the Internet as well as the EDS intranet. This will allow EDS to put information on its intranet and immediately communicate it to those individuals who need to see it.
- ◆ EDS is also working to add web interfaces to more of their legacy and client/server applications as well as develop many new applications that will run on the web. The web will become the primary interface for access into corporate applications.
- ◆ Much more information is being prepared for the intranet, including a corporate marketing site that provides look-and-feel templates, standards and guidelines for communications, and proposal-development support information.
- ◆ EDS is working to convert much of the information that exists today into knowledge. This involves taking the

information that exists and putting it within the context of processes. This makes the knowledge gained much more valuable to the person accessing the intranet.

EDS also uses Internet Relay Chat (IRC) sessions for real-time discussions within the corporation. In addition, the company pulls in a Usenet feed from the Internet and has internal news-groups for collaboration. It is adding processes to the intranet that work in concert with some of the MSExchange and Lotus Notes tools.

Results

The intranet at EDS has dramatically increased communications speed and improved the comprehension of information through a more intuitive interface and improved efficiency. There are many things that EDS delivered previously in paper form that it now delivers in electronic form. Numerous cost savings result from this new distribution method.

The intranet has also enabled EDS to leverage its intellectual capital more effectively. This has resulted in time savings, better-quality work, and reuse of information, processes, and software. It has also provided a mechanism for knowledge sharing that has now become critical within the company.

According to Carlson,

> the intranet has been a real competitive enabler. EDS is striving to reach an ambition of Any^5. This states that EDS will provide untethered, pervasive communications that will make any information available in any form, to anyone, anywhere at any time. EDS*WEB is helping us reach this ambition. In addition, the ability to open the silos of knowledge between organizations has provided EDS the opportunity to better leverage the intellectual capital of the organization.

Lessons Learned

Some of the issues EDS faced were:

- Completing the installation of TCP/IP on the internal WAN and implementing domain name services (DNS).
- Fear of the intranet not being secure. EDS had to convince groups that it was safe to put information on the intranet.
- Fear that people would spend all of their time *surfing the net.*
- The existing format of communications was very paper-oriented. EDS had to modify existing processes to begin preparing things for the intranet without adding a lot of extra work to the groups.
- Getting groups to take ownership of the information.

Things that worked well include the following:

- The intranet was pretty easy to sell because it was the right solution to provide access to information and was inexpensive to create and operate.
- Initially, EDS placed information on the intranet in native format (MSWord, MSExcel, etc.) with HTML card catalogs placed on top of the information for better searching. Also, converting many different formats into Adobe Acrobat PDF format allowed EDS to place much more information on the intranet.
- Many of the Systems Engineering and Communications groups took to this new communication vehicle very quickly. Each group was able to begin leveraging the new capabilities from the beginning.

Recommendations were as follows:

- Have a business architecture that drives the value of the intranet. The business benefits it can provide should be the driving force and continue to push future intranet development.
- Concentrate on compelling content in the beginning, not on fancy features. People want information that can ben-

efit them in their jobs. Although fancy features are nice, they shouldn't be the top priority.

◆ Creating content for the intranet should be part of each process that creates content for other media. One group shouldn't create the content and then *throw it over the fence* for another group to format for the intranet.

◆ Buying corporate licenses for products has also made it easier to implement the intranet.

The EDS intranet exploded much faster than the company anticipated. If allowed to do it over again, EDS would put a support structure of help desks and technical support staff in place earlier in the process.

Some other things mentioned included:

◆ Initially, the intranet security was separate from the other security in use in EDS. This caused confusion and a few headaches until EDS was able to migrate to a common security solution.

◆ It also took some time to clarify the differences in the evolution of on-line versus paper design. Authors had to consider many new things, such as colors, attention span, and access to the information, that were not as important in designing content for paper.

Future

In the future, EDS*WEB will become:

◆ *Application platform.* EDS*WEB is becoming the internal applications platform of choice for a corporate-wide, cross-platform, transaction-processing environment. Over the next few years, EDS will deploy more and more applications in this environment.

◆ *Distribution and communication vehicle.* EDS*WEB will become the distribution and communications vehicle within the company. EDS*WEB is recognized as a very cost effective method of communication that allows a greater degree of flexibility and speed than ever before. The addition of the PointCast product and the ability of employees to customize the information they receive will further enhance this.

◆ *Knowledge repository.*   More processes are being added to EDS*WEB that will turn currently available information into knowledge. This step dramatically increases the value that the intranet delivers to each employee.

JCPenney Company, Inc.

JCPenney, based in Plano, Texas, is the fifth-largest U.S. retailer, with over 1,200 retail stores and operations in 37 countries. Its Web site is at http://www.jcpenney.com.

Since I'll talk about JCPenney and its intranet in some of the remaining chapters, it would be redundant to include those details here.

Rockwell International Corporation

Rockwell International Corporation, based in Seal Beach, California, makes electronics, automotive, aerospace, and graphics products worldwide. It is the fifth-largest U.S. manufacturer of electronics and electrical equipment. Its Web site is at http://www.rockwell.com.

The information about Rockwell came from:

◆ Harry Meyer, Manager of Strategic Planning Administration

◆ Jim Sutter, Vice President and General Manager, Information Technology

◆ Dana Abrams, Director, Planning and Standards

Rockwell's intranet, Rweb, is accessible by 20,000 of its 80,000 employees at 60 locations. Rockwell has seven servers at major locations, and other sites use the corporate server.

The company initiated its intranet in 1995 when Corporate IT created a demonstration for Corporate Communications. Rockwell recognized a need to share information similar to what it was doing on the external Web site, but restricted to internal Rockwell access. The company established a Corporate IT project leader with a team and schedule, and similar activities at major business units.

Those involved in deploying the intranet were:

- Vice President and General Manager
- Director of Planning and Standards
- Director of Corporate Information Systems
- Division directors of Information Technology and Engineering

There was also a multifunctional work team with representatives from senior staffs, including communications, human resources, engineering, IT, and finance.

The champions for Rweb were the Vice President and General Manager IT, Human Resources, and Corporate Communications, including Media Relations.

Uses

Rockwell is in the early stages with its intranet. It is starting with a wide variety of basic uses related to the employee, the company, and the community. This includes the company vision, the corporate newspaper, open positions, the employee directory, information systems policies, business travel, links to business and financial news, and links to government sites. Many of Rockwell's organizations and departments are creating their own home pages describing who they are and what they do.

Later, the company will develop more sophisticated applications for targeted users with password protection and access to restricted information. Rockwell is also adding a search engine and internal newsgroups.

Results

Rockwell has not tracked total intranet cost for the enterprise. It recognizes the value of exploring the intranet's potential and moving through the learning curve at a logical pace. The value so far has come from saving time and improving communications, awareness, and responsiveness through information sharing. Meyer says that "Rweb provides a convenience store for knowledge and basic information." It facilitates the timely delivery of information. Rockwell believes that it's difficult to envision all of the potential benefits at this time.

So far, the impact on the organization has been largely one of sharing information across the enterprise. It helps to build a corporate consciousness.

Rweb impacts Rockwell employees by providing them with a valuable resource for ready access to a wide variety of information.

Lessons Learned

Issues they resolved included determining the design, layout, media, graphics, text, links, internal access only, and page format, such as PDF versus HTML.

Things that worked well for Rockwell included:

◆ Having the time to get started, show off the results, and receive favorable feedback
◆ The teamwork of committed staff resources

Recommendations are as follows:

◆ Get it done quickly. You can change it later, but you need to show results and value early.
◆ Don't expect to get it right the first time.
◆ Foster creativity.

The things Rockwell would do differently are as follows:

- Do more capacity planning and anticipation of volumes
- Provide a search engine

Future

For the future, Rockwell sees that it will become a standard practice to share information across a wide variety of organizations and distances. More important, the intranet is becoming the platform of choice for applications development and to modernize legacy systems.

SAS Institute Inc.

SAS Institute, based in Cary, North Carolina, produces integrated applications software. Its Web site is at http://www.sas.com.

Lauren Bednarcyk, Applications Developer, provided the information about SAS that appears in this book.

The SAS Institute intranet, SAS Wide Web or SWW, has been available to users since late 1993. SAS has approximately 3,000 employees worldwide, with 2,000 employees at its headquarters. Most of its 1,500 technical employees have access to SWW.

Bednarcyk explains how the SWW started:

> *Kevin Bond was doing some research using the Internet, and the other available search and retrieval tools (gopher, ftp, etc.) proved to be insufficient for his needs. More and more he found that the resources he needed were WWW accessible, so he downloaded the software and began to access it. He found it very useful and he found the interface (Mosaic) easy to work with. He immediately saw how it could be used within a company to circulate internal information easily. He started by setting up the server on his machine and bringing in HTML encoded files for public use. These early files were mainly about HTML, NCSA Mosaic, the WWW, etc. It was easier to download the HTML encoded files than to transform them to some other format and simply put them on the network.*

Bond requested and received approval to set up an external Web site and to recruit some help. In the process of developing the external site, Bond and his team developed some internal applications and showed them to others. Others took an interest and started publishing their own documents.

Those involved in actually deploying the SWW were from the Publications Technology Department, Web Technology Department, Computer-Based Training Department, and software development groups. Most of the people involved were programmers and software developers with an interest in documentation and information retrieval.

Uses

Anyone on the network can create content, and there are all kinds of information available on the intranet, such as:

- Sales and Marketing publishes strategies and directions for selling its software products, press releases, reviews of SAS Institute and SAS products, trade show information, and consumer information.

- Almost all organizations have a home page detailing the structure of the department or division, links to home pages of their subdivisions, links to personal home pages of the employees in the department or division, and general information about the function and projects of that organization.

- R&D documentation for software developers, such as requirements, specifications, and internal tools usage documentation.

- Planning and direction documents, such as documents outlining divisional and corporate goals.

- Production and release schedules.

- Comprehensive lists of internal tools and documentation on these tools.

- Descriptions of work processes.

- Downloaded resources for software developers, such as papers from conferences brought in from the Web.

- Software design team specifications.

- Department contacts (administrative assistants) maintain personnel lists for their departments.

- User manuals for products and internal tools.

- Individuals have their 15KB of fame by establishing home pages. These home pages may contain fun and personal material, and they may link to information about projects the person is working on.

- If a presentation is of general interest to the whole Institute, the speaker will often publish his or her notes on the SWW.

- The publications division has converted printed software manuals to HTML for on-line manuals.

- The Design and Production department of the publications division has a forms application to automate submitting design requests and business car requests

- The training division has created some basic tutorials about their internal software tools.

- SAS Institute has a mirror of the external Web site on the SWW for all to see. These pages also serve as a staging area for updates to its Web site.

- The facilities department publishes information about conference rooms and facilities contacts.

- The recreation and fitness center publishes its newsletter only on the SWW.

- Personnel posts job openings and publishes photos of new employees.

- The health care center publishes its newsletter on the intranet.

- One somewhat unique application is a clever use of CGI scripts to extract program structure dynamically and show class hierarchies (for object-oriented programmers) and link to documentation about those classes. This happens *on the fly,* which is necessary because it is documenting the structure of software while it is being developed.

Results

The cost of the intranet at SAS Institute has been very minimal. The company uses NCSA Mosaic for its browser and NCSA server, both of which are free. One person started this work on his own time, but soon it became more and more of a responsibility. Now it is much of his job, and another person also supports it part-time. This adds up to approximately one person's salary.

Savings have mainly been in the dissemination of information. As a worldwide company, getting news and communications out to all offices has been difficult. Now, SAS publishes widely distributed documents on the SWW. Thus, people in Cary, North Carolina, and in Japan can get the most current corporate information simultaneously.

According to Bednarcyk, *"the SWW has made the atmosphere around the workplace more open. The main impact is on our worklife, that it is easier to find documentation on various things without having to search blindly around the file system or ask others for access locations."* It has also facilitated cross-organization communication.

Another impact is that the intranet is becoming a de facto standard for publishing internal information. People are happier with only one browser to learn, and they can find documents fairly easily on them.

Lessons Learned

Some of the things SAS shared:

- ◆ They recommend having a single server because it definitely makes life easier.
- ◆ Sometimes people get possessive of their data, its display, and its organization. Everyone has an opinion

about how to structure the *entry point* to the web.
Employees have had some heated discussions about this.

Future

In the future, SAS Institute expects that the intranet will become even more firmly entrenched in its corporate culture. People like the interface, so the company expects to develop even more applications using web technology. It also hopes to implement some sophisticated search tools.

Silicon Graphics, Inc. (SGI)

SGI, based in Mountain View, California, makes high-performance workstations and software. Its Web site is at http://www.sgi.com.

Michael Graves, CIO, provided the information about SGI for this book.

SGI's intranet, Silicon Junction, is accessible by all 11,000 SGI employees in 195 locations. Silicon Junction has over 2,000 servers.

It started in early 1994 as a grassroots project. In early 1995, the Information Services organization officially created a team of five people to run and administer Silicon Junction.

The CIO is responsible for the operation of Silicon Junction. Originally, there wasn't a steering committee, but they have created one to guide the effort in moving forward. This committee consists of five key VPs.

Uses

Silicon Junction is an organizational structure for the information contained within the environment. The hit rate on Silicon Junction's home page is almost two hits per person per day. This usage is in addition to direct access to URLs via bookmarks and WEB-jumpers. Silicon Junction provides access to over 150,000 URLs.

In addition to the Silicon Junction team, many groups across SGI create and maintain content. Almost every department and organization has information on Silicon Junction. Applications cover a wide range of functions.

The next release of Silicon Junction will focus on an enhanced search engine, improved bookmark processing, and information management.

Results

SGI doesn't break out the cost of the intranet. These costs are part of the daily operations of the company. Beyond the budget of the Silicon Junction team, the cost of people and hardware to support the intranet hasn't added incremental cost to the operational costs of the organization.

SGI also hasn't measured the cost savings—it hasn't needed to because the productivity increase is evident. Graves says, "*In our company, technology is not used just because it's neat. It must add value!*"

The initial benefit was in information dissemination. SGI has several hundred thousand pages of information for sharing operational data and ideas. In addition, the company is progressively implementing applications to increase organizational productivity. An example of this is the Electronic Requisition System, which SGI uses to manage purchase orders and the approval process. This workflow application reduces the time it takes to process and track requisitions.

According to Graves, "*SGI's culture and people are very open. The intranet has helped us facilitate our open culture and communication. The intranet has changed the way we work and how people feel about their work. It has changed the way we manage Silicon Graphics. It has changed the way we run our company.*"

Lessons Learned

The major issue SGI faced was one of fantastic growth. Silicon Junction has been a huge success and the growth of content has been fantastic. Says Graves, "*That was a great problem to have!*"

Future

Graves feels that *"the intranet provides the foundation for Information Age companies. It will be a key component of our worklife within SGI for years to come."*

Texas Instruments Incorporated (TI)

Dallas-based TI is one of the world's largest manufacturers of computer chips and other electronic products for commercial, military, and consumer use. Its Web site is at http://www.ti.com.

Gene Phifer, Senior IT Manager, provided the information about TI for this book.

TI's intranet serves more than 20,000 out of 56,000 employees at over 100 locations. The company currently has more than 100 web servers, mostly located in larger U.S. sites.

TI's end users started the intranet many years ago. It started as a grassroots effort by engineers and scientists who brought up web servers to house workgroup-specific information. They also brought up news servers, which they use extensively for newsgroup-based collaboration. Eventually, this activity involved hundreds of engineers and scientists from all of TI's business units.

The IT department took a leadership role with the intranet in 1994. It formally provided Internet gateway support in 1992 and web browser support in 1994. Now, they provide web services and web servers.

Initially, the intranet didn't have a champion, but the CIO has now championed Internet technologies. When the IT department took a leadership role in 1994, it formed a steering committee consisting of representatives from every business unit, as well as the IT department. This committee still operates.

Nobody is actually *in charge of* TI's intranet, which Phifer notes is fitting for the Internet. The IT department provides the backbone network for running the intranet, and will provide web servers and web services to users who request them. No one person or group controls the intranet. The IT department also ensures that TI's Acceptable Usage Policy and other policies and procedures are in place.

Uses

The information on the TI intranet is primarily workgroup reference information. The company uses web servers as information and document repositories for the workgroups. Some web servers serve entire business units, and a few serve the entire TI community. Information on the intranet includes design guides, engineering reference material, and source pages. Some workgroups use the web to spread the news about who they are, what they do, the members of the workgroup, current activities, and plans. Every business unit has some information on the intranet. There are screen shots and a discussion of TI's intranet in Chapter 4.

TI's initial applications are the TI white pages and front ends to legacy applications. TI will invest heavily in web-based applications over the next year or two. It will also deploy many more IT-supported web servers, and it expects the end users to deploy a large number of web servers, as well. It will also create a TI-wide information repository composed of Saros Mezzanine document repositories, web servers, and Lotus Notes servers. These will all be front-ended by web browsers, with search and retrieval capabilities across all servers.

Results

Cost and savings information were not available. However, other benefits from the intranet are:

- ◆ It has provided excellent sharing of information.
- ◆ It allows collaboration via newsgroups so TI employees spread across the world can work as teams.
- ◆ It provides an excellent platform for future applications.

The impact on TI's employees has been to empower end users to provide their own information management solutions, which means less dependence on the IT department.

Lessons Learned

Some of the issues that TI dealt with included:

1. Ownership of the environment—deciding which parts the users wanted IT to manage and which parts they wanted to manage themselves
2. Network performance issues
3. Lack of TCP/IP connectivity until recently
4. Inadequate awareness of intranet possibilities

One of the things that worked well at TI was that since web technology is so easy to deploy and support, the end users did most of it themselves without the help of the IT department. Recommendations included:

1. Let end users drive the strategies, or at least involve them heavily.
2. Have some guidelines, recommendations, and standards around the intranet.
3. Be aware of the load on the network and plan ahead of demand.
4. The hardest part of installing the client is enabling TCP/IP. Spend a quality effort getting IP to the desktops of all users. After that, the web browser will go in with no difficulty.
5. Getting an initial home page on the intranet is easy. Keeping it alive and full of current, relevant information is the challenge.
6. If the IT department doesn't have R&D funds, let your end users fund it for you, and then leverage and share that knowledge. TI calls this "vicarious R&D."

If TI were doing this over again, it would:

♦ Get the IT department into a leadership position sooner.

- ◆ Provide more solutions in the web server area sooner for those workgroups that don't have the technical skills to get their own server going.
- ◆ Do a better job of staying ahead of the demand curve on the network.

One of the stories TI shared was that in such a highly technical company, *everybody knows the right answer.* With Internet technologies, just about everybody can implement and run the technology. In this kind of environment, you must let the end users chart the waters for you in many cases. The IT department then becomes the provider of basic services, such as the network, and communicator and coordinator of technologies. At some point, the users will agree enough on a technology so that the IT department can then officially provide support for it. The worst thing an IT department can do in this environment is to go out and study or evaluate a technology with the intent of providing support eventually. By the time they complete the study, the technology has changed, and the end users have gone on to the new stuff anyway.

Future

For the future, TI sees that the web browser will become the ubiquitous interface. Says Phifer, "*All applications will be web-enabled or will be entered via the web, and information delivery via the web will proliferate.*" He adds, "*Our use of the Intranet is exploding. It is causing us to completely rethink how we share information within TI.*"

Turner Broadcasting System, Inc.

Turner Broadcasting System, based in Atlanta, is one of the world's most progressive news and entertainment companies. It owns TV networks and professional sports teams. Its Web site is at http://www.turner.com.

Jimi Stricklin, Director of Employee Services Development, provided the information about Turner Broadcasting for this book.

Turner Broadcasting's intranet, Turner Employee Services Network (TESN), serves 3,000 of nearly 10,000 employees at 36 locations. The company started working on TESN in September of 1995, and rolled it out on March 29, 1996.

Turner Broadcasting started TESN to provide employees with access to HR information. TESN grew from a project chartered by Allan DeNiro, Vice President of Human Resources. Jimi Stricklin, Director of Employee Services Development, headed the intranet project. The project also involved Melissa Hoberg, Coordinator of Employee Services, and team members from HR, Purchasing and Logistics, Benefits, and Turner Reciprocal Advertising Corporation (TRAC). In addition, outside companies helped create TESN, did focus groups among employees, and developed the ad campaign to promote TESN to employees. They spent countless hours deciding what information to make available and how to present it so that the employees could relate to it.

Uses

TESN has applications for HR, HRIS, Benefits, Purchasing and Logistics, and TRAC. I talked about these applications in Chapter 4 when I discussed the Turner screen shots.

In addition, TESN has information to help employees with the changes required during the Olympics in Atlanta. TESN also contains the entire policy manual, as well as the Executive Message, which gives employees direct access to executives. The company has added job postings and a map index to make sure that information is available for specific locations.

Results

The major impact so far has been to give employees direct access to current information. Turner Broadcasting feels that each employee who learns to use the tool will become more effective. TESN is also making employees in other locations around the world feel like part of the team.

Lessons Learned

Some of the things Turner Broadcasting learned included:

- Its unique mix of companies needed a format that was cross-functional and fun to use.
- Its advertising campaign and creating TESN as a network worked extremely well.

Recommendations included the following:

- Involve many, but appoint a leader.
- Just get it going—don't keep trying to please everyone.
- Be more concerned about how to maintain the internal web and keep it current than what is initially on the site.
- Learn more about the technology before getting started. Create a plan for the project before moving on it or going back and writing it in the middle.

In addition, Stricklin talked about what was really unique about TESN:

TESN is a very unique web site in that it offers many new tools and not just the web. We took a view of our employees as customers and created an ad campaign around what was relevant to our population. We are in the business of television and entertainment and news and our people understand networks. So with TESN, the positioning was as a true broadcast network which led us to the types of marketing and to the look of our web site which is done in a program format. Human resources information is the HR Review, TRAC is The Price You'll Like with Bob Barter, Benefits is Inside Employee Benefits, and so on. We also have seen where the network aspect has more practical applications. Our other networks like TNT, TBS, CNN, etc., all use the ratings systems of Nielsen to understand what programming the audience is interested in seeing. With the web, we can have a much more accurate way to capture this information than anything our networks utilize. We know for a fact how many times each program is viewed. This enables us to update the programming to meet customer demand.

Future

For the future, Turner Broadcasting feels that more and more interaction will be possible with this tool. The company looks to TESN to become the number one source for information in their company worldwide.

United Parcel Service of America, Inc. (UPS)

Atlanta-based UPS is the world's largest package delivery company. Its Web site is at http://www.ups.com.

Marc Dodge provided the information about the UPS intranet for this book.

The UPS intranet, http://www.inside.ups.com/, is accessible by about 3,000 out of 55,000 employees.

UPS started development of its intranet in September, 1994, and gave access to users in January, 1995, because it felt the need to give its employees better and more timely access to information. The company put software on an existing workstation, along with some departmental information, and its intranet was born.

Those involved initially were in the Telecom area. Soon afterward, other departments followed their lead.

Uses

Information on the UPS intranet includes company news, group projects, contact people, employee phone book, terms glossary, and other such information. There is a lot of department-specific information as well. Groups that have information on the UPS intranet include Telecom, Distributed Systems, Marketing, Corporate, and R&D sites.

At the time of this writing UPS is working on some test Java applications and some interesting database querying. It plans to add more departments and more applications in the future.

Results

The intranet has helped cut costs by avoiding continual paper handouts and circulation. In addition, UPS must maintain only a single database in one location for this kind of information. Because of the intranet, UPS has seen increased communication, more timely information, and ease of getting and updating information. As a result, many groups want to put information on the intranet.

Lessons Learned

The issues dealt with included finding the right software and hardware to get it going and planning future development.
Recommendations are as follows:

♦ Start small and be prepared for major growth.
♦ Put procedures and standards in place ahead of the growth.

Future

For the future, UPS is planning more applications and more departmental information. It expects the intranet to be the main source of information company wide.

An Anonymous Company

There is one company that willingly shared information for this book, but requested that they not be listed by name. Their experiences were very valuable in preparing this book.

At this company, there has been a significant amount of Internet activity for many years. This activity resulted in the development of a lot of interest, technical capability, and skill. As a result, intranet web pages appeared very soon after the introduction of web technology. As with the Internet generally, the arrival of the Web generated significant interest outside the research community. Businesses and functions other than R&D soon produced intranet web pages. The R&D community facilitated this development by willingly sharing its experience and knowledge, and even assisting in the development of many of the early intranet pages.

Because TCP/IP is this company's networking protocol of choice, access to the intranet is an integral part of most standard desktop implementations. In a broad sense, though, users had access to the intranet even before the development of web pages.

The intranet got started because a lot of very capable people developed a keen interest in exploring its possibilities. They developed internal Web pages that were of value to themselves and the functions they were part of. There was no formal program or project whose objective was *to implement an intranet.* Even now, individual groups, functions, and businesses decide that the intranet is an appropriate technology for achieving some objective and then act upon that. More information and guidance are available now, and resources are available that weren't in the early days.

The company put an Internet Team in place, sponsored by their CIO and VPs of Corporate Communications and Corporate R&D. This group ensures that the company makes strategic use of the Internet, and has expanded its charter to include the intranet. The Internet Team has people from IS, Communications, R&D, and business and functional units.

One of the subteams sponsored by the Internet Team is creating an internal corporate home page. It will provide a home for applications and services of general interest and value to all employees. More important, it will implement a search strategy that provides a point from which to find any information.

Uses

A lot of different people, ranging from clerical staff to researchers, develop content for the intranet. The groups that have applications on the intranet include R&D, business units, Engineering, HR, IS, Communications, regional offices, and plants. In addition, there are a number of personal home pages.

One of the most well received applications on the intranet is the stock price, which is updated every 20 minutes. This is very important to senior executives. Also, IS network managers use the intranet to manage their environment and to distribute that information. There are also a lot of very interesting R&D applications.

Lessons Learned

The issues faced included the following:

- *Organizational.*   Beyond the users of the technology, many groups correctly feel that they have a stake in the implementation and development of both the Internet and intranet. Bringing these groups together in a network that could get things done was a challenge.
- *Technical.*   The last 100 yards—in some instances, locations are on the TCP/IP network but individual desktops are not. To reach its potential, the intranet must be widely available, and covering those last 100 yards to those desktops can be difficult.
- *Other.*   Senior managers need to be more fully educated about the possibilities of both the Internet and intranet in order to ensure support to continue moving ahead quickly.

Among the things that worked very well were:

- Allowing the intranet to grow in much the same way the Internet did—somewhat chaotically—resulted in a critical mass of servers and applications being developed more quickly than would have been the case had a formal project/program been put in place.
- The cross-functional network that is the Internet Team has worked very well and may be a model for other endeavors of this sort.

The recommendation was to start earlier. Without being controlling, this company believes it's important to have standards and guidelines in place to prevent people from wandering around looking for consulting and development skills. The sooner you can put these in place, the better.

Future

The company projects that future use of the intranet as a front end to legacy systems will be commonplace. It will be the primary vehicle for delivery of employee and company news.

In Part 2, we looked at how you use an intranet and who is using them.

1. Chapter 4 looked at lots of uses for intranets and showed examples of intranets from five companies.
2. Chapter 5 gave profiles of each of the 13 companies involved in this book.

In Part 3, we'll look at how you create your intranet.

1. Chapter 6 will look at two different ways to sell the intranet to your organization, including all the steps involved in doing so.
2. Chapters 7 through 12 will take a detailed look at some of the specific steps used to create your intranet and sell it to your organization.

PART THREE
How Do You Create Your Intranet?

chapter six

Two Different Ways to Sell the Intranet to Your Organization

Why and How Did Companies Create Their Intranets?

Why did companies start their intranets, and how did they start them? From talking with a variety of companies, it is clear that a lot of intranets started as *grassroots* efforts, though some were formal initiatives. Many started with the IT group, and some started in R&D, engineering, and HR. Before we plunge into the steps involved in creating an intranet, let's take time to look at why and how some of these companies started them. From this, you'll see that there is *no one right way* to create an intranet. The right way for you is the one that suits your organization and its culture. Reasons companies created intranets include the following:

- Because of the power and possibilities for the tools to solve business problems
- To meet communications needs
- To access information
- To share information and support mobile users

Because of the Power and Possibilities for the Tools to Solve Business Problems

At JCPenney, several of us saw the power of the Internet and realized what those same tools could do for us inside the company.

Our CIO also saw the power and quickly committed to making it happen. He asked me to collaborate with my colleagues to develop an Internet presence and an internal web. My charter was to involve every area of the company on a team to make it all happen. We started by building a demo and showing it throughout our organization. We used the demos to build enthusiasm and commitment, spread browsers, and attract to our team anyone who wanted to publish web content. Once we had representation from throughout the business, we started our Internet Team. We focused on what we wanted to accomplish with the Internet and jWeb, our internal web. Once we established our goals, we set about working to accomplish them. Although our champion, the CIO, sanctioned and supported our team, we were a grassroots effort in that we set the direction for jWeb, rather than him dictating it to us.

Several other organizations created their intranets because they also saw the power and possibilities of the tools. Because of that, these were mostly grassroots efforts. SAS Institute was one of those. It was one of the first businesses to create an intranet. They started the *SAS Wide Web* several years ago when Kevin Bond discovered that some of the resources he needed were accessible on the World Wide Web. He downloaded Mosaic, set up a server, and received approval to set up an external Web site. He also developed some small internal applications and demonstrated them. As word spread, people throughout the company started teaching themselves HTML and creating documents.

The SGI intranet, Silicon Junction, started as a grassroots effort, as well. The Information Services organization formalized it by creating a Silicon Junction team. A group of individuals at Bell Atlantic created their original intranet applications. The CIO formalized it by creating the Internet Services organization. At TI, the intranet also started as a grassroots effort. Hundreds of scientists and engineers throughout the organization saw the usefulness of the tools and deployed them. The IT organization then took on the responsibility for maintaining the infrastructure.

At EDS, the Technology Architecture group began researching Internet technologies in late 1993. In early 1994, it developed and presented a business plan and prototype to the CIO. With his approval, the group implemented its first intranet site immediately. In the beginning, the project was basically technology-driven by the *rank and file.* In the following months more groups implemented servers on EDS*WEB and the corporate repository grew and matured.

As you can see, some companies started by seeing the power of the tools and realizing that they could solve a problem or meet a need. Next, we'll look at companies that started with a specific need and realized that an intranet was the way to meet that need.

To Meet Communications Needs

Rockwell International created its intranet, *Rweb,* to fill a recognized internal communication need to share information. IT created the intranet to demonstrate the possibilities to Corporate Communications.

To Access Information

Amgen Pharmaceuticals created its intranet to address a need to access specific information. The company realized that it needed a way to store information so that it could be easily accessible when needed. An internal web was a perfect solution for Amgen, especially since many of its users were already using browsers to access the external Web. A cross-departmental team was formed to plan and pilot the internal web.

Turner Broadcasting created Turner Employee Services Network (TESN) to supply employees with the HR information they needed. Turner Broadcasting used a more formal approach to creating an intranet. The need for better access to information drove the creation of the intranet at UPS as well. It started simply by putting software and some departmental information on an existing workstation, and the UPS intranet grew from there.

To Share Information and Support Mobile Users

At Booz Allen & Hamilton, the intranet came about as the result of a formal effort to capture and share intellectual capital and to support mobile users anywhere in the world. The firm had deployed a web server on the Internet and realized that the architecture was appropriate for its intellectual capital program. Booz Allen determined how to collect and maintain the information, implemented a proof of concept, and then developed the final product.

Two Different Ways You Can Get Started

You have seen how several different kinds of companies started their intranets. Every company has taken a different approach, but there are some similarities. Some started with a formal program, whereas others started as an informal, grassroots effort. These grassroots efforts spread as people saw the intranet and got excited about it. Now, how do you start *your* intranet?

The two approaches to creating your intranet are similar to those used by our example companies:

1. *Traditional model*—The formal approach
2. *Internet model*—The grassroots approach

Traditional Model

This approach is quite familiar to anyone who has been around IT. It's the way that you do expensive IT projects. It requires a formal request for funding, a specific plan, a cost-benefit analysis, and return on investment (ROI) calculations. You present this to those who must approve and fund it. If approved, you move on to implementation. There are six steps in the Traditional model:

1. Do you need an intranet?
2. Are you ready?
3. Develop a project plan and proposal.
4. Present the proposal and sell the concept.
5. Implement it.
6. Measure the results.

Step 1: Do You Need an Intranet?

The first step is to determine if you need or want an intranet. What is compelling you to have one? At the time of this writing, you can hardly pick up a magazine without seeing articles about how companies use intranets. It's enough to make you want to run out and get one of your own, whether you need it or not!

Have your internal customers been reading those same articles? Are they starting to ask you for an intranet? Do you see a need in your organization that's not being met and for which an intranet is a perfect solution? Does your organization need better tools for communicating information, and maybe even for collaborating on projects? These are all reasons that compel many companies to consider creating an intranet.

As you saw, often the intranet started from a grassroots effort when some employees saw a need that an internal web could fill. They put together a prototype, and top management soon heard about it. They then created a team to do something about it. If you see needs that an intranet can solve, maybe it's time for you to get moving!

What about Business Goals?

Part of determining if you need an intranet is in figuring out the goals of your organization. Is there something an intranet can do to help meet those goals? Unless you focus on meeting the needs and goals of your organization, then you're looking at this backward. There really should be a reason that you need an intranet or you needn't get started on it.

This part isn't as hard as it sounds. Can an intranet help meet competitive threats? Can it help you do things faster, better, and cheaper? Intranets can provide lots of ways to do these things.

What problems and opportunities do you have because of the rapidly changing business environment? Are you reengineering a business process that requires information technology as part of the new process? What are the specific requirements? How does an intranet compare with other possible solutions?

Do some looking around—it shouldn't be too hard to spot potential opportunities where an intranet can make a big difference.

Step 2: Are You Ready?

Once you've determined that you have a need that an intranet can fulfill, then it's time to determine what it would take to create an intranet. There are five major areas of concern. Each area has its own set of steps.

1. What is the scope of the project? In other words, what area or areas of the organization should be part of the initial intranet project? This could be enterprise wide, or just a workgroup or department.

2. Do you have the infrastructure you need?

   - What are the computer needs of the area of your organization that you have chosen? Do they have PCs, Macintoshes, Unix machines, mainframe terminals, or no desktop machines at all? Will you need any computers?

   - Is that area on a LAN or WAN? If not, what is necessary to put it on one?

   - Does the LAN or WAN use TCP/IP? Today, most organizations have some mixture of protocols, but IT has recently been moving toward TCP/IP as a single standard. If a protocol other than TCP/IP is in use, such as IBM's SNA or Novell's IPX, what do you need to do to change to TCP/IP? Through some workarounds, it's possible to have an intranet without TCP/IP, but in doing so, you won't be able to provide your employees with the wealth of resources available on the Internet.

   To change to TCP/IP, you can:

   - Load an Internet Protocol (IP) stack on each machine.
   - Have IP reside on a gateway server.

If you're missing any of these components, you'll need to plunk down some serious money to change that. We'll talk about this in step 4.

If you already have TCP/IP in use on your LAN or WAN, you're in good shape and ready to move on to the next question.

3. Do you have the skills and resources you need? Are you willing to acquire the expertise to set up web technology, e-mail, and all the other intranet tools?

  ◆ Do you have expertise in setting up and running TCP/IP on the networks?

  ◆ Do you have expertise in Unix or Windows NT? In the early days of internal webs, Unix expertise was mandatory. That's changing somewhat. In the past year, more servers ran on Windows NT, and even Windows 95. If you intend to use Unix-based servers, you'll still need Unix expertise in-house or available for purchase. If NT is your chosen platform, then knowledge of NT is helpful. Recent research has shown that while Unix servers have been predominant for external servers, NT has been coming on strongly for internal servers.

You can hire the skills you need, if necessary. In our case, we were fortunate enough to have a new graduate with a Masters degree in Computer Science who was real sharp when it came to the tools we needed. New grads can be a good source of these skills.

4. Do you have the people resources to take on the extra workload of an intranet? Once up and running, the impact may be fairly small, but to get started requires someone to evaluate, select, acquire, install, and maintain server hardware, software, browsers, and content and management tools.

5. Do you have someone who can take the lead in developing and maintaining applications for the internal web? You may need additional resources. Some organizations have added only a single staffer, while others have found that they didn't need additional people. In some cases, someone was already doing some or all of these things for other systems and was moved into these responsibilities. As intranets have grown, people have moved into this from other areas of systems development.

Step 3: Develop a Project Plan and Proposal

By step 3, you have figured out what you require to create your intranet and what value it will bring to your organization. You have identified what your company should do with an intranet, what problems it will solve, and what goals it will meet. The next step is to detail the problems the intranet will solve, determine the cost of building an intranet, and detail the benefits you will derive from it. This information will go into the proposal you will create and present to whomever approves the funding of capital expenditures. You may wish to bring in a consultant at this stage to help you identify all the pieces that go into developing this proposal.

Technology projects often emerge from business process improvement (BPI) projects. Let's say, just for illustration purposes, that you're working on an HR human resources BPI project for the Benefits Department and that your team is recommending an intranet. We will use this premise to create our proposal. This is a highly simplistic example used for illustration purposes only. In your own proposal, you'll want to go into much more detail, including lots of facts and real numbers. If you already have experience in developing proposals you should skip this part and move on to step 4.

Sample Proposal: Benefits BPI Project

Figure 6.1 is a sample proposal for an intranet related to your Benefits BPI project. You may wish to look over each section of the sample proposal as I discuss it here. This proposal focuses on the four BPI steps that come before the request for funding:

The Benefits BPI Team has reviewed the benefits process in great detail. We have talked with employees and members of the Benefits Department staff to discover the problems with the current process. We have looked at the best practices of other companies and have created a new process based upon implementation of an intranet.

Problems with the Benefits Process

There are two major problems with the benefits process which led us to investigate it. We interviewed members of the Benefits staff and other employees and verified these problems. They are:

1. The Benefits staff feels that the current process of printing and distributing manuals is just too expensive, especially since changes are coming faster and faster these days. As soon as they get a manual updated, something else changes and they must start all over. They just don't seem to be able to catch up.

2. Employees feel that they have a hard time getting the benefits information they need. Their manuals are always outdated, and they can never find anyone in HR to answer their questions when they need help.

The Current Process and Why the Problems Occur

The current process flow (documented in the appendix of this proposal) shows some of the process steps that are part of the problem. For example:

◆ When there are major changes in benefits, the company rewrites the benefits manuals, prints them, mails copies to all locations, and warehouses sufficient copies to last until the next printing. This usually happens once per year per manual.

- When there are *minor* changes in benefits, the company publishes and mails revision letters with a page outlining the changes. Employees must insert these pages in their benefits manuals. Extra copies go to the warehouse for distribution with any manuals shipped in the future. This usually happens about three times per year per manual.
- Locations order extra copies of manuals and revisions from the warehouse to give to new employees.

The major process problems are:

- The process of making changes is very time-consuming.
- Things are changing faster and faster each year, and Benefits just can't seem to keep up.
- Because of the speed of these changes, manuals quickly become obsolete.
- The current process is very expensive because we have to print, distribute, and warehouse these manuals.
- Employees don't have easy access to this information, and they need the most current information.
- Employees can't always find someone to answer their questions or to update them on their status.
- It's hard for people to follow the manuals due to all the insert sheets detailing changes to the plan.

These problems occur because the Benefits Department just doesn't have a better way to distribute benefits information.

The Future Process That Will Solve the Problems

The BPI team proposes creating a new process (detailed in the appendix) for Benefits, including implementing an intranet, to solve the problem. An *intranet* is a private network that exists totally inside the company. A computer, called a *server,* will store all the benefits documents and make them readily available anytime someone needs access to them. We will place a piece of software, called a *browser,* on every computer. It will allow easy access to the benefits documents, regardless of the user's location.

An intranet will provide access for everyone to the latest information, and will be far less costly than the current process. Benefits can do updates quickly and easily, and everyone will have access immediately. The consequence of *not* doing this is that Benefits will fall further and further behind in disseminating changes, and employees won't have the most current information. Time lags in informing employees of changes could be costly to the company or to employees.

Implementation Plan for the Future Process

The team created a detailed implementation plan, complete with cost justification and a time line. You will find the detailed exhibits in the appendix.

Detailed Implementation Plan

The major steps in our implementation plan are:

1. Acquire and install server hardware and software.
2. Train administrators.
3. Acquire and install browser software.
4. Acquire and install publishing software.
5. Train Benefits staff on publishing software.
6. Convert benefits manuals and add revisions.
7. Create tutorials on the internal web.
8. Hold rollout meetings.

You can find the details of this implementation plan in the appendix.

Cost Justification

The cost justification consists of three parts:

1. Benefits and savings
2. Cost and expenditures
3. Summary and calculation of ROI

Benefits and Savings

The tangible cost savings from implementing an intranet will be approximately $199,000 the first year, as detailed in the appendix. (Figure 6.2 contains the cost justification that would normally appear in the appendix.) In addition, we expect to see intangible benefits in providing easy access to current information to all our employees. Not included are the savings to the Benefits Department from answering fewer phone calls. The time saved should allow them to do a better job of serving their existing customers. In addition, once the infrastructure for an intranet is in place, the entire organization can use it to achieve other significant cost savings.

Cost and Expenditures

The computing infrastructure and TCP/IP are already in place so the major expenditures are for servers and browsers. The costs of implementing the intranet total $79,500, as detailed in the appendix. (See Figure 6.2.)

Summary and Calculation of ROI

The first year cost savings of $199,000 less implementation expenditures of $79,500 provide total savings of $119,500 the first year. (See Figure 6.2.) This yields an ROI of 150 percent.

Time Line

We will start immediately upon approval of this project. The detailed time line appears in the appendix. (Figure 6.3 contains the time line that would appear in the appendix.) We will order all hardware and software and begin training the first month. The process of converting benefits documents will begin immediately upon installation of the publishing software and completion of the training. The conversion process will be complete by the end of month 3, and rollout meetings will take place in month 4 to roll out the new benefits documentation to all employees.

Figure 6.1   Sample proposal: Benefits BPI project.

1. Identify the problems with the process.
2. Define the current process and why the problems occur.
3. Create a future process that will solve the problems.
4. Develop an implementation plan for creating the future process, complete with a cost justification and a time line.

Identify the Problems with the Process   In this part of the proposal, we talk about the initial problems that led us to investigate the process. In the proposal we can see that the team has identified the two major problems with the benefits process:

1. The process of printing and distributing manuals is very expensive, and continues to get worse.
2. Employees aren't able to get the benefits information they need.

Define the Current Process and Why the Problems Occur   Next we talk about how the current process works and why it doesn't work anymore. You should put process flowcharts and steps in the appendix of your proposal and refer your readers there for the details. For the sake of simplicity, I didn't include an appendix in the sample proposal. In the proposal, the team detailed the process for doing major and minor revisions to benefits manuals, which included writing, printing, and distributing the changes. Major revisions happen once per year per manual, and minor ones happen three times per year per manual. In addition, copies go to the warehouse to accommodate the addition of new employees.

Among the major process problems we detailed are that the changes are coming increasingly faster, making it difficult for the Benefits staff to catch up. Manuals are expensive to print and distribute, and become obsolete faster. This means that employees don't have the most current information. Benefits just needs a better way to distribute information.

Create a Future Process That Will Solve the Problems   In this part of the proposal we talk about the recommendations, explain what they are, and mention the consequences of not implementing them. In the proposal, the BPI team recommends creating an intranet to make benefits information available to everyone. The proposal contains a very simple explanation of what an intranet is. The proposal indicates that an intranet will provide the latest information to everyone, and that Benefits can quickly and easily update this information. The consequence of not implementing an intranet is that Benefits will continue to get further behind and employees won't have accurate information.

Develop an Implementation Plan for the Future Process   Next we talk about the implementation plan for the future process, including the cost justification and the time line. The plan should contain complete details about implementation, the benefits from having an intranet, the cost, and the time line for implementing it.

Detailed Implementation Plan   The implementation plan shows the eight high-level steps of the implementation and refers the reader to the detailed plan in the appendix.

Cost Justification   The cost justification section has the following three parts:

1. Benefits and savings
2. Cost and expenditures
3. Summary and calculation of ROI

Benefits and Savings   In Figure 6.2, you can see the cost savings of $199,000 from implementing an intranet. In Figure 6.1, the proposal mentions additional cost savings. These include the potential created by having the intranet infrastructure already in place. Other areas of the organization can obtain similar savings with very little additional expenditure. If you need to review the benefits of having an intranet, Chapters 2 and 3 can give you lots of them.

Cost and Expenditures   Figure 6.2 also shows the required expenditures to implement the intranet. The premise used is that the network infrastructure already exists and that TCP/IP is already on each machine. The required expenditure for server hardware and software, browsers, publishing software, and training amounts to $79,500.

Summary and Calculation of ROI   Figure 6.2 shows that the result is an ROI of 150 percent!

Time Line   Figure 6.3 shows the time line for implementing the intranet. The executives will pay close attention to this and will want to know when the project will be complete so you can start generating those cost savings. Make sure that your plan is realistic in this regard because if they remember nothing else, they'll remember your projected completion date.

Executive Summary: Benefits BPI Project

When you've completed your proposal, go back and distill it into a concise executive summary to attach to the front of your proposal. Executives won't have time to read the entire proposal, so give them a summary of what's most important. It should be no more than one or two pages: Give them the facts and sell them on the project.

Cost Savings from New Benefits Process

Annual savings on the cost of preparing, printing, and mailing
benefits manuals

    Major changes to manuals:

        4 manuals/yr. @ $12 per manual   96,000
           × 2,000 employees

    Minor changes to manuals:

        4 manuals × 3 changes/yr   78,000
           @ $3.25 per change × 2,000
           employees

Eliminate one person from warehousing   25,000
   and mailing operation

    Total cost savings in year 1 $199,000

Expenditures for New Benefits Process

Server hardware and software   25,000
Browser software @ $25 × 2,000   50,000
Publishing software   1,000
Training   3,500

    Total expenditures $79,500

Summary

    Cost savings in year 1   199,000
    Expenditures   79,500
    Net savings in year 1   119,500
    ROI   150%

Figure 6.2   Sample cost justification: Benefits BPI project.

Steps	Month 1	Month 2	Month 3	Month 4
Acquire and install server hardware and software	■			
Train administrators	■			
Acquire and install browser software	■	■	■	
Acquire and install publishing software	■			
Train benefits employees on publishing software	■			
Convert benefits manuals and add revisions	■	■	■	
Create web-based tutorials		■	■	
Hold rollout meetings				■

Figure 6.3   Sample time line: Benefits BPI project.

Step 4: Present the Proposal and Sell the Concept

Once you've prepared your proposal, you'll need to present it to the executives who make the funding decisions. When presenting the proposal, remember to use simple and clear language to explain your findings and recommendations. Make your presentation short and to the point. Always stick to the facts. With the kind of ROIs that intranet projects can generate, it shouldn't be too hard to get approval, since the numbers speak for themselves.

Step 5: Implement It

When you have approval, you can proceed with your project plan. You may wish to pilot part of the implementation in order to work out the bugs before you move into a full-fledged rollout.

Step 6: Measure the Results

Once you have implemented the project, you should look back at the results and compare the actual results with what you projected. You can also review what you've learned from the implementation. This will come in handy as you move on to implement more sophisticated tools and applications, such as workflow and groupware, on your intranet. There is a lot more information in Chapter 11 about measuring results and in Chapter 12 about next steps for your intranet.

Internet Model

Now let's look at the second way you can implement your intranet. The Internet model is the informal, grassroots approach used by some companies to implement their intranets. It's unstructured and doesn't require all the formal approvals necessary in the Traditional model. It's based on allowing the intranet to grow in the rapid, and sometimes chaotic, manner in which the Internet itself has grown. This rapid growth allows the intranet to quickly reach critical mass. Your intranet will likely grow and become pervasive much faster if you choose the Internet model. If your network is already in place, you can choose to use the Internet model because cost won't be much of an issue and you won't have to get major funding in order to build it.

The Internet model encourages access and contributions. Anyone who wants access to the intranet can have it, and anyone who wants to create content can do so. Obviously, you can't have everyone contributing to an external Web site—someone has to manage its development or you'll confuse your customers. For an internal web site, you have lots more flexibility. You may wish to encourage everyone's contributions. You can encourage people, and even departments, to learn, experiment, and try new things that can yield wonderful ideas and insights. The end result may be things that help people do their jobs better.

The first two steps of the Internet model and the Traditional model are the same, so feel free to look back to the Traditional model for the details of these two steps. It's in the third step where the two models start to diverge. There are nine steps in the Internet model:

1. Do you need an intranet?
2. Are you ready?

3. How do you proceed?
4. Build your intranet.
5. Create your audience.
6. Promote your intranet.
7. Create widespread enthusiasm and capability.
8. Make your intranet pervasive.
9. What lessons have we learned, and where do we go from here?

Step 1: Do You Need an Intranet?

As before, in the Traditional model, you first need to determine why you need or want an intranet. If you determine that an intranet can help meet goals or specific business needs, then move on to the next step.

Step 2: Are You Ready?

Since you've determined that you need an intranet, it's time to move on to what's required to create it. Again, what areas of the organization need an intranet most? That's a good place to start promoting the concept. In step 2 in the Traditional model, you determined whether you had the necessary computers, networks, and network protocols. I'll presume that if the infrastructure isn't in place, you'll be going through the Traditional model approach to get the funding necessary to create it. For purposes of the Internet model, I'll presume for subsequent steps that you already have the infrastructure in place, or soon will.

Do you have the expertise you need to set up intranet technologies and do you have the people resources to do so?

Once you've answered these questions, you can move on to step 3.

Step 3: How Do You Proceed?

It's at this step that the two approaches start to diverge. You should be aware that in the Internet model, steps 3 through 6 can, and should, be done concurrently, and probably in an iterative fashion.

Champions and Steering Committees

Often, one or two people have the original vision of what an intranet will do for your organization. Once the CIO or someone high in the organization shares or catches your vision and is willing to become the champion, then it becomes easy to start deploying an intranet.

In most of the companies I spoke with, the champion or sponsor of the intranet was someone in IT, usually the CIO. In some companies, the role of champion and sponsor was held by several people, with the CIO being joined by his or her peers in corporate communications, HR, or occasionally R&D. Some companies also had steering committees, which often consisted of the CIO and top IT management.

The roles of the champion and the steering committee should be to create and spread the vision of how the intranet can help the organization and to eliminate obstacles. The goal of the champion and steering committee should be to determine where the intranet can best help the organization and to make sure it's deployed there. The champions will also be the sponsors for the intranet team, providing support, encouragement, and funding to get the team going.

In my situation, when our champion, the CIO, gave me responsibility for the Internet Team, he made me responsible to a steering committee. This committee consisted of himself and all of the top management in IS. The role of this steering committee was not only to make sure that I was moving fast enough at selling the Internet and intranet, but also to make sure that we addressed issues and took care of infrastructure needs. The clout of the steering committee overcame lots of obstacles. This support was critical to the successful deployment of jWeb.

A comment that I hear frequently in conjunction with intranets is that you must have support from the very top executives. That may be true in some organizations, but it may be counterproductive in others. In the Traditional model, you probably do need that kind of support to get the funding required. In the Internet model, all that may really be necessary is that the top executives are aware of, and in favor of, having an intranet.

They don't have to actively support it. In fact, if the CEO comes out and tells everybody that "intranets are wonderful," then everyone will get on the bandwagon. They may have a tendency, however, to stop and get approvals from every boss up the chain of command before putting anything on the web. Nobody wants to disappoint the CEO, and no boss wants to be responsible for something in his or her area being less than perfect. What this may do is slow it all down and stifle innovation. If the top executives and management are aware of the intranet and allow people to innovate and explore, the results may be amazing. A lot, however, depends on your culture, so it's up to you to make that call.

Should You Get Outside Help?

Once you have a champion and his or her budget, you need to decide how to proceed.

You should first identify your goals. What do you want an intranet to do? Once you've identified your goals, you can then identify things you don't have the experience or depth of knowledge to do. What things would you like someone else to do for you? What resources do you need that you don't have? This should dictate whether to hire some help or to go it alone.

- *Go it alone.* If you have people with the necessary skills and time to set up an intranet, then you can certainly do it yourself. If you make mistakes, you can just back up and try something different. Nobody gets the perfect intranet the first time out—*don't expect to.* The best implementation will come from learning what you like and don't like, and from trying new things until something works well for you. You may find yourself enhancing, or even redoing, it in a few months. You'll have to keep it fresh and new, or people just won't use it. It's harder to keep it new and interesting than it is to create it in the first place.

- *Bring in some help.* If you're running pretty *lean and mean,* and you're starting to get scared about what an intranet will require, then you may want to bring in some assistance. If you hire some help, you'll get up to speed faster and avoid the pitfalls others have encountered.

What Should a Consultant Do?   Here are some of the things a consultant can help with or do for you:

- Help you identify your goals for the intranet
- Help you work through any organizational issues
- Meet with areas throughout your organization to help identify needs for an intranet and the types of information that should be found on your intranet
- Help identify how people use the information and how you should provide it to them
- Help identify the sources and locations of information you need on your intranet
- Identify ways to get the information on the intranet and determine any conversion that's required
- Identify any network infrastructure you need and help with the procurement and installation required to get the network ready for the intranet
- Identify server hardware and server and browser software needed for the intranet and help with the installation
- Identify authoring and graphics tools for publishing web content
- Identify document databases, conversion tools, and any tools necessary to provide access to existing documents
- Assist with development of internal web structure and design
- Help develop guidelines and standards
- Help develop a publishing and approval process
- Help create demos

- ◆ Help promote the intranet throughout the organization
- ◆ Help form an intranet team and help them get focused
- ◆ Help develop applications and links to legacy databases
- ◆ Help figure out how to bring suppliers and customers into your intranet to provide opportunities for business partnerships
- ◆ Help identify and implement workflow and groupware
- ◆ Help identify and implement leading-edge technologies
- ◆ Help ensure you meet your intranet goals

With an intranet, you may not want to farm out quite as much as you would with an external Web site. You probably want more control over your proprietary information. You'll also want to make sure your intranet fits your culture. The intranet is just the medium. The communication and information are the important parts.

How Do You Select a Consultant? Once you've decided that you want help on this, how do you find and select a consultant or outsourcer to help you?

1. *What kind of assistance is available?* Hardware and software vendors, such as Sun, HP, IBM, Digital, and a host of others, offer intranet services and consulting. Then there are the systems integrators, such as EDS and others. There are partnerships that have sprung up, such as the teaming of HP and Netscape, to provide intranet services. There are also independent consultants who specialize in intranet and Internet consulting.

2. *How do you locate the kind of assistance you need?* Ask your hardware and software vendors about the services they provide. Keep in mind that they focus on selling products as well as consulting services. Call the systems integrators you know. They focus on the technology to give you the right solution. What about intranet and Internet consultants? You can find listings

for them on the Internet, so check out the search engines for consultants.

3. *How do you choose the right one for you?*   Ask whether these consultants can do the things for which you need assistance. If not, can they help you find the resources to do all these things? What are their capabilities and what alliances do they have? Large firms may have a depth of resources that can help you with just about any need, but they can be expensive. Small firms may not have the depth of resources, but if they have alliances with other firms they can often provide most of the things you need. Typically, they cost less, too. Finally, do you want one-stop shopping, or are you willing to do a little of the coordination yourself?

4. *Talk to the people who would be working with you, not just the person selling the services.*   What have their intranet experiences been? What is their perspective? Do they focus on the technology or on the solutions that an intranet can provide? Are you comfortable with them? Do they seem to know about your business and how it works? Do they understand your culture, and can they work within the constraints it imposes? Request the names of previous clients and talk with them. Were they pleased? Did the consultant understand their needs?

After you've assessed the answers to these questions, you will have narrowed your list of candidates. At this point, the selection may come down to *gut feel* as to which consultants will best fit with your culture and the people with whom they'll work.

Once you've chosen your consultant, identify what you expect from them and what they should expect from you and your organization. Also, make sure to define how you'll both know whether or not the project has been a success.

Step 4: Build Your Intranet

It's here at step 4 that the information for each step becomes far too much to include in this chapter. For each of the remaining steps of the Internet model, I'll give you a summary of the step here and refer you to the appropriate chapter for the details.

The role of the champion is to create and share the vision and sow the seeds for the intranet. Now it's time for the champion to make a modest investment to get the ball rolling. It's really important to get some applications going to prove the value of the project before anyone starts mentioning the dreaded *ROI*. Though you can measure ROIs for intranets, it seems that most companies just aren't bothering with that. They see intranets as *no-brainers* and are just doing it. In many cases, it's just so cheap that it doesn't make sense to go through the justification process. In some cases, they aren't measuring the results because they've already seen the impact. It's pretty obvious once you've shown people, but you do have to show them, not just talk about it. That's where funding by the champion comes in.

In Chapter 7, I'll talk in great detail about the specific things you'll need to do to build your intranet, which include the following:

1. Determine and develop infrastructure needs.
2. Determine security needs and implement security.
3. Evaluate and select an Internet service provider.
4. Select and install hardware and software.
5. Plan for maintenance of your intranet.

Step 5: Create Your Audience

Before people will be willing to publish content for the intranet, they'll want assurance that there will be an audience for their content. Your next step is to actually create that audience. One of the reasons you'll do your demos is to create demand. People will want browsers and access as a result of what they've seen. Prepare for rolling out browsers and other tools before you even start presenting the demos.

In Chapter 8, I'll talk in great detail about the specific things to do to create your audience, which include:

1. Identify and select the tools you will need.
2. Determine how to deploy these tools to your users.
3. Develop a plan for training and supporting users.

Step 6: Promote Your Intranet

The next step is to start doing demos to show people your intranet and what it can do. You have to have something to show customers in order for them to buy. People can't see what isn't there, so you have to build something to show them. You could describe it until you're blue in the face, and they just won't get it. Show them, and they'll understand.

There were two goals for our demos:

1. Recruit web publishers—those people in your company who have content they wish to publish on the intranet.
2. Recruit an audience of users—those people who will use the content the web publishers create.

There are two steps in promoting your intranet:

1. Build the demo
2. Present the demo

Build the Demo

You can build your demo very cheaply. My colleagues had already set up a server, but that's not necessary to create a demo for an intranet. All you really need is a spare computer, a browser, and an HTML tool, which you can download from the Internet for free. If you need to get access to the Internet cheaply, you can get by with a modem and an inexpensive dial-up account. When you get the tools, then you can start learning HTML. You can find lots of guidance on the Internet and in a variety of books. So it's really very inexpensive to create your demo.

While you're getting the computer and the tools, you can also figure out what to put in the demo. It seems that the standard first application for an intranet is the employee telephone directory. After that, you can get some employee benefits information and then find some kind of documentation to use. It helps if it's something that you print and distribute widely, and which you must update frequently. The more expensive the process of reprinting and distributing the information, the better candidate it is for a demo, and the greater the impact of your presentation. Once you have your material, you can start setting up HTML pages.

Next, start talking to your business partners in various parts of the business to find out what they would like to have in easily accessible electronic form. Every area has critical information that needs to be at everyone's fingertips. With a little research, you'll have more stuff for a demo than you can possibly have time to set up. You'll want to have enough variety in your demo to strike a chord with everyone who sees it. If you can't always get the data you need, there's nothing wrong with using mock data so that you can illustrate the concept.

A very fertile area is where the people using information have several different types of computers and operating systems. This makes the cost of creating a typical application much more expensive because it requires that it be built for multiple platforms. This kind of information is a good candidate for your demo, since Web browsers are available for almost every platform and you have to set up the data only once.

One more thing to look for: What kind of information do people need that is in databases but that they can't easily access? Use some of the web-to-database tools if you can get them before you start showing your demo. If not, you can create a mock-up simply to show the concept for your demo. The purpose of your demo is to help nontechnical people understand the concept, so you needn't be concerned that this isn't real database access.

Once you've set up a variety of information, you're ready to go, especially if you have hit on a lot of the *hot buttons* from different parts of your organization.

If you have the time and resources, add some glitz to your demo with fancy graphics, sound bites, and even video clips. You can probably already see their eyes lighting up! Be careful—a little goes a long way.

When you have the demo ready, it's time to start building the real intranet. Once it's ready, you can incorporate it into your presentations in place of the demo applications.

In Chapter 9, I'll talk in more detail about the specific steps involved in building the demo, which include:

1. Set up the computer.
2. Learn HTML.
3. Decide if you need an introduction.
4. Determine what to include in the demo.
5. Build sample applications.
6. Build the real intranet.

Present the Demo

Once you have the demo applications ready, you can start showing your demo. Who do you show it to first? What about some of the areas where you talked to people and got data that they really needed to access? Does your sponsor have someone in mind to show this to right away? Which goals did you use to create your vision and which area of the organization is involved in fulfilling those goals? We started with a few key executives. The choices of where to start are as individual as your organization, but it really doesn't matter. Just start somewhere. As soon as a few people have seen it, word will spread so quickly that people you don't even know will ask to see your demo.

Once we started showing the demo to some of the executives, they would typically get very excited about the prospects and would want a browser and access to the Internet and intranet right away. Usually, the next step was a demo for those executives' staffs, and then their whole departments. The excitement was contagious.

It was always fun to allow participants to brainstorm uses for the tools and then turn those ideas into applications for upcoming demos. It's especially neat for someone to see the demo for a second time with his or her staff and see the application they came up with. By giving them credit for the idea, you create an intranet evangelist.

Over several months, I did over 100 demos and presentations, including to the company's Management Council and the Board of Directors.

Through these demos, we recruited potential web publishers and invited them to join our Internet Team. People don't always volunteer to be on teams, but this was such a fun thing to do that the team grew to 55 web publishers and techies in just a few months.

The demos served not only to recruit web publishers and users, but also to build a great deal of enthusiasm for what an intranet could do for the company. The various functions of the business could see that the intranet could allow them to focus on their priorities and designate their own resources to accomplish them. They were also enthusiastic about having easy access to information. They were then quite supportive of those from their area who wanted to publish content for the internal web.

In Chapter 9, I'll go into a lot more detail about the specific steps involved in presenting the demo, which include:

1. Schedule the demos.
2. Tailor the demos to your audience.
3. Build enthusiasm.
4. Answer questions and address concerns about the Internet and intranet.

Step 7: Create Widespread Enthusiasm and Capability—The Role of the Intranet Team

As soon as we started showing our demo, people became enthusiastic and wanted to publish departmental information on the internal web or put information on the external Web. Because of that, the Internet Team included not only techies, but also graphics artists, communications people, and people from every area of the company. One of the reasons for which the Internet Team existed was to make it easy for publishers to get started. We created classes for them, helped them get the tools, and let them put their content on the IS server. Only when they wanted more control did they need to take the next step and put up their own server. This gave them time to walk before they ran.

Another function of the team was to increase the capabilities of these publishers. In our team meetings, technical experts kept the team apprised of the technical issues being discussed and resolved, new software being evaluated and approved, and tools and techniques that were available. We always included demos of the newest tools, such as the newest beta version of Netscape and how to use its new capabilities. Team members who attended conferences, seminars, and expos shared what they learned with the team. We always previewed new things that we were developing for the external site and showed the latest additions to the internal web. We kept the team aware of any new plans for either the intranet or the external Web site. Members of the team became invaluable resources to each other.

In Chapter 10, you'll find a lot more depth of information about creating widespread enthusiasm and capability through an intranet team, including:

1. Why you need an intranet team and who should be on that team
2. How the team works
3. What the team's objectives are
4. What impact the team has

Step 8: Make Your Intranet Pervasive

When publishers start moving from vanity pages to real and valuable content, you know you're getting where you want the intranet to be. Every department gets into the act by putting documentation, procedures, or whatever information it normally publishes on the internal web. Publishing starts taking place on the internal web rather than elsewhere. People start expecting to find the information they're looking for by going to the web. The intranet is starting to become ingrained in the culture, and it's creating an information democracy where users are in control of what they publish. You may even start to see changes in your culture.

How do you get your intranet to this stage? You do it by designing it for your users, keeping it fresh and new, reviewing your bandwidth needs frequently, adding new tools, and continuing to coordinate the team's efforts. Also, make sure the intranet provides value to your business and meets your business needs.

In Chapter 11, you'll find more details about making your intranet pervasive, including:

1. How do you make the intranet the universal user interface?
2. What are the critical success factors?
3. How do you measure the results?

Step 9: What Lessons Have We Learned, and Where Do We Go from Here?

Once your intranet has become pervasive throughout your organization, it's time to step back and see what you've learned. Then you can see how the lessons you've learned apply to what you'll do as you move forward with new phases of your intranet. Once you've done that, it's time to look at what you can do to enhance your intranet and its value to your organization. You can add tools and applications for workflow and groupware as the next step in the development of your intranet. In Chapter 12 I'll talk about the 20 lessons learned by the companies that participated in this book and I'll discuss what your next steps might be.

The Traditional Model or the Internet Model: To Bureaucratize or Not?

We've talked about the Internet model and the Traditional model, which I also refer to as the Bureaucratic model. Bureaucracy is a fact of life today in most established businesses. It lends order and control to what could otherwise be chaos. Rules enable everyone to know what they can and can't do. However, bureaucracy can stifle innovation and creativity. It makes businesses slow to react to customer needs and changing customer expectations. Many nimble new businesses are popping up to fill the voids created when customer needs change and bureaucratic companies aren't agile enough to accommodate those needs. This new competition is causing some businesses to realize that they must move away from bureaucracy and toward empowering their workers. That's why trying the Internet model for creating your intranet makes lots of sense.

Given a choice between the Traditional model and the Internet model, how do you decide which way to go?

1. *Traditional model.*   If you don't already have the infrastructure to support an intranet, you probably have to use the Traditional model because of the great expense involved. Getting the network infrastructure required for an intranet tends to be the hardest and most expensive part. It involves a more formal structure and organization to get it going. You can keep your infrastructure project separate and use the Internet model for the rest of your intranet project.

2. *Internet model.*   If you already have the necessary infrastructure for an intranet, the task is much easier and cheaper, and you can choose to use the Internet model. The decision probably depends on your culture. If your organization allows, or even encourages, grassroots efforts, then you should use the Internet model.

   How does your CIO want to approach this? If you have an open-minded CIO who doesn't want the intranet turned over to the bureaucracy, it should be pretty easy to use the Internet model. If you turn your intranet over to your bureaucracy, it will certainly slow it down. It's even possible that it won't get a chance to prove its value. I prefer the Internet model because of its impact on the culture.

For the remainder of this book I'll focus on steps 4 through 9 of the Internet model. That should not convey to you that the Traditional model is not important, because indeed it is. However, most companies are already familiar with the Traditional model and use it regularly. Many have their own standardized approach to doing so. The Internet model is new and different, and requires much more explanation. Also, the fact that I will devote most of the rest of this book to the Internet model should not convey to you the message that all 13 companies used it. That's not the case. These companies used both approaches and hybrid approaches of their own. However, the incorporation of intranets and the Internet into business seems to be the first time in recent memory that a technology has escaped our traditional bureaucratic approach.

Checklist: Ways to Sell the Intranet to Your Organization

Figure 6.4 summarizes the steps involved in selling an intranet to your organization.

---

1. Why companies have created intranets

    ◆ Because of the power and possibilities for the tools to solve business problems
    ◆ To meet communications needs
    ◆ To access information
    ◆ To share information and support mobile users

2. **Traditional Model** for building your intranet—the formal approach

    ◆ **Step 1: Do you need an intranet?**

        ◆ Why do you need or want an intranet?
        ◆ What are the goals of your organization?

- What are your problems and opportunities because of the rapidly changing business environment?
- Are you reengineering a business process that requires an intranet as part of the new process?

- **Step 2: Are you ready?**

  - What area or areas should you include?
  - Do you have the infrastructure?

    - What are your computer needs?
    - Is that area on a LAN or WAN?
    - Does the LAN or WAN use TCP/IP?

  - Do you have the skills and resources needed?

    - Do you have expertise in setting up and running TCP/IP?
    - Do you have expertise in Unix or Windows NT?

  - Do you have the people resources to take on the extra workload?
  - Do you have someone who can take the lead in developing and maintaining applications?

- **Step 3: Develop a project plan and proposal**

  - What's in the proposal?

    - Identify the problems with the process.
    - Define the current process and why the problems occur.

◆ Create a future process that will solve the problems.
◆ Develop an implementation plan for the future process.

  ◆ Detailed implementation plan
  ◆ Cost justification—benefits and savings, cost and expenditures, summary and calculation of ROI
  ◆ Time line

◆ Executive summary

◆ **Step 4: Present the proposal and sell the concept**

  ◆ Use simple and clear language.
  ◆ Make it short and to the point.
  ◆ Stick to the facts.

◆ **Step 5: Implement it.** Pilot and roll out.
◆ **Step 6: Measure the results**

3. **Internet model** for building your intranet—the grass-roots approach

   ◆ **Step 1: Do you need an intranet?** See step 1 of Traditional model.
   ◆ **Step 2: Are you ready?** See step 2 of Traditional model.
   ◆ **Step 3: How do you proceed?** Do steps 3 through 6 concurrently.

     ◆ Champions and steering committees—determine roles.

       ◆ Create and spread the vision of how the intranet can help.

- ◆ Eliminate obstacles.
- ◆ Sponsor and provide funding for the intranet team

◆ Support from the top executives can be counterproductive depending upon your culture.

◆ Should you get outside help?

- ◆ Identify your goals.
- ◆ What do you need?
- ◆ Should you get help?

  - ◆ Go it alone if you have the people with the necessary skills and time.
  - ◆ Bring in some help if you're running pretty lean and mean.

◆ What should a consultant do?

- ◆ Help you identify your goals for the intranet
- ◆ Help you work through any organizational issues
- ◆ Meet with areas throughout your organization to help identify needs for an intranet and the types of information that should be found on your intranet
- ◆ Help identify how people use the information and how you should provide it to them
- ◆ Help identify the sources and locations of information you need on your intranet

- Identify ways to get the information on the intranet and determine any conversion that's required
- Identify any network infrastructure you need and help with the procurement and installation required to get the network ready for the intranet
- Identify server hardware and server and browser software needed for the intranet and help with installation
- Identify authoring and graphics tools for publishing web content
- Identify document databases, conversion tools, and any tools necessary to provide access to existing documents
- Assist with development of internal web structure and design
- Help develop guidelines and standards
- Help develop a publishing and approval process
- Help create demos
- Help promote the intranet throughout the organization
- Help form an intranet team and help them get focused
- Help develop applications and links to legacy databases
- Help figure out how to bring suppliers and customers into your intranet to provide opportunities for business partnerships
- Help identify and implement workflow and groupware

- ◆ Help identify and implement leading-edge technologies
- ◆ Help to ensure you meet your intranet goals

◆ How do you select a consultant?

- ◆ Who—hardware and software vendors, systems integrators, independent consultants
- ◆ What are their capabilities?
- ◆ What alliances do they have?
- ◆ What is their intranet experience?
- ◆ Do they focus on solutions?
- ◆ Do they understand your culture?
- ◆ Who are their previous clients?

◆ Identify what you expect from consultants and what they should expect from you.

◆ Define how you'll both know when the project is a success.

- ◆ **Step 4: Build your intranet.** The champion funds initial development, which includes:

  - ◆ Determine and develop infrastructure needs.
  - ◆ Determine security needs and implement security.
  - ◆ Evaluate and select an Internet service provider.
  - ◆ Select and install hardware and software.
  - ◆ Plan for maintenance of your intranet.

- ◆ **Step 5: Create your audience**

  - ◆ Identify and select the tools you will need.

- ◆ Determine how to deploy these tools to your users.
- ◆ Develop a plan for training and supporting users.

- ◆ **Step 6: Promote your intranet.** Recruit web publishers and users.

  - ◆ Build the demo—steps include

    - ◆ Set up the computer.
    - ◆ Learn HTML.
    - ◆ Decide if you need an introduction.
    - ◆ Determine what to include in the demo.
    - ◆ Build sample applications.
    - ◆ Build the real intranet.

  - ◆ Present the demo—steps include

    - ◆ Schedule the demos.
    - ◆ Tailor the demos to your audience.
    - ◆ Build enthusiasm.
    - ◆ Answer questions and address concerns about the Internet and intranet.

- ◆ **Step 7: Create widespread enthusiasm and capability—the role of the intranet team**
- ◆ **Step 8: Make your intranet pervasive**
- ◆ **Step 9: What lessons have we learned and where do we go from here?**

  - ◆ What lessons have you learned?
  - ◆ Next steps

◆ Apply the lessons you've learned as you do new phases of your intranet.

◆ Identify new tools to add to your intranet.

4. Which way should you go—Traditional model or Internet model?

◆ *Traditional model.*   Use the Traditional model if you need to build the infrastructure for your intranet. You can keep your infrastructure project separate and use the Internet model for the rest of your intranet project.

◆ *Internet model.*   Use the Internet model if you already have the infrastructure and your culture allows grassroots efforts.

Figure 6.4   Ways to sell the intranet to your organization—checklist.

chapter seven

Build Your Intranet

Determine and Develop Infrastructure Needs

Now it's time to get the ball rolling. The champion must provide the initial funds to build a prototype or demo system, or even better, the real thing. The first thing you'll need to do is determine and develop your infrastructure needs. As we talked about in step 2 in Chapter 6, to run an intranet, you must generally have TCP/IP as the protocol used on the network. This may be either through having an IP stack on each desktop machine or through using an IP gateway server. At this point, you should either have TCP/IP or be implementing it.

Do you have people with the skills to administer and support TCP/IP on your network?

Do you have the network infrastructure to support the level of traffic you expect on your intranet? Do you need additional bandwidth? The larger your intranet becomes, and the more graphics, audio, and video you add, the more network bandwidth you'll need. Take time to forecast and analyze that now. Should you out-source this so you can get bandwidth on demand? Also, beware that bandwidth-hogging applications can shut down other applications and users on the network.

Once you move browsers out to the masses and you have a lot of content on your intranet, it's time to take another look at capacity issues. You may wish to consider a network management tool, such as Network Health or Command, to document and analyze your WANs. As intranets explode throughout organizations, bandwidth will be a major issue, and perhaps a major headache, for network administrators.

Intranets are a microcosm reflecting what happens on the Internet itself. We see lots of big graphics and other bandwidth-eating applications. The same can happen on your intranet. Just as we teach programmers to write efficient code, we should also teach web publishers how to create efficient web pages.

How Will You Serve Remote Locations and Remote Users?

If you're already linking your remote locations through a WAN, and the TCP/IP protocol is in use, then remote locations can access your intranet just as easily as those residing locally on your LAN. The major constraint will be the bandwidth between locations.

Some of your options for connecting your remote locations and users into your intranet include:

1. **Dedicated leased line:** Dedicated leased lines are digital phone lines that connect your locations. Their speeds range from 56 kilobits per second (Kbps) to T1 speed of 1.544 megabits per second (Mbps).

2. **Non-dedicated dial-up or switched access:** Options for non-dedicated access include:

   ◆ **Dial-up analog modem:** This is the cheapest and slowest way for remote locations or users to access your intranet. It involves using analog telephone lines and a modem, which can be at speeds of 9.6 Kbps, 14.4 Kbps, 28.8 Kbps, or 33.6 Kbps. Dial-up is for those who need occasional access to the network, and is fine for "road warriors" and those who sometimes access your LAN from home.

   ◆ **Integrated Services Digital Network (ISDN):** ISDN is similar to using a dial-up analog modem except that it's digital rather than analog. It's slightly more expensive but much faster. ISDN's speed ranges from 64 Kbps to 128 Kbps. You generally use ISDN for telecommuters and small remote offices.

◆ **Frame relay:** Frame relay is currently one of the most popular ways for connecting remote locations since it's the least expensive way to have a digital circuit. Frame relay speeds range from 56 Kbps to T1 speed of 1.544 Mbps.

◆ **Asynchronous Transfer Mode (ATM):** ATM is a new technology that's not yet in widespread use on corporate networks. Since it's available at speeds of up to 45 Mbps, it's ideal for multimedia and will become more widespread as organizations need more bandwidth on their networks.

There are three additional technologies to watch for possible future use for remote access:

1. **Asymmetric digital subscriber line (ADSL):** This and other related digital subscriber line technologies are just emerging. They use standard twisted-pair phone lines and special modems. What's unusual is that much of this technology provides a higher speed for receiving information than it does for sending it.

2. **Cable modem:** This is another emerging technology, and it uses television cable and a cable modem.

3. **Direct broadcast satellite (DBS):** This is an existing technology that's primarily for one-way communication, such as for massive downloads of information.

Your choice of speed will dictate the kind of router that you'll need on your network to connect remote locations and users into your network.

Virtual Private Networks

Virtual private networks (VPNs) are a way to use the Internet itself as the network. They will become quite prevalent over the next few years. A VPN is basically the use of compatible firewalls on each end of the network connection to encrypt transactions and permit access only to those with authorization. You can use them to link with your remote locations or to allow your suppliers and customers to transfer files to you or to access information on your intranet. VPNs are less expensive than dedicated lines, and can be more flexible as they come and go as needed.

Microsoft has recently announced that it will include a remote access protocol, point-to-point tunneling protocol (PPTP), in the next version of Windows NT Server. It will allow remote and mobile users to access their corporate networks via the Internet from wherever they are.

Determine Security Needs and Implement Security

Security should be a major concern for any organization accessing the Internet or using the Internet to create a VPN. You'll want to identify your security needs and determine how to implement the necessary security. There are several tools to consider as part of your security plan:

- *Firewalls.* The main purpose of a firewall is to protect your corporate data and networks from intrusion by outsiders. Firewalls do this by monitoring all packets of information and deciding which ones to allow to enter. You can also use a firewall internally to block unauthorized access to confidential areas of your intranet. At the time of this writing, some of the leading firewall vendors are CheckPoint Software Technologies, Raptor Systems, and Trusted Information Systems. Firewall software is also available for free over the Internet. Whichever way you go, make sure you understand how to configure it properly.

- *Encryption.* Encryption allows information to flow confidentially across the Internet. There are two basic types of encryption:

  1. *Encrypting firewalls* allow you to exchange information securely and confidentially across the Internet and turn it into a virtual private network with your remote offices.

2. *Message encryption* allows you to encrypt e-mail messages so they can securely and confidentially traverse the Internet.

Internet and intranet security are very important and they change quickly. My advice is to either read everything you can on the subject and proceed very carefully or hire good help to set up your Internet security. Here are some resources to check out for current information:

◆ You can find a good FAQ on Internet Firewalls, by Marcus J. Ranum, at http://www.v-one.com/pubs/fw-faq/faq.html.

◆ The World Wide Web Security FAQ is at http://www.genome.wi.mit.edu/WWW/faqs/www-security-faq.html.

◆ Eugene Spafford, an assistant professor of Computer Science at Purdue, has a computer security hot list with links to everything you could want to know about computer security. It also doubles as the official WWW hot list of the Computer Operations, Audit, and Security Technology (COAST) Laboratory at Purdue. Check it out at http://www.cs.purdue.edu/homes/spaf/hotlists/csec.html. It includes information about organizations, journals, newsletters, mailing lists, books, FAQs, cryptography resources, computer viruses, firewalls and firewall vendors, Web security, electronic commerce, and lots more. It is a most incredible list of computer security resources. You could spend weeks and weeks checking out all the sites listed. This is a great starting point in your quest to learn about firewalls and Internet security.

◆ For information on encryption technology, check out RSA Data Security, the company that set the standard for encryption technology, at http://www.rsa.com.

◆ If you decide to get help with your Internet security, you can find a list of companies that specialize in computer security on Yahoo at http://www.yahoo.com/

Business_and_Economy/Companies/Computers/
Security/Consulting/.

While firewalls keep out outsiders and encryption keeps your information confidential, keep in mind that having these doesn't mean that you're completely safe. I strongly urge you to have a firewall, but just be sure that it doesn't give you a false sense of security. It's easy for someone to get inside your company and plug in their own computer or use an existing computer to access your confidential information. Firewalls and encryption can't prevent this. Another vulnerability is through computer viruses, which can come in from the Internet, or more commonly, *walk in* on floppy disks. One of the most important parts of your Internet security plan is to have a clearly stated Internet security policy so your employees understand what things they should and shouldn't do. This should also include regular use of virus-scanning and virus-protection tools.

Evaluate and Select an Internet Service Provider

There are many advantages to allowing access to the Internet from your intranet. If you plan to do so, then you'll need an Internet service provider (ISP). If you wish to provide your employees with Internet e-mail, but not Internet access, you'll still need an ISP. If you wish to create a virtual private network, then you'll also need an ISP. If, however, you have only a single site and don't wish to connect to the Internet for any reason, then you won't need an ISP.

You can begin evaluating ISPs while you're still defining your security needs. How do you find an ISP? The best resources are on the Internet. To do your initial research, consider getting a temporary dial-up account or use an on-line service, such as CompuServe, that provides access to the Web. The most popular source of ISPs on the Internet seems to be *The List* at http://thelist.com. According to The List, at the time of this writing, there are 2,245 Internet service providers, and there will undoubtedly be many more by the time you check into it. The List provides a variety of searches to help you locate ISPs. For instance, for the United States and Canada, you can search for national providers, or search by state, province, or area code. You can also use the graphic map to click on the area that interests you. For the rest of the world, you can search by country or by country code. The List provides ISP information such as names, area codes served, phone and fax numbers, e-mail addresses, URL, services they provide, and the fees for their services.

Until recently, The List also provided an opportunity for users to post comments and evaluations of the services of the various ISPs. They have removed those comments because apparently some ISPs used them to trash their competitors. If you want to find out more about specific ISPs, you can ask for feedback on the Usenet group, alt.internet.services.

An additional place to look for an ISP is in Commerce Net's ISP Directory, which you'll find at http://www.commerce.net/directories/products/isp/isp.html/.

Once you've located potential ISPs, how do you evaluate them? You must ask them lots of questions. UUNET Technologies provides an excellent list of criteria to use to select an ISP for your business. You can find this list, entitled *Selecting an Internet Provider,* at http://www.uu.net/busguide.htm#selecting. They list eight criteria, which for the sake of brevity, I have paraphrased here.

1. *Orientation.*   Does this provider focus on the needs of businesses?

2. *Quality of service.*   Is the service reliable, available, and high-performance?

    ◆ *Reliability.*   Does the provider have redundant equipment at all major switching hubs and redundant backbone links? Does the Network Operation Center (NOC) have an Uninterruptible Power Supply (UPS) for backup? Does it include a self-contained (gas or diesel) generator?

    ◆ *Availability.*   If you will be using a dial-up connection, what is their "p-grade" of service? A p-grade of p.05 means that no more than 5 calls out of 100 get a busy signal. Avoid ISPs that are higher than p.05.

- ◆ *Performance.*   Examine a diagram of their network. Look for a high-speed, high-capacity backbone to ensure minimal delays. What is the speed of the backbone? The maximum available is 45 Mbps. What is the speed at which large and small nodes connect to the backbone? For large nodes, 10 Mbps or higher is best, and for small nodes, T-1 is preferable to 56 Kbps.

3. *Points of Presence.*   Is the network Point of Presence (POP) close to your site? It will be less expensive to connect into if it's close to you. It's best to find a provider with direct connections to national and international components of the Internet.

4. *Service product range.*   Does the ISP provide a wide range of services that will meet all of your needs? If you need dial-up service and dedicated high-speed links, do they offer both? A good provider should offer dedicated lines at speeds from 56 Kbps, up to T-1, and on up to T-3 (45 Mbps), so you can upgrade when you need to.

5. *Value-added capabilities.*   What value-added capabilities do they offer? Some of the ones that may interest you are:

- ◆ **Security options.**   Can they help you set up the appropriate security?
- ◆ **Domain names.**   Can they provide you with your own domain name? Can they register your domain name for you?

6. *Support.*   Do they have a 24-hour-per-day, 7-day-per-week Network Operation Center? Do they have personnel who focus only on the needs of business customers? Do they provide all the services you need?

7. *Experience.*   How long have they been an ISP? Is this their main business? How many business customers do they have and are those customers happy?

8. *Cost.* While cost is important, it is only one of the criteria upon which to judge an ISP. It's best to avoid the cheapest provider because they must obviously scrimp somewhere to save on costs. Determine the range of prices and select a provider that isn't at either extreme.

These eight criteria should help you select an ISP. Before you do, make sure you talk to other customers of that ISP before making your final decision.

Acquire an Internet Domain

As I mentioned in step 5 above, your ISP should be able to provide you a domain name and get it registered for you. A domain name is nothing more than your address on the Internet. An example might be *yourcompany.com.* You will need a domain name to have either an Internet Web site or Internet e-mail.

In the United States, you acquire domain names through an organization called InterNIC Registration Services. InterNIC is also handling Canadian registration temporarily. For other countries, you can check out Yahoo's Domain Registration list at http://www.yahoo.com/Computers_and_Internet/Domain_Registration/ to find the registration services for the various countries and regions of the world.

In the United States, InterNIC will register your domain name for a $100 initial setup fee, which is good for two years. Renewals are $50 per year thereafter for each domain name.

U.S. domain names (Table 7.1) end in a three-character code called a top-level domain name. These include **COM** for businesses, **EDU** for educational institutions, **GOV** for governmental organizations, **MIL** for military organizations, **NET** for network providers, and **ORG** for nonprofit organizations. Addresses for other countries have a two-character country code for the top-level domain name. Table 7.1 includes a sampling of country codes, such as **AU** for Australia, **CA** for Canada, and **DE** for Germany.

In the example above, *yourcompany.com, com* is the top-level domain name and *yourcompany* is the second-level domain name. This domain name is part of both your WWW address and your Internet e-mail address.

TABLE 7.1 Top-Level Internet Domain Names: United States and Selected Countries

Domain Name	Description
COM	U.S. Commercial
EDU	U.S. Educational
GOV	U.S. Government
MIL	U.S. Military
NET	Network
ORG	Nonprofit Organization
AU	Australia
CA	Canada
DE	Germany
FI	Finland
FR	France
JP	Japan
NL	Netherlands
SE	Sweden
UK	United Kingdom

Select and Install Hardware and Software

Since this book is more about how to build an intranet and what to use it for rather than what to use to build it, I won't go into much detail about the hardware and software you need. Besides, if I talk much about specific hardware and software, that information will be obsolete by the time you read this book. So let's focus on the things you need and how to find out which tools to consider at the time you're ready to do so. I'll talk about:

- Servers
- Browsers
- Search tools
- Document authoring tools
- Document conversion tools
- Document databases
- Database query tools

Servers

As I said earlier, you can start pretty cheaply by using a spare or borrowed computer and downloaded software from the Internet to run it. This will give you a chance to prove the concept. This will get you started, but since intranets grow like wildfire, you will outgrow it pretty quickly and will need some real commitments. The free software that's available on the Internet is generally good, and has been pretty extensively debugged due to the volumes of users that have used it. However, support can be an issue if the person or persons that created the software have gone on to something else or somewhere else. So let's talk mostly about commercial products.

Several surveys have shown that for external Webs, Unix servers seem to command the marketplace. However, Windows NT and Windows 95 have made lots of headway and are starting to command an ever larger portion of the external server market. For intranets, Windows NT appears to be leading the pack. That was even before Microsoft started giving away its Internet Information Server.

When you select your server hardware, make sure that response time is a major consideration. Select a server that will meet your needs as intranet traffic gets heavier. Get the biggest server you can afford at the time because it won't take long before you'll use every bit of its capacity.

As you get into server software, you'll need several different kinds of servers. You can acquire them separately and put them on different machines, or you can acquire them in a single package and put them on the same machine. Keep in mind that performance may not be as good if you have them all on the same machine. The types of servers you may need are:

- *Domain name server (DNS).* Sometimes called an Internet server, to handle domain names and other Internet services.
- *Web HTTP server.* To provide HTML pages to web browsers, and possibly to provide secure Web transactions. Security comes in several varieties:

1. *Secure HTTP (SHTTP),* incorporated in servers from Open Market.
2. *Secure Sockets Layer (SSL),* incorporated in servers from Netscape, Microsoft, IBM, and Open Market.
3. *Private Communications Technology (PCT),* Microsoft's enhanced version of SSL.
4. *Secure Transport Layer Protocol (STLP),* which Microsoft has just submitted as a draft proposal to the Internet Engineering Task Force (IETF). This protocol combines Netscape's SSL 3.0 with Microsoft's PCT 2.0, and is an attempt to forge an encryption standard from the competing protocols.
5. *Secure Electronic Transaction* (SET), a joint standard developed by MasterCard and Visa. It should be in use soon after this book reaches the stores.

♦ *Proxy server.* To allow access to the Internet from your intranet, while keeping the two systems separate. The proxy server will take requests from internal clients and request a specific address from the external server. This provides security because you don't reveal internal network addresses to the outside world.

♦ *Simple Mail Transfer Protocol (SMTP) Server.* For e-mail. This server may also support the Internet's Post Office Protocol 3 (POP3) and Internet Message Access Protocol 4 (IMAP4).

♦ *Gopher server.*

♦ *File Transfer Protocol (FTP) Server.*

♦ *Transaction server.* For access to databases.

Some servers include other features and functions, such as firewalls, search applications, utilities for creating and authoring Web pages, and a graphical user interface (GUI) for managing web page files.

Some of the major players in the server market include:

◆ **Microsoft,** with their Internet Information Server (IIS). IIS is easy to install and free. NT Server 4.0 will have IIS bundled with a domain name server and will provide a web server, gopher server, and an FTP server. It will also allow you to deny or permit FTP access based on a user's IP address.

◆ **Netscape,** with a variety of server products, both secured and unsecured.

◆ SGI

◆ Sun

◆ IBM

◆ Hewlett-Packard

Server hardware and software change quickly, so how do you get the latest information about servers when you're ready for it? Here are some resources to check out when you start researching intranet tools. They apply not just to servers, but also to all the categories of software discussed in this section. These resources include:

◆ The World Wide Web FAQ at http://www.boutell.com/faq/. This is a great starting point for researching Web servers and other things related to the WWW. It contains information on obtaining and using Web browsers, establishing and using Web servers, authoring Web pages, images and scripts, and other resources about the Web.

◆ Web Compare at http://www.webcompare.com/. Web Compare lists servers and browsers and includes comparisons and charts of features.

◆ Intranet Soundings, the Web's only moderated message exchange dedicated to intranets, at the Intranet Journal at http://www.brill.com/intranet/ijx/.

◆ Network World Fusion at http://www.nwfusion.com/.

- WebMaster Magazine's Technology Notes at http://www.cio.com/WebMaster/wm_tech_notes.html.
- The Complete Intranet Resources at http://control.cga.sc.edu/intranet.htm.
- PC Magazine at http://www.pcmag.com/, which includes:

    - Intranet Tools Directory at http://www.pcmag.com/IU/intranet/reviews/ir-dir.htm
    - Product Index at http://www.pcmag.com/IU/index.htm

- Search engines such as Yahoo at http://www.yahoo.com.

Since many computer magazines do reviews and benchmarks, you may want to check them out on the Net or on the newsstand.

Browsers

In addition to servers, you also need browsers. The browser you choose should be available for all the platforms you have to support. To make it easy for you to deploy, it should include all the features you need so you don't have to install lots of additional tools. These features may include e-mail, newsgroups. FTP, Telnet, plug-ins, add-ons, security, and maybe even virtual reality tools. You should also consider whether the browser supports the latest version of HTML, ActiveX controls, and scripting languages, such as JavaScript and VBScript. Since Microsoft has jumped into the Internet fray by giving away its Internet Explorer browser, Microsoft and Netscape are now battling for control of the browser market. Check out the latest on browsers at the sites listed in the previous section. I'll also talk more about browsers in Chapter 8.

Search Tools

Several of the companies that I spoke with said that they wished they had provided a search tool to their users sooner. Most were using Lycos, PLS, Verity, and WAIS. It will be a good idea to go ahead and evaluate search tools, whether or not you plan to install one initially. Currently, there are quite a few search tools available, such as:

- Alta Vista
- Excite
- Open Text
- Lycos
- Personal Library Software
- Verity
- WAIS

Document Authoring Tools

When choosing HTML authoring tools, keep in mind who your web publishers are and what their preferences will be. For instance, publishers may prefer WYSIWYG (What You See Is What You Get) authoring tools, such as NavigatorGold, PageMill, FrontPage, or GNNpress, which show what a page will look like as you create it. However, most HTML authoring tools are not WYSIWYG. Select tools that are easy to use and robust enough to do all the things that your publishers will want to do.

A good resource to check out for current information on authoring tools and conversion tools is the HTML resource at NCSA. You'll find it at http://union.ncsa.uiuc.edu/HyperNews/get/www/html.html.

Document Conversion Tools

There are many tools emerging for converting existing documents to HTML, with more on the way. These should prove to be popular products as companies seek to convert their huge investments in existing documentation and manuals for use on their internal webs. Some examples include:

- **Microsoft Internet Assistants.** Convert Word, Excel, and Power Point files into HTML documents.

◆ **HTML Transit.**   Converts a wide variety of formats, including Word and Word Perfect, to HTML.
◆ **Web Publisher.**   Converts Word, Word Perfect, and other documents to HTML.

Document Databases

Document databases store existing documents and can convert them to HTML *on the fly* for display in a web browser. Some representative document database tools are:

◆ **Basis Document Manager** by Information Dimensions
◆ **DynaWeb** by Electronic Book Technologies
◆ **Folio Infobase Web Server** by Folio
◆ **InterNotes Web Publisher** by Lotus

Database Query Tools

Database query tools are in their infancy, but you'll definitely want to start evaluating and selecting some if you wish to offer access to your databases from your intranet. Some of the tools that allow you to program web-to-database queries include:

◆ **Cold Fusion** by Allaire
◆ **WebServer** by Oracle
◆ **web.sql** by Sybase
◆ **Internet Information Server** by Microsoft

Plan for Maintenance of Your Intranet

As you select and install hardware and software, make sure to consider your needs for monitoring and maintenance of your intranet. Make sure that those who will administer your intranet have the tools and training they need to properly set up and maintain your intranet.

Checklist: Build Your Intranet

Figure 7.1 summarizes the steps involved in building your intranet.

---

1. Determine and develop infrastructure needs

   - Identify needs

     - Do you have TCP/IP?
     - Do you have people with the skills to administer and support TCP/IP?
     - Do you have the network infrastructure to support the level of traffic you expect?
     - Do you need additional bandwidth?
     - Should you outsource this so you can get bandwidth on demand?
     - Do you need a network management tool to document and analyze your WANs?

   - How will you serve remote locations and remote users?

     - Ways for remote locations and users to access your intranet

       - Dedicated leased line
       - Non-dedicated dial-up or switched access
         - Dial-up analog modem
         - ISDN
         - Frame relay
         - ATM
       - Other technologies for remote access

- ◆ ADSL
- ◆ Cable modem
- ◆ DBS

◆ Virtual private networks (VPNs)

- ◆ To link remote locations
- ◆ To allow suppliers and customers to access your intranet

2. Determine security needs and implement security

◆ Security methods

- ◆ Firewalls
- ◆ Encryption

◆ Have a clearly stated Internet security policy, which should include regular virus scanning and virus protection tools.

3. Evaluate and select an ISP

◆ Locate

- ◆ *The List*
- ◆ Ask for feedback on the Usenet group, alt.internet.services
- ◆ Commerce Net's ISP directory

◆ Evaluate—eight criteria

- ◆ Orientation: Does this provider focus on the needs of businesses?
- ◆ Quality of service: Is the service reliable, available, and high performance?

- Points of presence: Is the network point of presence close to your site?
- Service product range: Does the ISP provide a wide range of services that will meet all of your needs?
- Value-added capabilities: What value-added capabilities do they offer?
- Support: Do they have a 24-hour-per-day, 7-day-per-week network operation center? Do they have personnel who focus only on the needs of business customers? Do they provide all the services you need?
- Experience: How long have they been an ISP? Is this their main business? How many business customers do they have and are those customers happy?
- Cost: Determine the range of prices and select a provider that isn't at either extreme.

- Talk to other customers of that ISP
- Acquire an Internet domain

4. Select and install hardware and software

- Servers

  - Hardware—get the biggest server you can afford
  - Software—types of servers you may need:

    - Domain name server (DNS)
    - Web HTTP server
    - Proxy server
    - Simple Mail Transfer Protocol (SMTP) server

- ◆ Gopher server
- ◆ File transfer protocol (FTP) server
- ◆ Transaction server

- ◆ Browsers

    - ◆ Should be available for all the platforms you have to support
    - ◆ Should include all the features you need, such as:

        - ◆ E-mail
        - ◆ Newsgroups
        - ◆ FTP
        - ◆ Telnet
        - ◆ Plug-ins and add-ons
        - ◆ Security
        - ◆ Virtual reality tools
        - ◆ Latest version of HTML
        - ◆ ActiveX controls, JavaScript, and VBScript

- ◆ Search tools
- ◆ Document authoring tools—WYSIWYG or not?
- ◆ Document conversion tools
- ◆ Document databases
- ◆ Database query tools

5. Plan for maintenance of your intranet

    - ◆ Consider your needs for monitoring and maintenance of your intranet
    - ◆ Provide tools and training for administrators

Figure 7.1　Build your intranet—checklist.

chapter eight

Create Your Audience

Why Should You Create Your Audience?

Why should web publishers even bother to publish content on the internal web if they have no audience for it? The answer is that they *won't*. So, if you want content, you must have an audience first. Otherwise, nobody will bother to publish or to use your internal web.

It's not hard to create the audience first. Actually, it's pretty easy if you already have TCP/IP on the desktop. To create an audience, simply set up a web server, put a browser on each computer, and turn people loose. If users have Internet access, they can surf the Net while your publishers start to create content for the internal web. All you really need to start your internal web is a simple, but useful, application. Set up your phone directory or employee locator as a starter application to get people coming to the internal web. If you give them some value, they'll come.

What Tools Will Users Need?

When you do your demos, people will want access for themselves, and they'll want it now! You should prepare for this before you start doing your demos. Once you start those demos, you'll have an avalanche of demand for browsers. It's very easy for it to get ahead of you.

When we started our demos, the browser scene was very user-*un*friendly. We worked with Mosaic on an X-terminal, which was dreadful for nontechies. Even so, people were clamoring for access. Fortunately, within just a few weeks, a much more user-friendly environment, Netscape, became available, and we were able to start deploying it. Netscape was very easy to use. People showed the internal web to their friends, who saw how easy it was to use and wanted it for themselves. It was like a grass fire—one spark started an inferno. Be fully prepared to roll out browsers *before* you start presenting your demo.

Which tools should you choose? There are so many tools to choose from that I couldn't possibly go into all of them here. Besides, by the time you get this book, many of the tools will have changed significantly. There are lots of sites on the Web where you can find reviews of tools and links to specific product information. I've listed some of these sites in the Appendix.

You'll need a browser, or client, to provide users with access to the information on the internal web. There are lots of things to consider in choosing a browser, such as:

- *User-friendliness.* Is it user-friendly? Is it easy to configure and easy to use?

- *Security.* Does it provide the type and amount of security that you need?

- *Cost.* How much does it cost? Though this is important, it shouldn't influence your choice, since the cost of most browsers is minimal.

- *Features and tools.* Does it include or support the features and tools you need? Some of the things to consider are:

- *HTML.* Does it support the latest version of HTML? Do you need the features of the latest version?

- *E-mail and newsgroups.* If you don't have e-mail, you should certainly consider providing it for your users. Newsgroups are very useful, too, and you may want to consider providing them, as well. Some browsers have e-mail and newsgroups built in, which makes it a little easier to set these up.

- *FTP and Telnet.* Will your users need FTP to do file transfers, or Telnet to access mainframes? If so, do these tools come with the browser you're considering or will you need to provide them separately?
- *Plug-ins, add-ons, and special features.* Some browsers support plug-ins, add-ons, and special features, while others don't. If you have a need for some of them, you'll want to choose a browser that supports them.

  You may want to consider what 3D, phone, audio, video, whiteboarding, chat, and plug-ins could do for your users. Is there a business reason for which your users need them? For example, could your product development engineers in different locations use phone, whiteboarding, and chat to discuss technical issues related to a specific technology? Could you deliver technical seminars via streaming audio feeds? Could you deliver training by video? Could your chemists use 3D to view molecular structures? The uses are almost endless.

  If there is some real value your users could get from accessing and playing with some of these tools, you might consider piloting some with different groups of users. That way, you can learn what business uses they can come up with and deploy these tools based on what you learn.
- *Java scripting, and ActiveX controls.* Do you plan to move beyond static pages to support applications? If so, some browsers support Java scripting, and ActiveX and others don't. You should be aware of this in selecting your browser.
- *VRML tools.* At some point you may also consider tools that use Virtual Reality Modeling Language (VRML). Does the browser you're considering support these tools? Just imagine what using these tools could do for your business.

Which Way Should You Go—Free or Purchased?

To quickly create your audience, you should make browsers and other intranet tools easily available and inexpensive. If you can use free tools, or if your champion is willing to absorb the cost, you can make these tools free to users, which is even better.

There are a lot of free Internet tools you can use to build your intranet. Should you go with them or should you buy tools? If the free tools meet all of your needs, by all means go with them. If you need extra features that aren't available in the freebies, such as Netscape's security or special features, that's worth careful consideration. Netscape is quite inexpensive. For a small organization, the cost of licenses is fairly small. However, for an organization with thousands of users, Netscape can add up to some serious money. That's why the very large organizations that are deploying Netscape have negotiated worldwide, corporate licenses. This move toward corporate licenses has made it less expensive overall, but it's not cheap to bite the bullet and pay for it all up front. That's where the champion and his or her budget can help.

How Will Your Users Get the Software?

How can you make it easy for people to acquire the software? I'll talk first about how they get it initially, and then about how they get upgrades. I'll assume that your users already have computers that are on a network and that they may or may not have TCP/IP.

Initial Installation

You can do the initial installations in three different ways.

1. You can have a person or group responsible for doing installations if you have to install a TCP/IP stack on each machine, or if you have to install browsers and tools individually. Some companies have an infrastructure group or desktop services group that handles both of these tasks.

2. You can let people download their own software if everyone already has TCP/IP and you have a corporate license for your browser, or if it's free. For example, EDS

developed installation kits for the client software. It added the installation kit to FTP servers and to the product catalog for its desktop computing environment. Once in the product catalog, an EDS employee could install the software simply by selecting it from a menu of options. In addition to placing the client software in the desktop product catalog, each business unit rolled out the software throughout its organization.

3. You can let the system do the installations if you have an automated system.

Upgrades

You can handle upgrades to browsers, e-mail, and other tools similarly. Once the software is already on the individual desktop computers, users can download upgrades simply by clicking on an icon. You can announce browser upgrades on your internal web so people know that they're available. A handy feature to add to your internal web is information about the new features in the browser and how people can use them to get more value from the tools.

How Will You Provide User Training and Support?

How will you provide the training? Fortunately, browsers are so easy to use that we structured our demos to also function as a tutorial. In the demo we showed how to use the browser and what you could do with it. We also showed how to access and use both the internal and external webs, and we spent a few minutes talking about how to use e-mail and newsgroups. When people left the demo and got their browsers, they already knew what to do.

You may also want to have a way to refresh their memory. You can put a tutorial on your internal web site as one of your first pieces of content. It can be one of the options you put on your home page. You should make it very easy for users to locate.

How will you provide support for intranet users when using the browsers and applications you provide? Do you have a help desk already? If so, it may be easiest to train the help desk staff to support the intranet.

If you create a Web Services group, will it have responsibility for support? If so, you can post its phone number and an e-mail *mailto* address on the intranet home page. You can add a FAQ page and a newsgroup for posting questions. This can engage the help of your *power users* for support.

As you continue to do your demos, you may find the audiences getting larger and larger. In our case, we even had several *standing-room-only* demos. According to Bob Metcalfe, the *Father of Ethernet,* the power of the network increases exponentially according to the number of users connected to it. This is *Metcalfe's Law* and is especially relevant to the Internet and intranets. We were growing more and more powerful every day! When potential publishers saw the size of the audience they would have, they immediately got busy publishing.

Checklist: Create Your Audience

Figure 8.1 summarizes the steps involved in creating your audience.

---

1. Why should you create your audience?

   ◆ To get web publishers to publish content
   ◆ Set up your phone directory or employee locator as a starter application for users

2. Which tools will users need?

   ◆ Prepare before you start presenting your demos
   ◆ See resources listed in Appendix B
   ◆ Select a browser—things to consider:

      ◆ **User-friendliness:** Is it user-friendly? Is it easy to configure and easy to use?

- **Security:** Does it provide the type and amount of security that you need?
- **Cost:** How much does it cost?
- **Features and tools:** Does it include or support the features and tools you need?

    - HTML
    - E-mail and newsgroups
    - FTP and Telnet
    - Plug-ins, add-ons, and special features
    - Java scripting, and ActiveX controls
    - VRML tools

- Which way should you go—purchased or free software?

    - Do the free tools meet all your needs?

        - Is there a feature you need that is only available in a specific commercial browser?
        - Should you negotiate a corporate license?

3. How can you make it easy for your users to get the software?

    - Initial installation

        - Group to take responsibility for installing TCP/IP stack and browsers
        - Let people download their own copy
        - Let the system automatically do the installations

- Upgrades

  - Announce browser upgrades on internal web
  - Users download upgrades themselves simply by clicking on an icon.
  - Put information about new features on the internal web

4. How will you provide user training and support?

- Training

  - Demos as tutorials
  - Tutorials on the internal web

- Support

  - Help desk—train the help desk staff
  - Web services group—post its phone number and an e-mail *mailto* address on the home page
  - FAQ page
  - Newsgroup for posting questions—engage help from power users

Figure 8.1 Create your audience—checklist.

chapter nine

Promote Your Intranet

What Are Your Goals for Your Demo?

To get people interested in your intranet, you have to promote it and show people the power it brings them. James Cash Penney used to say that you can't sell from an empty wagon. It's important to show them what you're selling.

You should have some goals in mind before you even start to build your demo. What do you want to accomplish? In our case, we had two major goals. We wanted to show people the Internet and intranet so we could:

1. Recruit users as an audience for web publishers
2. Recruit web publishers and others for the team

Recruit Users As an Audience for Web Publishers

Web publishers won't set up anything until they know they have an audience ready for their information. After you've decided the browser for your users, you can start to promote the intranet to them. Once they've seen it, they'll want it. You'll want to get browsers on their computers immediately to capitalize on their enthusiasm. The demos are an integral part of the strategy to create an audience for your publishers. As the audience grows, the content will grow as well, and the intranet will become more valuable.

Recruit Web Publishers and Others for the Team

Our Internet Team consisted mostly of people working to put their departmental information on the Web and jWeb. Other members of the team were those who worked on the technical side of web servers and services.

In the demos, people would become so enthusiastic that they were ready to start publishing departmental information immediately. The Internet Team was the means to develop and support these publishers. It provided them with tools to get started, help in learning how to use those tools, and a means to support their efforts. As I gave demos, I asked for volunteers to join the Internet Team. When we were ready to kick off the team, the group had grown so large that we had a hard time finding a room to meet in. As we continued the demos, the team grew even larger. That's a *good* problem to have.

Build the Demo

After you've set your goals for the demo, then you're ready to start building it. What are the steps you should follow? How long should they take?

To make it easy for you to gauge the time frames involved in these steps, I've included a time line (Figure 9.1). It shows the first six months of our intranet project and how the steps fit together the way we did them. The steps and time frames to build the demo are:

1. *Set up the computer.*   Accomplished in month 1.
2. *Learn HTML and other tools.*   Accomplished in month 1.
3. *Decide if you need an introduction.*   Accomplished in month 1.
4. *Determine what to include in the demo.*   Spanned months 1 and 2.

Steps	Month 1	Month 2	Month 3	Month 4	Month 5	Month 6
Build the demo						
Set up the computer	▨					
Learn HTML and other tools	▨					
Decide if you need an introduction	▨					
Determine what to include in the demo	▨	▨				
Build sample applications	▨	▨				
Build the real intranet		▨	▨	▨	▨	▨
Present the demo						
Schedule the demos						
Top executives	▨	▨	▨			
Managers in key areas	▨	▨	▨			
Information systems		▨	▨			
Management council/board of directors				▨		
Word of mouth		▨	▨	▨	▨	▨
Open demos				▨	▨	▨
Tailor the demos to your audience	▨	▨	▨	▨	▨	▨
Build enthusiasm	▨	▨	▨	▨	▨	▨
Answer questions and address concerns	▨	▨	▨	▨	▨	▨

Figure 9.1   Demo time line—promote the intranet.

5. *Build sample applications.*   Spanned months 1 and 2.
6. *Build the real intranet.*   Started in month 2. We rolled out the real intranet in month 4, and continued to expand it through month 6 and beyond.

I don't necessarily advise that you build and present your demo the way we did. We had to start presenting demos before we had that much to show for an internal web. I advise waiting to start your demos until after you have them *built.* It was a challenge to present demos, build demos, create the Internet Team, and do everything else, all at the same time. The project got so much momentum going that I often felt like I was trying to jump on board a speeding freight train. It was difficult, and sometimes messy, but it was also fun. In retrospect, I don't think that I'd do it any differently if I had it to do over again. For your own sanity, however, you might consider taking it a step at a time.

Set Up the Computer

Once you've determined the goals for your demo, it's time to start building it. You can build a demo *on the cheap.* You really need very little more than a browser on a computer. You need:

1. *Computer.*   You probably already have one you can use, or you can borrow a spare computer to use.
2. *Internet access.*   My colleagues had already arranged for Internet access and set up a server, but you can also get on the Internet cheaply by using a modem and a dial-up account.
3. *Browser.*   You can download Mosaic or Microsoft's Internet Explorer from the Internet for free, or you can purchase Netscape directly over the Internet.
4. *HTML authoring tool.*   When we started there were really only a few HTML authoring tools, such as HTML Assistant, HTML Edit, and Hot Metal. Today there are so many more. Some HTML authoring tools are free, some are shareware, and you must purchase others. Appendix B has some references to links to HTML authoring tool resources.
5. *Graphics tool.*   You can purchase a commercial graphics package for up to a few hundred dollars, or you can acquire shareware graphics tools, such as Lview, from the Internet. Again, check out the Appendix for some references to graphics and authoring resources.

6. *Caching tool.* If your demo will include the Internet, you may want to acquire a tool that allows you to cache pages from the Internet in case you lose your connection during a demo. There are now tools, such as Web-Whacker and WebEx, that will automate this process for you. When we created our demos, the only way to have a backup in case of a lost connection was to individually save every page, graphic, and icon to the hard disk. Then we had to change the HTML to reassemble the pages from all the pieces on our hard disk, and change the addresses of links. This was not fun.

Learn HTML and Other Tools

Once you have the tools, it's time to learn some HTML and how to use the tools. When we started in 1994, which is ancient by Internet standards, things were much different from today. When we started learning HTML to build demo pages, there weren't even any books on HTML authoring. We had to learn from the information on the Web or from a few pages in one of the Mosaic books. Today, there are lots of good books on the subject and numerous resources on the Internet. Tools today make it much easier to build your demo. Many of these tools do conversions for you, check HTML syntax, and even feature WYSIWYG editing. Besides, this is the easy stuff.

Decide If You Need an Introduction

Before you build your sample applications, you need to decide how you wish to help your audience understand the basic concepts. You may need a simple introduction to explain what the Internet and the WWW are all about.

When I became involved with our Internet project, I inherited some previously scheduled demos to do in the first few days. We started demos before we were really ready to do them. For my introduction, I inherited the Power Point slides my colleague had used to show the Internet to the CIO. These slides were much too "*techie*" for business audiences, so I didn't use them. I quickly built some HTML pages giving a short introduction in very simple language. These pages covered:

◆ The Internet and its history
◆ The World Wide Web and where it came from
◆ Browsers
◆ Hypertext linking and HTML

I used the browser to display these pages. The audience saw and understood the concept of browser and hypertext linking before I ever explained them.

Today you have more options when you build your presentation. You can use a package, such as Power Point or Freelance, and view slides in your browser. When we initially set up our demo, the only way to use Power Point slides in a browser was to go through individually converting each slide, which was a very time-consuming process.

Do you need an introduction? Call or have lunch with some of the people who will be in your demos, and find out how much they know about the Internet. This may dictate whether or not to take the time to create a good introduction. If your organization already has Internet access, then you may not need one, and can go straight to the meat of your demo. I started leaving out our introduction in my later demos. People had started to read about the Internet and the Web in the business press and popular media, such as *Business Week* and *Time.*

Determine What to Include in the Demo

Next you'll want to identify what to put in your demo. You should identify and incorporate the needs of your business so you can show people what they can do with an intranet.

Identify Needs

The first step is to start to identify some of those needs and contact business partners to supply you with information for the demo. These steps include:

1. *Brainstorm.*   Identify as many things as you can that would add value if they were on the intranet. The CIO and I brainstormed a list of things we could save money on if we put them on the intranet.

   ◆ *Paper.*   You can start with information in paper form which costs the company lots of money to print and distribute. This might include telephone directories, procedures manuals, and benefits information. There are very few areas of a business that don't have this problem. Most companies are not in the business of warehousing paper, but that's what companies have done so people could have what they needed when they needed it.

   ◆ *Disparate systems.*   Another problem to look for is when you have information accessed by many folks using different types of equipment and operating systems. Web browsers are available for virtually every platform available in business and cost much less than the numerous proprietary solutions that are available.

2. *Identify contacts.*   I used the brainstormed list as a starting point. I called my IS colleagues who worked with specific areas of the business to find out who to contact. For example, Distribution owned one of the applications, so I called the Distribution systems manager to find out the name of the business partner responsible for it.

3. *Contact business partners.*   Once I knew which business partners to contact, I called them and explained what we were doing and how an intranet could help with their applications. I asked for copies of real information to use in the demo. No one ever turned down my request, and furthermore, they wanted to get on the list to see the demo. I used this list when it was time to set up the demos.

Involve Others

The next step is to involve everyone who can help you determine the critical business needs. Talk to everyone you know who can tell you what's critical in their part of the organization. Is there something that you can do with an intranet to solve one of their problems?

1. *Informally.*   We knew our business partners were aware of critical business needs, so I talked to everybody I knew.

    - I stopped friends in the hall and told them about the intranet and how it could be of value to their department. I asked what applications they thought would be of value to have on the intranet.
    - Over lunch with friends, I always asked about what kinds of things would be of value to them. I asked what kind of information they had difficulty accessing, and what information they needed to access often and easily.
    - Before long, people I didn't even know were seeking me out to tell me about information they wanted to put on the intranet.

2. *Formally.*   In addition to the informal approach I used, you might consider assembling Joint Application Design (JAD) sessions to brainstorm and identify uses.

It didn't take long to get a long list of specific business needs and lots of data. With that, it was easy to start putting pieces in the demo.

Build Sample Applications

For your demos, you'll need a wide variety of information—something to hit the *hot buttons* of every area of your organization. Here are some of the things you can do:

1. *Create a home page for your department.* Put up lots of useful information as an example of what other departments might do.

2. *Create an employee locator.* Show an employee search for locations, telephone numbers, e-mail addresses, and organization for employees.

3. *Set up a variety of HTML pages.* Create lots of different HTML pages showing procedures manuals, benefits information, and samples of all the other information you have gleaned.

4. *Tie HTML pages to databases.* You can show how people can have timely and easy-to-use access to information that resides in databases. If you don't yet have the tools or resources to tie the web to databases, you can create a mock-up simply to show the concept. There's nothing deceptive in telling people that what they're seeing is a mock-up—it's just to illustrate the concept since you don't yet have the tools or resources. Access to live databases is very doable and easier and cheaper than with proprietary tools. It just takes time.

5. *Add some graphics, sound, and video clips.* It is so much better to illustrate a concept than to simply talk about it. If you add some graphics, sound, and video clips, you'll catch people's attention and communicate your message more effectively. For example, when IBM brought out the *butterfly keyboard* on their portable computers, they could explain it, but people just didn't understand. IBM put a short video on their web site and they were able to show you how the keyboard worked. Yes, a picture is worth thousands of words. Just be careful that you don't overdo it.

Don't worry about any of the pieces that you need to mock up. The purpose of your demo is to help nontechnical people understand what you can do with the Internet and intranet. It's most important for them to see it.

Build the Real Intranet

As soon as we had built the demo, we started building the real intranet. Many of the sample applications used in the demo were real information. All we had to do was to incorporate them into the new look for jWeb. In the demos, we received feedback that we used to create the new look and navigation for jWeb.

Pretty soon, we had a real web site with lots of applications to roll out to the company. We then changed the demo over to using those real applications. We really used the demo applications only for a month or two before we had real jWeb screens that we could use in the demo.

A few of these early applications on jWeb included:

♦ *Phone directory.*   This was one of the first things on jWeb. It made it easy for people to look up an individual's phone number, e-mail address, location, organization, and so forth. This information was already available in other systems, but wasn't universally accessible.

♦ *IS information.*   Shortly after jWeb came up, various departments in IS created their own home pages and information resources. We used those pages in the demos, as they provided ideas to help other departments get started. The first IS information was who to contact with specific types of technical questions and problems. You could search on specific hardware, software, or area of interest to get a listing of who supported that area and how to contact them. Soon there were also organization charts for the various departments in Information Systems. You could click on the name of an individual to go to their home page and find out about their areas of expertise. In addition, we quickly added lots of documentation to jWeb.

♦ *Training schedules and registration.*   You could see the schedules for training classes and click on a *mail-to* to send a message requesting registration for a certain class.

♦ *Software downloads.*   You could click on the name or icon for in-house-created software, and it would install itself on your computer. Later, you could download site-licensed software. When upgrades were available, clicking on the icon would download them as well. There was also information to tell you what was new in the latest version and what to expect from it. Of course, this required prior testing and approval to make sure that it would work with the different operating systems and configurations. If, as you were downloading, something unusual happened, the phone number and a clickable hyperlink *mail-to* address for the person supporting the installation were both available on the screen.

Present the Demo

Once you have sufficient applications for a demo, it's time to start the dog and pony shows. Over about six months, I did over 100 demos and presentations to groups of various sizes, ranging from small groups of two or three to large groups of several hundred. The steps to present the demo are:

1. Schedule the demos.
2. Tailor the demos to your audience.
3. Build enthusiasm.
4. Answer questions and address concerns about the Internet and intranet.

Our demos started the day after I started the project and ran through month 6, depending on the specific audience for each. (See Figure 9.1.)

Schedule the Demos

Where do you start? How do you decide who to show the demo to first? How do you schedule them?

We started by having senior IS management arrange demos for us. The CIO lined up demos for the top executives, and senior IS managers lined up demos with their customers who were responsible for Catalog, Stores, and Merchandising. Here's how our demos proceeded, along with the times from Figure 9.1.

1. *Top executives.* It was important for the top executives to be aware of the Internet, so we invited them to take a look at it. This included the CEO and those who reported directly to him. These demos mostly took place in months 1, 2, and 3.

2. *Managers in key areas.* There were some areas that were really important to line up in support of the external Web site. These included Catalog, Stores, and Merchandising. We scheduled key managers in these areas to be among the first to see the demo. Most were enthusiastic, so we gave them browsers to help them get started surfing the Net. They quickly asked us to provide demos for their staffs and supply them with browsers. In this way, the Internet and intranet quickly spread to the entire departments of the key managers. Since this was before the mainstream periodicals had picked up on the Net, we had to provide a lot of education to help people understand what the Net was about. These demos mostly took place in months 1, 2, and 3, and occurred simultaneously with the demos to top executives.

3. *Information Systems.* We provided a lot of demos for groups of IS folks. One of our goals was to get systems folks thinking in terms of how they could use the web. These demos also took place in months 1, 2, and 3 and were simultaneous with the demos for top executives and key managers.

4. *Management Council and the Board of Directors.* When we gave a demo for our CEO, he asked us to do a presentation to the Management Council—the top executives of the company. This presentation was early in month four. After the presentation to the Management Council, the Chairman of the Board asked us to give the presentation to the Board of Directors. This presentation took place early in month 5.

5. *Word of mouth.*   The more people who saw the demo, the more there were who wanted to see it. The excitement was contagious, and word began to get around. Pretty soon, people were calling to say that a friend told them about the demo and they'd schedule one for their department. After the Management Council presentation, we had even more requests. The requests for demos started in month 1 and continued throughout the whole time we were doing demos.

6. *Open demos.*   By month 4, the requests for demos were coming faster than we could fulfill them. The best way to deal with this was to create a schedule of open demos and invite the whole company. We scheduled and presented numerous open demos during months 5 and 6.

Tailor the Demos to Your Audience

For each demo, we customized the presentation to the interests of the group or department we were working with. It was important to tailor each and every presentation so the audience could see what was of value for them. We generally set up interesting and useful Web sites as links on a page on our intranet to make it easy for our audience to find these locations later. For example:

1. *Finance.*   For Financial audiences, such as controllers, auditing, financial planning, and others, we visited financial resources and sites, such as the SEC's Edgar Project and FinWeb's Links to Financial Resources.

2. *Catalog, Merchandising, and Marketing.*   For Catalog, Merchandising, and Marketing, we visited early retailers, catalog companies, and shopping malls on the Internet, such as Burlington Coat Factory, L. L. Bean, Whole Foods, Service Merchandise, and Shopping 2000.

3. *Human Resources.*   For Human Resources, we visited early recruiting sites, such as Career Mosaic and the Online Career Center, as well as other personnel-related sites.

4. *Information Systems.*   For Information Systems audiences, we visited vendor sites, such as IBM and Microsoft, and early computer magazine sites.

5. *Management Council and the Board of Directors.*   The CIO sent articles to the Management Council in advance of our demo to get them familiar with the Internet so that we could *cut to the chase* and not waste their time. We were careful to communicate in their language, and to choose sites in which they would have an interest.

   When we did the presentation to the Management Council and the Board of Directors, we discovered a great way to get their attention. We decided to show the home page of the alma mater of someone prominent in our organization. We were very fortunate in what we found at the alma mater of our Chairman of the Board, W. R. Howell. It just so happened that there was a page about the Oklahoma Business Conference, at which the featured speakers were W. R. Howell and Dan Quayle. Their pictures appeared prominently on the page that told about the conference. During our presentation, when we showed the Internet page with the Chairman's picture, the murmur in the room told me that we made the right impact. Who could argue about the Internet when the Chairman was already on it?

Sample Presentation

What follows is a sample of the kinds of things we generally covered in a demo. It's more of an overview and doesn't go into great detail. I based this sample presentation upon the one we gave to the Management Council, though it isn't exactly the same. I've included this sample presentation to give you an idea of how you may want to structure your demo.

We started off by focusing on the World Wide Web, and then moved on to the internal web. I'm including both the external and internal parts in the sample presentation for several reasons:

- Many of you may be selling both concepts as well and this gives a feel for how to weave together both parts into a single presentation.
- Having both an external and internal presentation can give you a feel for selling the concept and tailoring it to the audience.

I'm including pictures of some of the most interesting of the actual screens we used with the sample presentation. It's not feasible to include them all so don't be concerned that there isn't a screen for everything mentioned. Keep in mind that Web sites change frequently and will probably not look like they do in these pictures. These screens are merely to give you ideas as to how to do your demo. You should use the current version of these screens for your demo.

In very formal presentations, I did the talking and my colleague drove the mouse. In less formal presentations, I usually did both. Prior to presenting this to the Management Council, we rehearsed several times to perfectly choreograph the words with the mouse clicks. That way, nothing distracted from the message we were delivering. When you present to a group of very high level executives, remember to speak their language. One of the most important things I've learned is that *it's more important to communicate than to be technically correct.* In this presentation I describe the Internet simply as a network of computers. It's more correct to describe it as a network of networks, but that would only confuse a non-technical audience. Your goal is to communicate so that they understand.

The presentation contains the following sections:

1. Opening and Introduction to the Internet and the World Wide Web
2. Business Sites
3. Education Sites
4. Government Sites
5. Shopping Sites

6. JCPenney Site

7. jWeb

Opening and Introduction to the Internet and the World Wide Web   We usually started by introducing ourselves. For formal presentations such as this, an executive usually introduced us.

> *Good morning.*
>
> *Today we're going to show you the Internet, what some call the Information Superhighway. We'll illustrate different ways that companies and organizations communicate with their stakeholders. The Internet is a global network of computers. The World Wide Web is a part of the Internet. It contains words, pictures, movies, and sound. When a company wants to participate in the World Wide Web (or Web for short), they establish a home page.*
>
> *That's like hanging up a shingle for the rest of the world to see. Various organizations—business, government, and education—use the Web to present information they want to publish. Once a home page is published, it can be viewed by anyone.*

Business Sites   This is AT&T's home page (Figure 9.2). Here are some of the things AT&T wanted to make public, such as their annual report and their press releases.

Here's General Electric's home page (Figure 9.3). They've chosen to publish information about their products and services and to put out their annual report. From here, you can go to the home pages of some of GE's business units.

IBM's home page (Figures 9.4 and 9.5) also has information on products and services, as well as technology and research. They've devoted a lot of effort to talking about their commitment to the Internet.

Here's an example of a retailer—Burlington Coat Factory (Figure 9.6). They've chosen to publish a store locator for the convenience of their customers.

On a map of the United States (Figure 9.7), you can click on Texas and view a list of stores in the area (Figure 9.8). They've

Figure 9.2   AT&T home page.

decided to publish addresses and phone numbers. Obviously, one could choose to publish such information as store hours and types of merchandise and services available.

Here's Whole Foods (Figure 9.9). They use the Internet to communicate with their customers by talking about their mission statement and quality standards.

They provide information guides and recipes (Figure 9.10), show financial reports, and even ask for suggestions from their customers.

Whole Foods is doing customer service (Figure 9.11) via the Internet by using electronic mail. They get information about their customers, and customers can make suggestions or give feedback.

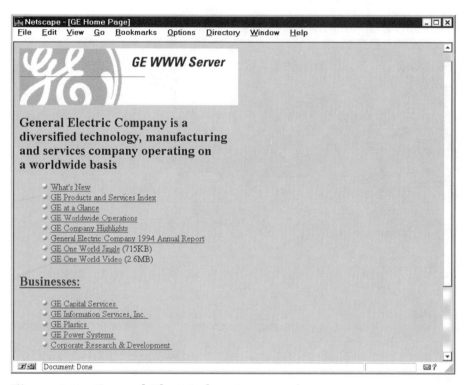

Figure 9.3   General Electric home page.

Let's move on from businesses to education and look at how universities communicate with their customers.

Education Sites   Here's MIT's home page (Figure 9.12). It provides information for students and potential students.

Under Libraries (Figure 9.13), we can access the hours, locations, and phone numbers for the libraries.

Under Publications (Figure 9.14), we can see information about MIT's publications and the document distributions centers from which we can acquire them.

Here's the home page of the University of Oklahoma (Figure 9.15).

And here's information about the Oklahoma Business Conference (Figure 9.16), which featured W. R. Howell and Dan Quayle.

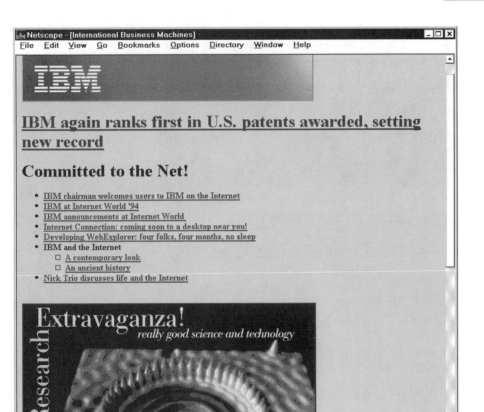

Figure 9.4   IBM home page.

Government Sites   Let's move on and look at government organizations and how they communicate with their customers.

Here's the home page of the U.S. Bureau of the Census (Figure 9.17). It has a news flash announcing that at the beginning of the year, the U.S. population exceeded 261 million. From here, we can access their Main Data Bank, which provides access to all kinds of census data.

Here's Thomas (Figure 9.18), the home page of the U.S. Congress, which is named after Thomas Jefferson. If we look

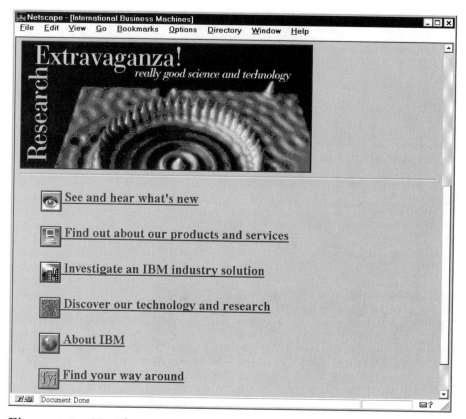

Figure 9.5   IBM home page—continued.

under the 104th Congress, we have access to all House and Senate bills, which are searchable by keyword or by bill number.

Here's the home page of the Securities and Exchange Commission's EDGAR Database (Figure 9.19). It holds the SEC filings of public companies. We'll search the EDGAR archives for JCPenney. We found 25 filings.

Here's our latest form 10Q, which is a quarterly financial report to the SEC.

Shopping Sites   Let's move back to business and look at some examples of shopping on the Internet.

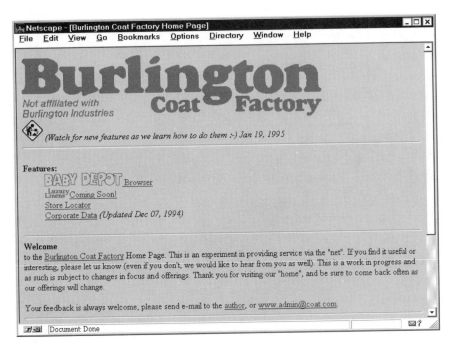

Figure 9.6   Burlington Coat Factory home page.

First is FTD (Figure 9.20), which has a free personal reminder ser-vice (Figure 9.21) to alert you of any holiday or personal occasion.

Here's where you register—simply select the holidays you wish to be reminded of (Figure 9.22), identify personal occasions (Figure 9.23), and submit it. Shortly before the occasion, you'll receive an electronic mail message. It will include flowers and gifts which may be ordered by returning the electronic mail message.

FTD also makes it easy to order flowers for Valentine's Day (Fig-ure 9.24). Simply select roses or flower arrangements.

We'll select roses (Figure 9.25). Select what you want to order, type in a message, indicate how you want to pay, and submit the order. That's it! It's taken care of for you!

Let's look at another shopping example.

Here's Shopping 2000 (Figure 9.26)—a virtual shopping mall that is an offshoot from a CD-ROM catalog. It includes JCPenney and many other retailers.

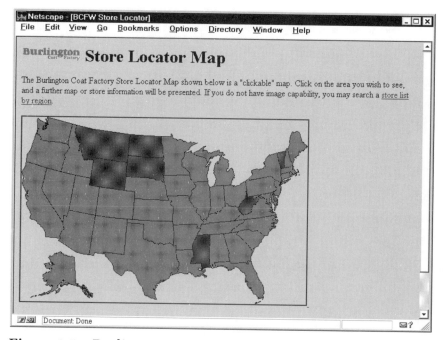

Figure 9.7 Burlington Coat Factory Store Locator.

In the JCPenney section (Figure 9.27), we offer men's wear, bedding, housewares, and specialty catalogs.

We'll select men's Hunt Club loose-fit jeans (Figure 9.28). Here's a picture, as well as all the information you need to place an order.

JCPenney Site Here's JCPenney's home page (Figure 9.29) from just prior to Christmas, featuring the popular Christmas toy, the Power Rangers.

Catalog came up with a last-minute shipment of Power Rangers (Figure 9.30). We put them on the Internet and made some sales.

This was our next home page (Figure 9.31).

We had an About JCPenney section (Figure 9.32), which included the *Penney Idea* (the company's values statement) and a picture of J. C. Penney.

We also used the home page to publicize special events, in this case the *Seventeen Magazine* Cover Model Search (Figure 9.33).

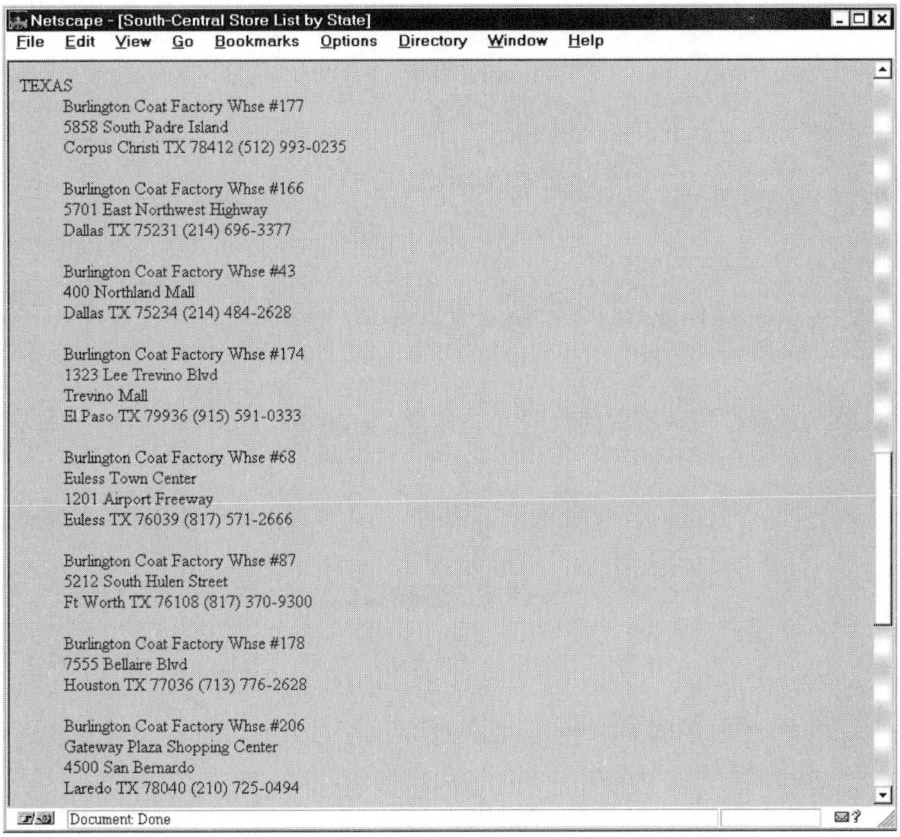

Figure 9.8   Burlington Coat Factory stores in Texas.

Here is the information about the kickoff event, which was held at Southfork Ranch and broadcast live to the stores. It featured celebrities, including Jamie Walters from the TV show *Beverly Hills 90210*. To find out more about Jamie, we'll click on his name.

Here we see the multimedia capabilities of the Internet. We can see information about Jamie (Figure 9.34) and can listen to a sound clip of a song he performed at Southfork. (We clicked on *Hold On,* Jamie's hit record, and played a short sound clip—you should have seen their eyes light up!) We received that clip from Atlantic Records via *electronic mail* and then we put it on the Internet.

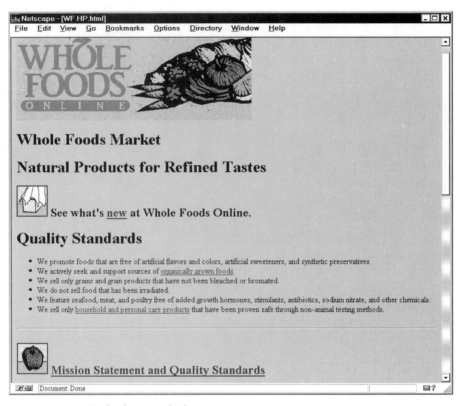

Figure 9.9   Whole Foods home page.

We also had details about the Cover Model Search, such as how to enter, what you could win, and that the deadline was March 13. Customers could submit questions or comments to the communications department. When you click on their e-mail address, a screen pops up, already addressed to them. Simply type in a message and send it, and it goes directly to their mailbox.

And here's the current home page, which people now see on the Internet. (You have the idea now, so there really isn't much need to continue with the screen shots. Besides, I don't have the remainder of the screens, but that part isn't important. From here on, you can substitute your own screens into a format similar to what I used. The point is to show you an example of what the presentation is like.)

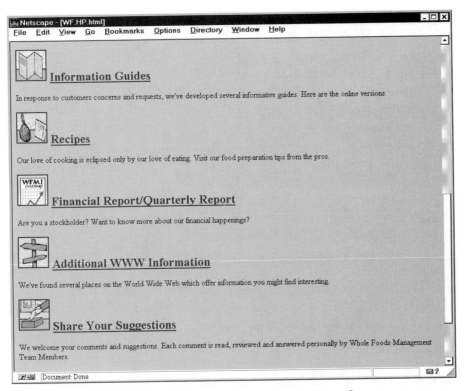

Figure 9.10 Whole Foods home page—continued.

Of course, we have to have shopping. Here's our new Internet Store.

Under shopping, there are products from Women's Department, Men's Department, and Sports & Fitness, including a wide selection of catalogs to order. Also, here is Catalog's toll-free number.

In Women's Department, let's look at a Worthington Tunic. We have a small picture of the item. Click on the picture to enlarge it. Here are the sizes available as well as a list of colors, prices, and catalog numbers.

To look at the next item, click the Next button, and we see Hunt Club leggings.

By clicking on the Customer Service button, we see delivery information, warranties, shipping charges, and other information.

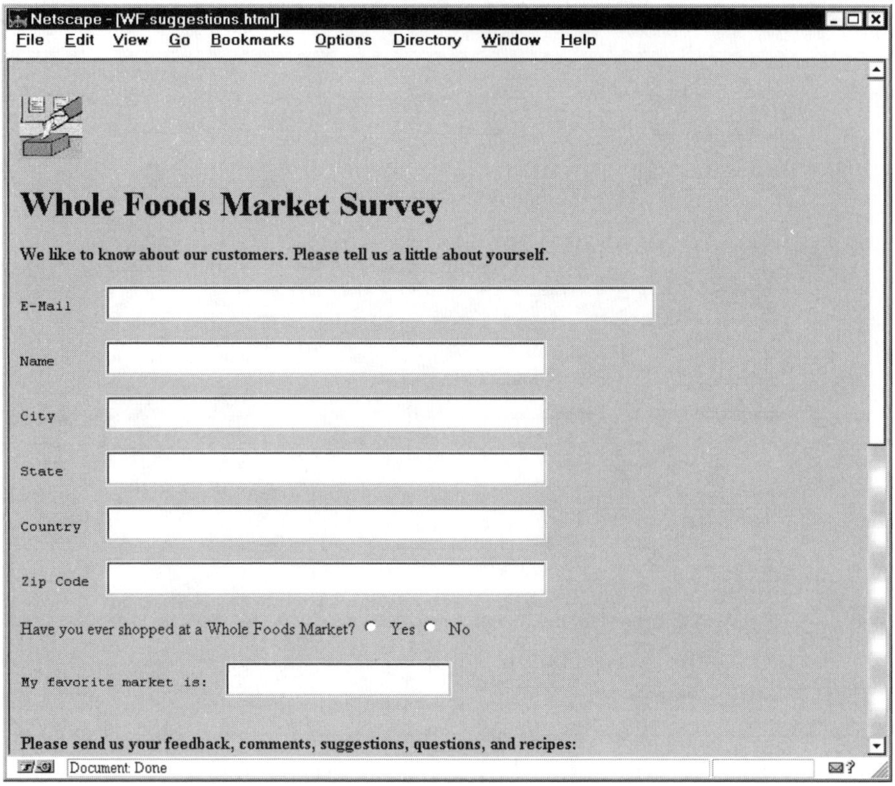

Figure 9.11 Whole Foods market survey.

Here's the Gift Registry. We can click on Highlights to find out more about the program, or click on Wedding or Baby to see the brands available. And here's how you can get a Gift Registry catalog.

We also have college recruiting on the Internet in a section called A World of Opportunity.

First, we see that JCPenney won the 1995 Catalyst Award.

Then, there's a section with information about the Store Management Trainee program, what backgrounds are sought for that, and how to apply. For areas such as Information Systems, there's an e-mail address to click on for sending résumés electronically. There is also benefits information.

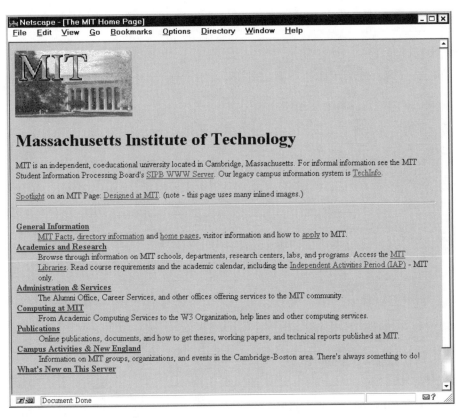

Figure 9.12   MIT home page.

jWeb   Now let's move on to something equally exciting—jWeb. (Refer to Figure 4.12 for a peek at what jWeb currently looks like.) We'll look at some ways we could use the Internet just for associates (employees). jWeb is only accessible by associates.

When you get Netscape, your computer will be set such that jWeb is your home page and will come up automatically when you open Netscape.

First, let's click on What's New to show what is either new or has been updated recently on jWeb.

(For confidentiality reasons, I can't talk about those applications on jWeb that are different from those commonly found on most intranets.)

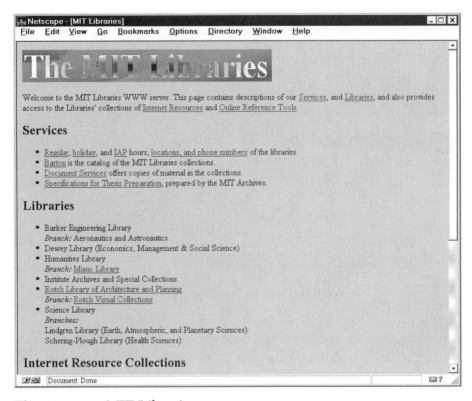

Figure 9.13   MIT Libraries.

Here's a list of home-office departments. First, we'll click on Information Systems.

On the Information Systems home page, we find the IS mission statement and links to the various areas of IS.

Here's the Advanced Technology Group. They have their mission statement, an organization chart, home pages of managers and their people, downloadable software, support contacts, and vendor contacts.

For those interested in building web pages, here's the HTML class, with a way to sign up for it right here.

In the reference manuals area, here are the materials for the HTML class. You can refer back to them after taking the class, or use them to learn HTML if you can't attend.

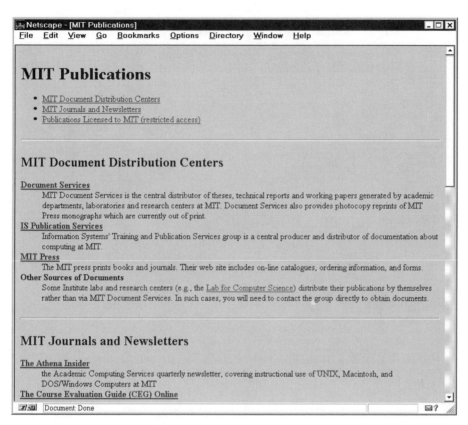

Figure 9.14 MIT Publications.

The jWeb Document Guide gives you the document format and detailed syntax guidance.

jWeb is a great place to put procedures manuals. When information changes it can easily be updated and is available to everyone. A What's New section can list the changes and link you directly to where those changes are found. A real advantage to putting procedures in jWeb is that you can include pictures, tables, charts, sound, and even video to clarify difficult procedures.

Construction Services was the first non-IS area to put information on jWeb. Here's their mission statement, as well as a variety of information. Here's a copy of their department newsletter, plus

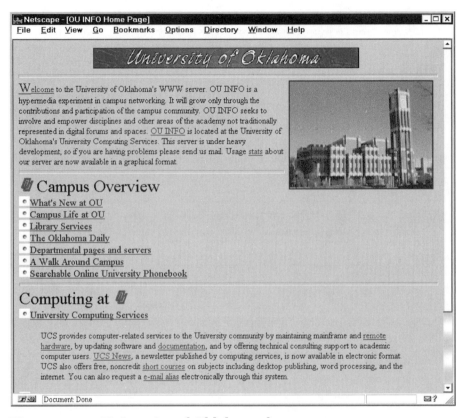

Figure 9.15   University of Oklahoma home page.

links to places of interest to their department. They even have pictures of new stores under construction.

The Stores department provides a store locator map and other applications (which must remain confidential).

Subsidiaries, such as Life Insurance, have also created their own home pages and added lots of content.

Web Services, the group which supports jWeb, provides an associate telephone and e-mail directory search, a place for organization charts, and Interesting and Informative Places on the Web.

When you get Netscape, Interesting and Informative Places on the Web is the tool to help you get out on the Web and find what you need. It contains links to government resources, media,

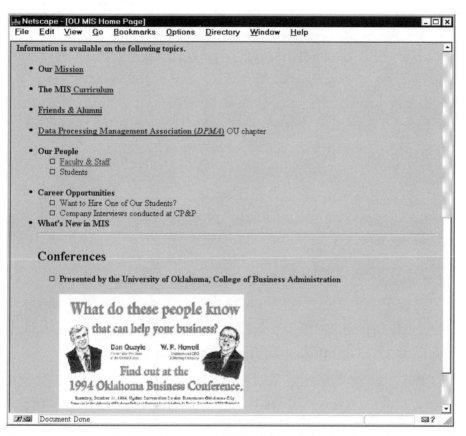

Figure 9.16 University of Oklahoma MIS Department home page—Oklahoma Business Conference.

finance, retailers, catalog companies, and companies we do business with.

(Before closing, I talked about how to use Netscape, including mentioning how to print and save. I also talked about how to use bookmarks. In addition, I gave a short presentation on how to use Internet e-mail and showed and discussed both external and internal newsgroups.)

Closing Comments In closing, the Internet and the internal web will be important for us in communicating with customers, suppliers, associates, shareholders, analysts, the press, potential asso-

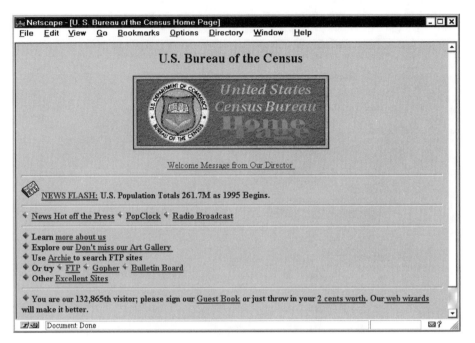

Figure 9.17   U.S. Bureau of the Census home page.

ciates, and even retirees. We're in the process of learning more and more about how to use them, and expect that you'll be hearing lots more about them in the future.

Build Enthusiasm

You have scheduled the demos, tailored them to each audience, and have been presenting them. At every demo you'll find that you hear more and more ideas of ways you could use the intranet. So what do you do with those ideas?

Brainstorm Ideas

As we showed the demos, enthusiasm continued to grow. The potential of the Internet and intranet fascinated nearly everyone who saw the demo. Part of the fun of the early demos was to encourage people to brainstorm about how we could use the tools.

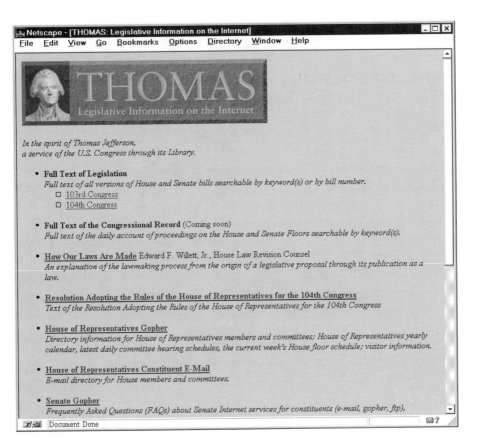

Figure 9.18   Thomas—the home page of the U.S. Congress.

This brainstorming resulted in long lists of ideas for both the intranet and the Internet.

Use These Ideas to Enhance the Demo

We used the brainstormed lists to develop new applications for the demo, and later for the real intranet. As people start spouting ideas for using the intranet, it's important to start turning these ideas into real applications for the next set of demos. The contributors will be really proud if by the next time they see the demo, you've incorporated their ideas into it. Make sure to give them credit.

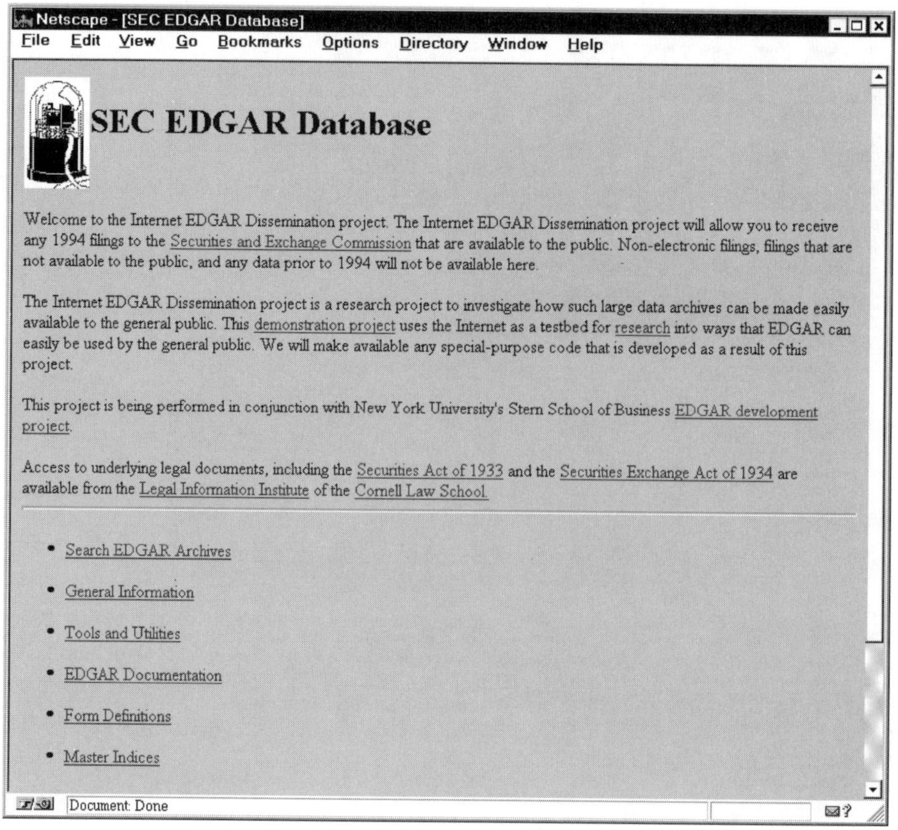

Figure 9.19   Securities and Exchange Commission EDGAR Database.

Most of the ideas that people came up with, and that we used to enhance the demo, were proprietary, so I can't talk about them here. However, there's one example related to the external Web site that illustrates this point. In one of our earliest demos, just before Christmas, we showed our brand-new external Web site and talked about how we could use it. One of our executives mentioned that Catalog had a new shipment of Power Rangers, the most popular Christmas toy at the time. It was too late to get them into the catalog, so he suggested that we put them on the Internet. With a wink of our CIO's eye, one of my colleagues left the demo to go see the person in charge of the Power Ranger figures. He received approval and got

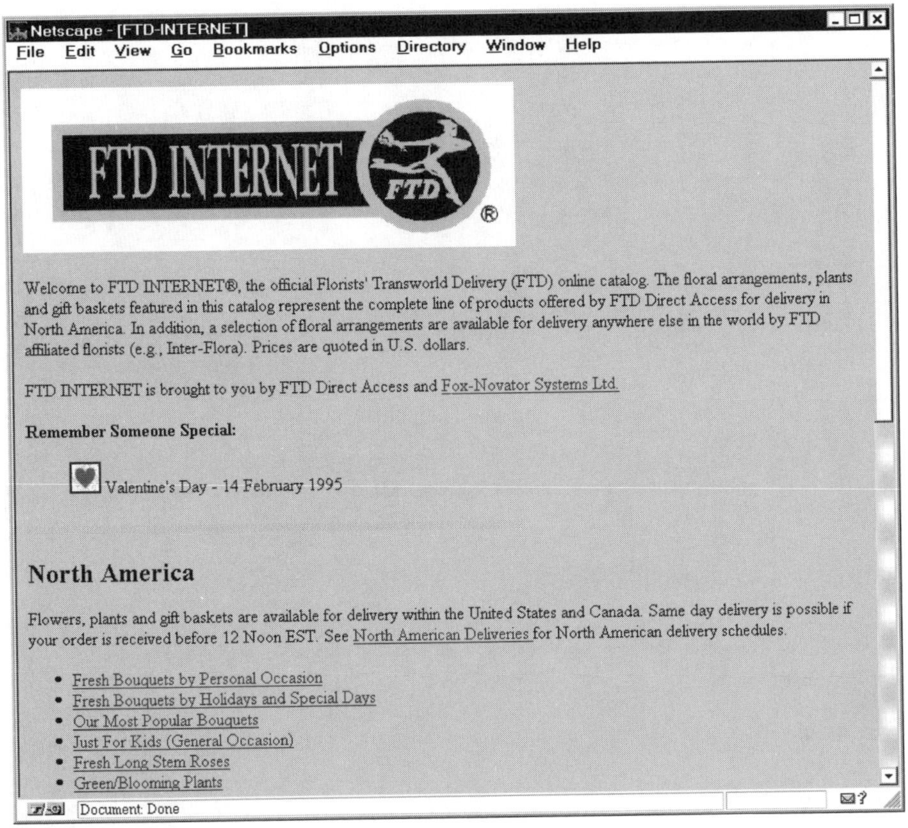

Figure 9.20   FTD home page.

a set of the toys to have photographed. He created the HTML page while he waited for the photo. When the photo was ready, he got everybody together for approvals, and it was up on the Internet in under three hours from the time it was first mentioned.

As we presented our demos, we repeated this story to convey the point of just how quickly you can utilize this technology. We always gave credit for the idea to the executive who came up with it.

What Excited Users?

As you go around doing demos, it's important to take note of those things that users become the most excited about. These are the

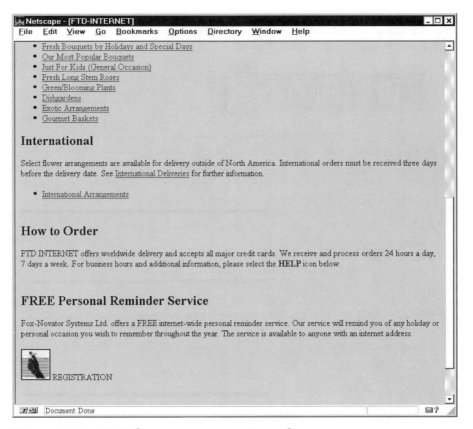

Figure 9.21   FTD home page—continued.

things you'll want to focus on first. Some examples from our presentations were:

◆ Ability to address the dynamic business environment
◆ Puts the user in control
◆ Ability to communicate and share knowledge

Ability to Address the Dynamic Business Environment   One of the things that got the most attention was the ability to do things quickly to address the dynamic business environment. Since the

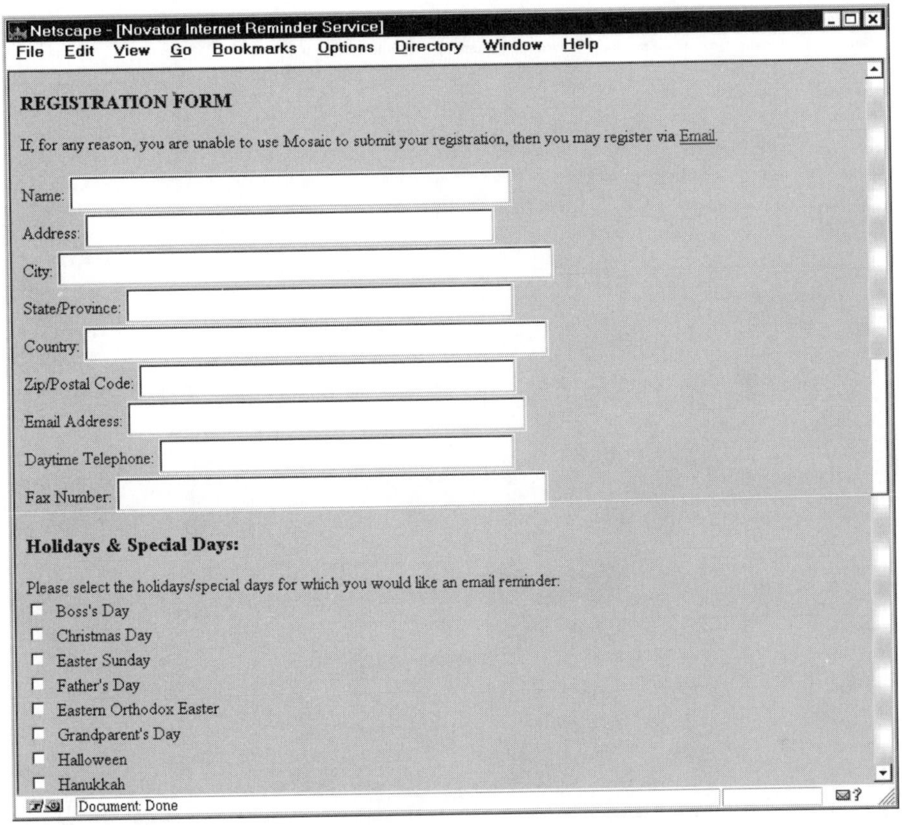

Figure 9.22 FTD Personal Reminder Service.

company was emphasizing doing things faster, cheaper, and better, our CEO made a *big deal* over our Power Ranger story when we presented the demo to the Management Council. If we can put Power Rangers on the Web in just three hours, when it's necessary to get approvals and graphics, think of how quickly we can get things onto the intranet.

Even though people thought the Internet was neat, their real enthusiasm was for the internal web. There were so many things they saw that they had uses for immediately and were ready to start on. No other medium, short of e-mail, could get the word out so quickly. With an intranet, you have only a single copy, unlike

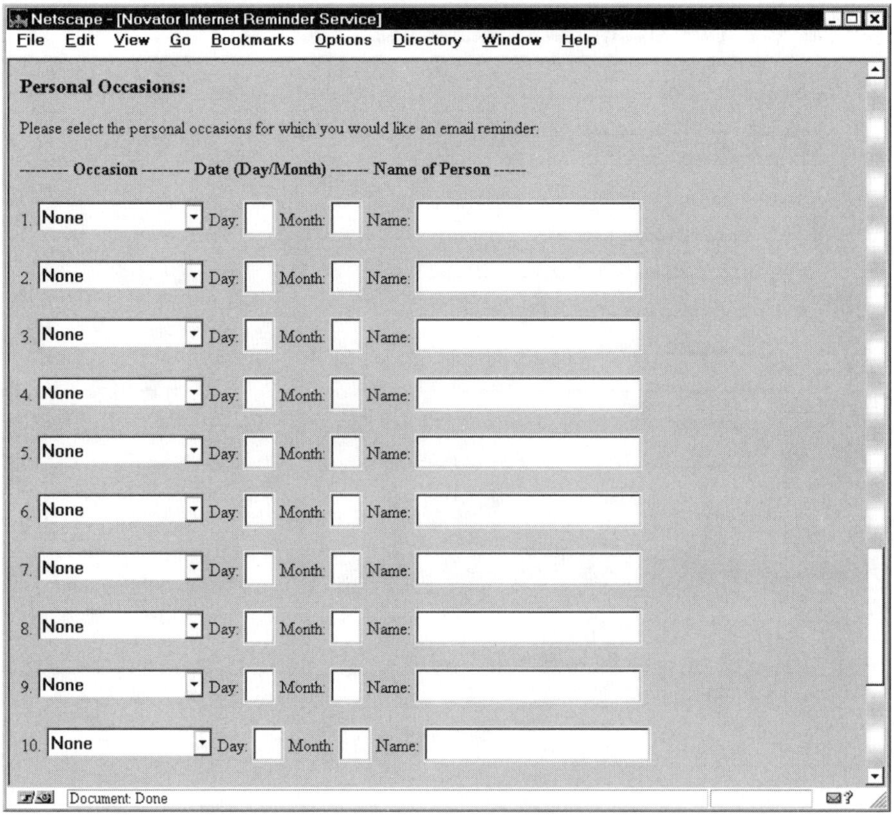

Figure 9.23   FTD Personal Reminder Service—continued.

e-mail's multiple messages. If you need something communicated quickly, the intranet is obviously the way to go. If something is new, you can put an alert on the web to let people know there is a bulletin or new information to check. This ability to move faster and do things cheaper is fueling the rapid assimilation of intranets in organizations. When compared to current technologies, intranets are extremely cost-effective. What is there not to like about intranets?

The greatest excitement was over having an easy and inexpensive answer to problems that had been plaguing lots of users. It wasn't that Information Systems hadn't been addressing their

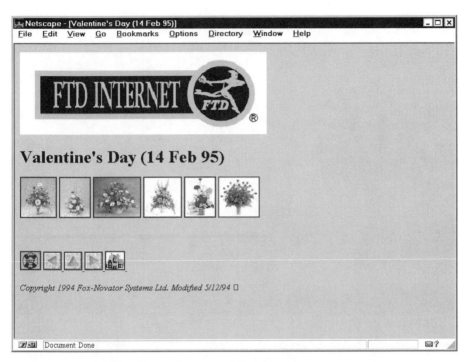

Figure 9.24 FTD for Valentine's Day.

needs, because indeed they had been. It was just that in a dynamic business environment, new needs come along all the time. It's not always easy to get these new needs met.

Puts the User in Control With an intranet, you don't have to be a programmer to put things on it. People with any kind of technical ability can easily and quickly learn HTML and the other skills. Departments can use their own people and resources to address their systems needs. In other words, users are in control of their own destinies.

Another problem for users was that in some cases they already had the information on-line. To get it changed, they had to get a programmer to change it, particularly in the case of help files and on-line documentation. With the intranet, the creator of the content takes responsibility for making sure that the information is

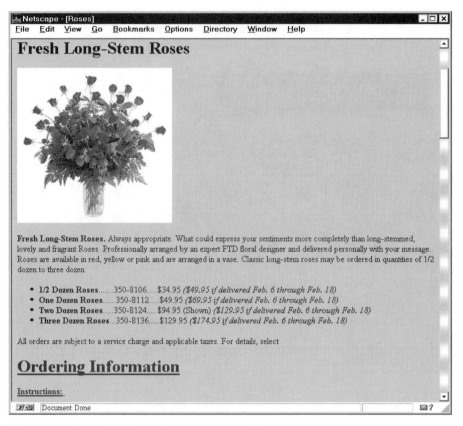

Figure 9.25   FTD Fresh Long-Stem Roses.

always up-to-date. Again, users are in control of their own destiny. They set their own priorities without having to negotiate with IS.

Ability to Communicate and Share Knowledge   Of great interest to people was the ability to communicate knowledge. Newsgroups, for instance, are an important part of the intranet. There are many experts in the company whose information other areas need. Sharing that knowledge enables an organization to better compete in an increasingly dynamic marketplace. Many corporations are investing millions of dollars to build knowledge-based

Figure 9.26   Shopping 2000 home page.

systems and groupware. In doing so, they use more sophisticated tools than you find on an intranet; however, an intranet provides a great start.

For example, if someone has a question or problem, he or she can post a question or query on an internal newsgroup related to the problem. Anyone with solutions or information that can help can post an answer to the newsgroup. Within as little as a few minutes, the person can have an answer to the question. Not only does this help the individual with the question, but the answer is out on the newsgroup for all who subsequently have the same problem. The newsgroup provides a ready source of knowledge

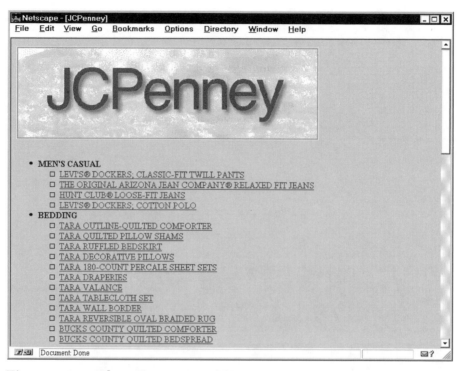

Figure 9.27 Shopping 2000—JCPenney.

right at your fingertips. It's searchable by those seeking answers to specific questions, so there's no need to ask the same question repeatedly. This was a feature of the intranet that generated a lot of enthusiasm in the demos.

Answer Questions and Address Concerns about the Internet and Intranet

Any good demo should stimulate lots of questions. It never hurts to anticipate what these questions will be and have answers ready for them. It doesn't take many presentations before you start to hear the same questions over and over. When I had a rather tight time frame for a demo, I would often make sure to answer the most commonly asked questions during the demo or at the closing of it in order to save some time. Then I would open up the discus-

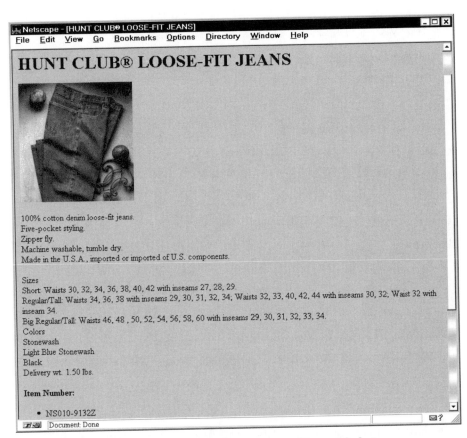

Figure 9.28   Shopping 2000—JCPenney, Hunt Club jeans.

sion for questions, which were usually more technical in nature. I made sure the audience knew they could leave if they didn't have questions. Here are some of the questions that I, and those I spoke with at other companies, encountered most frequently.

- What will happen to productivity if we give employees access to the Internet?
- How secure is the intranet?
- If we give employees access to all this information, won't they be harder to deal with?

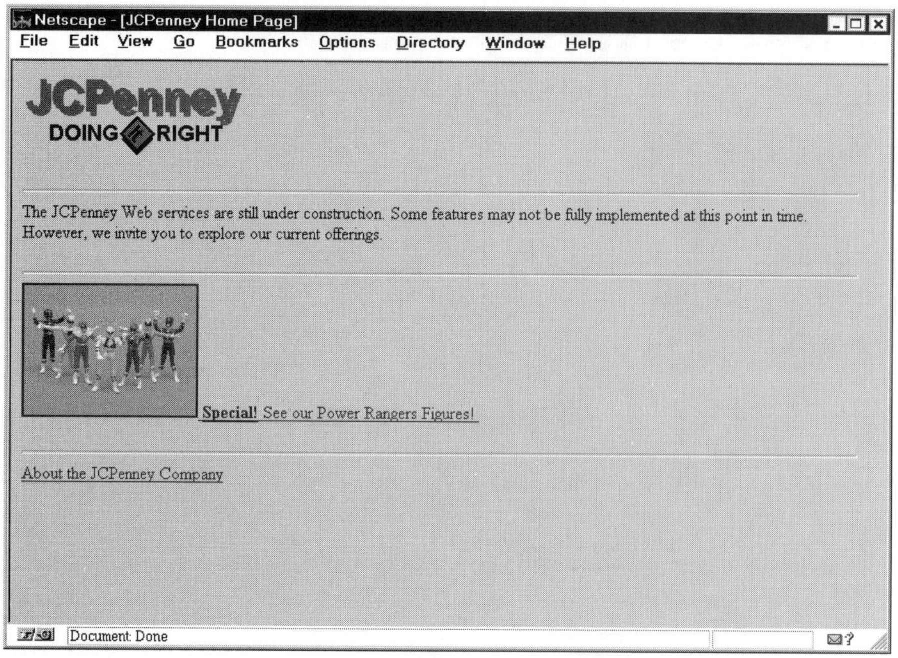

Figure 9.29   JCPenney home page before Christmas.

+ If we access the Internet, won't we bring in viruses?
+ How much does it cost the company to access the Internet?
+ How do I get my department on the intranet?

What Will Happen to Productivity If We Give Employees Access to the Internet?

Because the concept was so new and different, we had several questions and concerns that came up in virtually every demo. Since we were selling the concept of both the Internet and an internal web from the very beginning, we had to deal with the issue of whether to allow intranet users to access the Internet. This is a subject that seems to be fraught with lots of emotion in every company that deals with it. Despite the enthusiasm for the Internet, there was a lot of fear and concern from managers over opening up the company to access to the Internet. What will happen when we get out on the Internet and everyone starts to play?

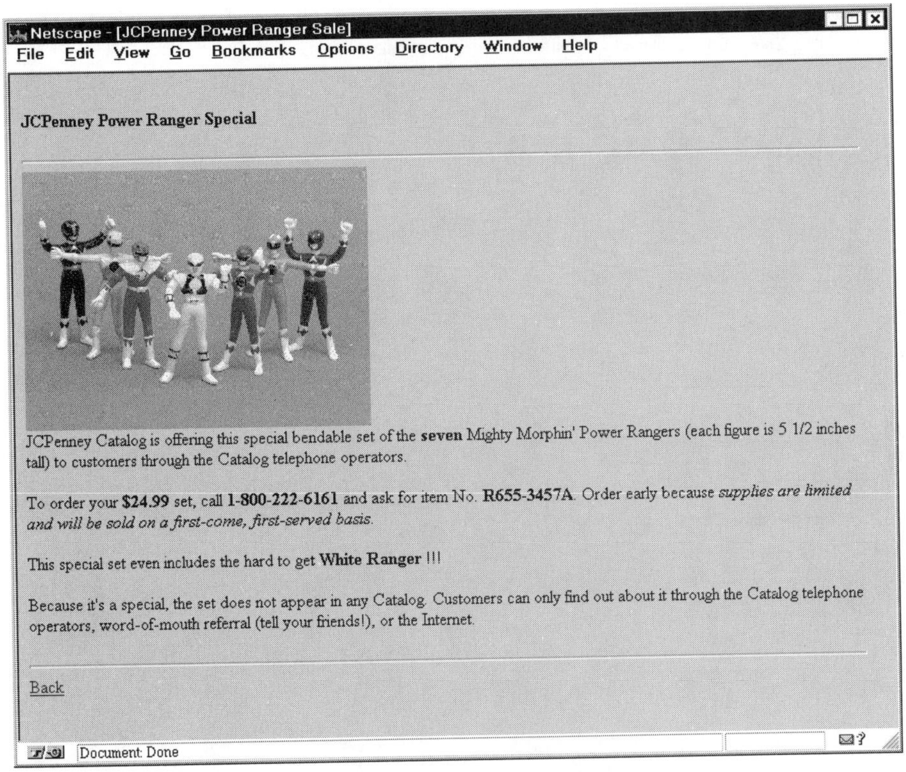

Figure 9.30   JCPenney Power Ranger special.

What will happen to our productivity? We soon determined that really wasn't much of an issue. You go through a few weeks where people are in the fascination stage, like overwhelmed children on Christmas morning flitting from toy to toy. As soon as the novelty wears off, people settle in to using the Internet to find what they need. In the process, they find that the fascination stage has trained them to find what they need, making them better prepared to use the Internet when they have a real need.

How Secure Is the Intranet?

People frequently asked if those outside on the Internet could access our sensitive, internal information. Our demos focused on both intranet and Internet, and were created with the premise that

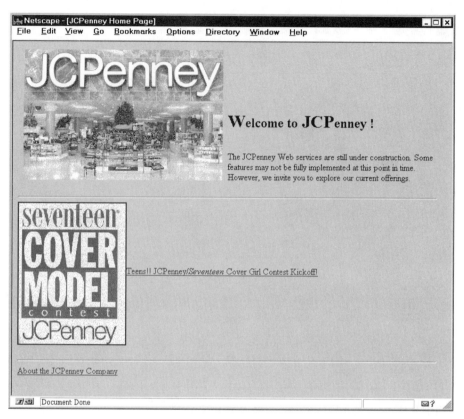

Figure 9.31 JCPenney home page after Christmas.

employees could access the Internet from our internal web. There-fore, we took the time in our demos to differentiate between the Internet and the intranet. We stressed that they were physically separate in order to keep out unwanted access. We didn't want some executive getting paranoid that people on the outside could access our sensitive corporate information. That would have killed the project before it really started, so we dealt with that concern right up front.

If We Give Employees Access to All This Information, Won't They Be Harder to Deal With?

One company I spoke with heard the question of whether giving employees all this information would make them harder to deal

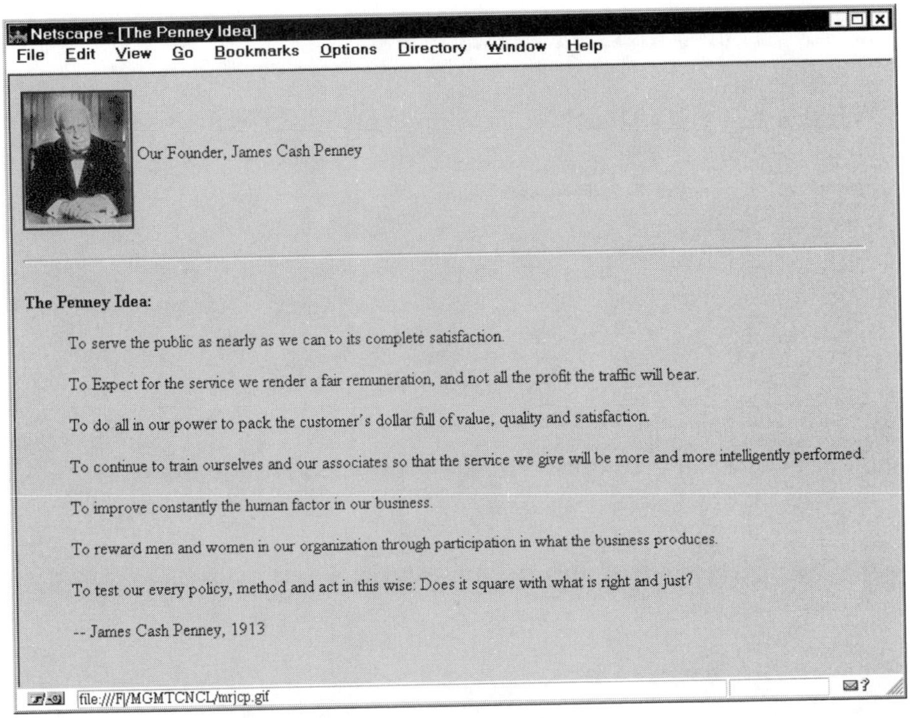

Figure 9.32   JCPenney—about JCPenney.

with. This question is a big shock because it lets us know that we still have some dinosaurs around in management. All I can really say to this is that if you want to keep people in the dark, then you'll still have to manage them. If you're willing to give them information, then you can empower them to accomplish their own results. With what's happening in business today, that's really your only reasonable alternative.

If We Access the Internet, Won't We Bring in Viruses?

With anything, there is a certain degree of risk. You need to control that risk as much as possible by making people aware of the risk, making virus-protection software available, and encouraging people to use it. Today there's even software that will catch viruses before they get through your firewall.

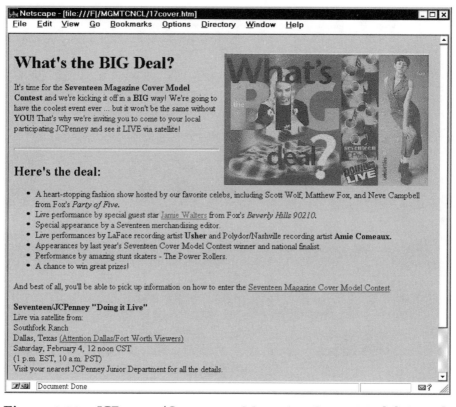

Figure 9.33   JCPenney/*Seventeen Magazine* Cover Model Search kickoff event.

How Much Does It Cost the Company to Access the Internet?

Executives frequently wanted to know how much it cost the company to access the Internet and to build an intranet. We reassured them that the cost was quite minimal. The major cost was a small amount of hardware and software for getting it set up, and a minimal amount for software for each user. On top of that, it cost a few thousand dollars a month for our access to the Internet, and that primarily depended on the size of data pipe we needed. We also mentioned that we believed the company was spending more money than that simply to access proprietary

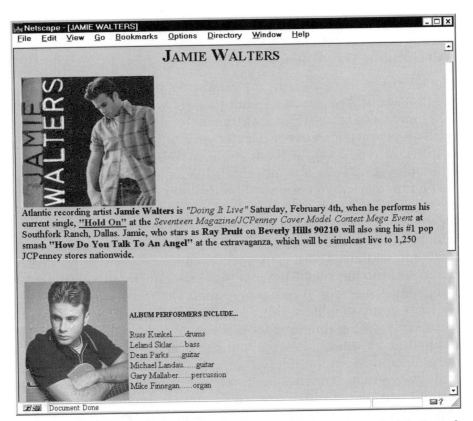

Netscape - [JAMIE WALTERS]

File Edit View Go Bookmarks Options Directory Window Help

JAMIE WALTERS

Atlantic recording artist **Jamie Walters** is *"Doing It Live"* Saturday, February 4th, when he performs his current single, **"Hold On"** at the *Seventeen Magazine/JCPenney Cover Model Contest Mega Event* at Southfork Ranch, Dallas. Jamie, who stars as **Ray Pruit** on **Beverly Hills 90210** will also sing his #1 pop smash **"How Do You Talk To An Angel"** at the extravaganza, which will be simulcast live to 1,250 JCPenney stores nationwide.

ALBUM PERFORMERS INCLUDE...

Russ Kunkel.....drums
Leland Sklar......bass
Dean Parks......guitar
Michael Landau.....guitar
Gary Mallaber......percussion
Mike Finnegan......organ

Document: Done

Figure 9.34 JCPenney/*Seventeen Magazine* Cover Model Search kickoff event, with Jamie Walters.

dial-up information each month, and some of that could go away through use of the Internet. Once they heard this, cost was no longer a concern.

How Do I Get My Department on the Intranet?

Part of our purpose in selling our audience on jWeb was to get them interested in putting their departmental information and lots more on it. We told them about the classes we offered in HTML and jWeb and invited them to sign up. Most important, we told them about the Internet Team and invited them to join. I suggested they see me afterward to sign up.

Other Ways to Promote Your Intranet

Web Fair

Since I did so many demos, the number of people reached was in the thousands. You reach a point, though, where it's time to use other means to promote your intranet. To make browsers and the intranet pervasive on every desktop and to further heighten the enthusiasm, the Internet Team staged a Web Fair. It was open to all employees. It was a wonderfully lively, all-day event, with a surfing theme. There were surfboards and other props all over the auditorium, and some Internet Team members dressed casually for the event. There were computers all around the auditorium which showcased the various departments' web sites and any new applications. There were several computers set up for people to surf the Internet. There were mini–training sessions running simultaneously in adjacent rooms. The folks from the Web Services group taught sessions on HTML, CGI coding, and how to use various web publishing tools. People could sign up for web publishing classes on the spot using a form on the internal web. Several vendors, including Netscape, had booths, complete with trade show–type drawings for T-shirts, books and software. The turnout was incredible—so much so that all the refreshments disappeared in the first hour, and replenishments came several times. People came in waves, and every time we saw the CIO, he had a different senior executive with him. The excitement was incredible and spread browsers and the intranet to thousands of employees.

Advertising Campaign

Turner Broadcasting had a very interesting way to promote their intranet. TESN grew from a project where the VP of Human Resources created and sanctioned a cross-functional team to develop ideas on better ways to serve internal customers. They held focus groups with employees to identify what employees needed and worked with an outside company to design the internal web site and create the content. To promote TESN to their employees, they worked with an ad agency to build an ad campaign. The ad agency came up with the network idea and created a teaser campaign.

The campaign consisted of the following features:

1. *Posters.*   They created posters, which they hung in the break rooms at all locations. The caption said *"Turner Network Stars,"* and the poster had four pictures illustrating Turner networks.

   ◆ For TBS, there was a picture of David Justice of the Atlanta Braves.
   ◆ For CNN, a picture of Larry King of *Larry King Live.*
   ◆ For Cartoon Network, a picture of Fred Flintstone of *The Flintstones.*
   ◆ For TESN, a picture of Michelle Thomas of Human Resources.

   At the bottom of the poster, there was a simple logo for TESN and the message *"Turner's Newest Network Launches March 29, 1996."*

2. *Mailing.*   They treated the ad campaign like a consumer campaign for a network. They sent a small copy of the posters to employee's homes with a message from Allan DeNiro, Vice President of Human Resources, and an invitation to the launch meetings. The message said:

   Turner Broadcasting has launched many great networks including TBS, CNN, Headline News, the Cartoon Network, TNT, TCM, and most recently, CNNfn.

   Today our Company is launching its newest network. It is our smallest network, in that it reaches an audience of less than 10,000 people. But it is our most important audience because all 10,000 are employees of Turner Broadcasting System, Inc.

   The network is TESN, Turner Employee Services Network. TESN represents our first step towards giving you, our "cus-

tomers," a new level of service from Human Resources, Bene-fits, Purchasing and Logistics, and TRAC.

TESN's mission is to provide you with information that makes your life at Turner easier and better. TESN will give you information you need to know when you want it, how you want it, and where you want it.

TESN premiere meetings will be held in Atlanta, Los Ange-les, New York, and Washington, D.C., starting the last week of March. So, look for more information coming your way soon.

TESN will launch worldwide on Friday, March 29, 1996.

It will be like nothing you ever expected. . . .

3. *Launch meetings.* Turner held launch meetings at the CNN Center in Atlanta on March 29. There were launch meetings in other Turner locations over the next few weeks. The meetings featured a wonderful, professional videotape which showed:

- ◆ Allan DeNiro talking about how he had created the team to come up with ways to treat each employee as a customer. He had challenged them to create the greatest customer-service organization.

- ◆ The team talking about how they had talked to employees to find out what they wanted and needed, and decided to:

  - ◆ Create an internal web to serve employees as customers.
  - ◆ Offer kiosks for those employees who don't have computers.
  - ◆ Provide a 24-hour service hotline for employees.
  - ◆ Give each employee a personal service repre-sentative in HR.

- ◆ A special report about TESN by CNN news anchor, Lynne Russell. She introduced TESN and gave employees an overview of what they would find there. Then she introduced Allan DeNiro and Jimi

Stricklin, Director of Employee Services Development, and turned the meeting over to them to do a live demo of TESN and answer questions.

They had a great turnout for these launch meetings. According to Jimi Stricklin, the ad campaign worked extremely well, and *people came in droves, and were excited because it was for them.*

Checklist: Promote Your Intranet

Figure 9.35 summarizes the steps involved in promoting your intranet.

1. What are your goals for the demo?

    - Recruit users as an audience for web publishers
    - Recruit web publishers and others for the team
    - Other?

2. Build the demo

    - Set up the computer—you need

        - Computer
        - Internet access
        - Browser
        - HTML authoring tool
        - Graphics tool
        - Caching tool

    - Learn HTML and other tools
    - Decide if you need an introduction

- Call or have lunch with people to find out how much they know about the Internet—determine whether you need an introduction
- Build HTML pages or presentation slides giving a short introduction covering

  - The Internet and its history
  - The World Wide Web and where it came from
  - Browsers
  - Hypertext linking and HTML

- Determine what to include in the demo

  - Identify needs

    - Brainstorm—think about

      - Information in paper form
      - Information that resides in disparate systems

    - Identify business partner contacts
    - Contact them

  - Involve others to find out about critical business needs and problems

    - Informally—stop people in the halls, have lunch with friends, let people seek you out
    - Formally—JAD sessions to brainstorm and identify uses

- Build sample applications—you can illustrate the concept if you

    - Create a home page for your department
    - Create an employee locator
    - Set up a variety of HTML pages—procedures manuals, benefits information, and samples of lots of other information
    - Tie HTML pages to databases—create a mock-up, if necessary
    - Add some graphics, sound, and video clips, but don't overdo

- Build the real intranet

    - Design the look and navigation
    - Possible applications

        - Phone directory
        - IS information—contact lists, organization charts, and documentation
        - Training schedules and registration
        - Downloadable software

3. Present the demo

    - Schedule demos

        - Top executives
        - Managers in key areas
        - Information systems

- Word of mouth
- Open demos

- Tailor the demos to your audience

  - What are some relevant sites? Create an intranet page of Interesting and Useful Web sites for users to access after the demo.
  - What is the appropriate language to use with this audience?
  - It's more important to communicate than to be technically correct.
  - Potential sequence for presentations

    - Introduce colleagues and yourself
    - Introduce the Internet and the World Wide Web
    - Visit business sites
    - Visit education sites
    - Visit government sites
    - Visit sites relevant to your business or industry
    - Show your external site
    - Talk about the intranet
    - Show your intranet demo
    - Closing—what is the impact of the Internet and intranet on your business, and what are you doing about it?

- Build enthusiasm

  - Brainstorm ideas for using the tools
  - Use these ideas to enhance the demo and the real intranet

- ◆ Use the brainstormed ideas to build new applications
- ◆ In the demos, share stories about where the ideas came from and give credit to the originator of each idea

- ◆ What excites your users? Take note of these and use them for your applications.

- ◆ Answer questions and address concerns—anticipate these questions and have answers ready for them

  - ◆ What will happen to productivity if we give employees access to the Internet?
  - ◆ How secure is the intranet?
  - ◆ If we give employees access to all this information, won't they be harder to deal with?
  - ◆ If we access the Internet, won't we bring in viruses?
  - ◆ How much does it cost the company to access the Internet?

    - ◆ How do I get my department on the intranet?

4. Other ways to promote your intranet

  - ◆ Web fair

    - ◆ Surfing theme
    - ◆ Showcase departments' web sites and any new applications
    - ◆ Surf the Internet
    - ◆ Mini–training sessions

- Sign up for classes on the intranet
- Vendor booths and drawings
- Advertising campaign
  - Posters
  - Mailings
  - Launch meetings

Figure 9.35 Promote your intranet—checklist.

chapter ten

Create Widespread Enthusiasm and Capability: The Role of Your Intranet Team

Why Do You Need an Intranet Team?

When you build an intranet, there are lots of things you must do, some of which include:

- Set the organization's direction for the intranet.
- Guide the intranet in moving in that set direction.
- Create the infrastructure.
- Evaluate and select hardware and software.
- Install and maintain servers.
- Install intranet tools for people.
- Create training for web publishers.
- Design the structure of the internal web site.
- Design the home page.
- Develop content and design.
- Create publishing guidelines.
- Encourage web publishers to publish.
- Approve content for the intranet.
- Advertise and promote the intranet.

- Encourage and support people in their use of the intranet.
- Create applications.
- Update publishers on new tools.
- Keep it all moving forward.

These things require lots of different people and lots of different skills. You need programmers, systems administrators, communicators, artists and graphic designers, marketers, technical support, trainers, and others. You don't usually find these skills in a single department. You'll need people from all across the organization. That being the case, how do you coordinate all these activities and get them accomplished? That's the role of the intranet team. The team sets the direction and coordinates and communicates all the necessary steps required to start up and maintain your intranet. The team does everything on the list. In my own experience, we called ourselves an Internet Team because we focused on both the external Internet and our internal internet, jWeb.

Without the Internet Team, jWeb wouldn't have grown as quickly as it did. Recently I spoke with Cathy Mills, VP and Director of Company Communications at JCPenney. Cathy is the owner of jWeb. She said that the Internet Team was the driving force in the development of jWeb. She belongs to several organizations of directors of corporate communications. Others often ask her how JCPenney created its intranet and how they should create theirs. She tells them to put some young people together in a room—some young communicators, young artists, and young information systems folks—and to lock the door so they can't get away, because they won't enjoy this interaction until they find a common ground. Getting them all together is absolutely crucial to developing an intranet. She also said that a facilitator is valuable to keep them from spending huge amounts of time flailing around and to promote constructive communication. She believes the team is the only place folks from such different areas of the company can come together and work on something of common interest, and that this was really critical to the development of jWeb.

Should the Intranet Team Be Combined with or Separate from the Internet Team?

Does it matter whether the team deals with both the Internet and intranet, or just the intranet? Not in any significant way. However, the companies I talked with that had teams in place had generally vested the responsibility for both with the single team.

The advantage of a single team is that since many of the issues are the same or overlap, you don't have two competing bodies trying to make decisions about the same thing. Also, since the tools are essentially the same for both, you get leverage rather than duplication when you train publishers and share new tools and techniques.

The disadvantage is that sometimes things can seem a bit fragmented because you focus on several different audiences. Do you want the same standards and approvals for the different audiences, or do you wish to treat them differently? You can overcome this confusion by having subgroups focus on the different audiences and different issues.

Again, there is no right or wrong way, so it depends on what seems right for your organization.

Composition of the Team

How do you get people on an intranet team? In our case, when the CIO created the team, he sent out an e-mail announcing it to Information Systems. He suggested that anyone who wanted to be on the team should contact me, and within hours, I had several volunteers. More came in over the next few days. We invited those who worked on the technical parts of the web to join the team.

Then, when we started doing demos, we invited everyone who wanted to publish content on the web and wanted to join the team to let me know. We got lots of volunteers from all areas of the company, as well as two or three appointees. I believe that the team was so enthusiastic and accomplished so much because most were volunteers.

The team should be a cross-functional team with representatives from all areas of the organization. Who makes up the Intranet Team? Where do they come from and what do they do?

- *Team leader.*   The team leader is the representative of the champion and keeps communication flowing between the team, the champion, and the steering committee. The team leader has responsibility and authority to keep everything moving, resolve issues, and ensure that the team meets its goals.

- *Web architects.*   These folks develop the structure and flow of the internal web.

- *Web services.*   These are the ones who evaluate and select Internet and intranet tools, build web applications, train and support web publishers, and keep everyone up-to-date. They keep the team apprised of the technical issues being discussed and resolved, of new software being evaluated, and tools and techniques available to web publishers and developers.

- *Webmasters.*   They are the ones who set up and administer web servers and maintain the content of those servers. Their role is to keep the team aware of capacity issues and what is being done in that area as well as changes that will impact the publishers of content.

- *Programmers and applications developers.*   These folks hook the databases to documents and forms and do fancy things like develop Java applications.

- *Graphic artists and designers.*   These folks develop the home pages and graphics for the internal web. They may create libraries of graphics, icons, bullets, and navigational tools for use by all web publishers.

- *Communicators.*   These are the folks who are responsible for the image and message of the company and have responsibility for all internal communications with employees. They already know how to communicate with employees, including what to say and how to say it.

- *Web publishers.*   These folks generally come from all areas of the organization. They're enthusiastic about the web and are responsible for developing and overseeing the content of their departmental web sites.

- *Technical support.*   These folks install, or help with installation of, TCP/IP, browsers, and other applications for users.

- *Trainers.*   These folks develop and deliver training for web publishers and end users.

- *Help desk and support.*   These folks support your audience as it grows, and should be brought into the planning early in the process.

- *Legal.*   These folks deal primarily with the external Web site, but need to be aware of anywhere the intranet interfaces with suppliers, customers, or others outside the company. Have them involved but make sure they understand that their role is not to delay everything.

- *Facilitator.*   The facilitator plans for and runs the team meetings to ensure that they are as productive as possible.

Does the Team Really Need a Facilitator?

What is a facilitator? A *facilitator* is someone specially trained to run meetings effectively. Facilitators may also be skilled in team building and other aspects of team dynamics; in other words, some of the warm and fuzzy stuff that IT professionals typically disdain. The facilitator gets everyone to participate and ensures that you use all input. Facilitators are skilled in bringing teams to consensus, allowing everyone to buy into the decisions.

Why do you need a facilitator? It seems like a frivolous job that's not very useful. That's what people might think if they've never attended a meeting run by an experienced facilitator. The facilitator makes sure that meetings are productive and run smoothly, which isn't an easy task for team meetings of 40 to 50 people.

I believe that facilitators are very valuable; but then, I've been a facilitator, so I'm biased. To facilitate the Internet Team, I was able to line up my co-facilitator from a previous Business Process Improvement project. He wanted to do web publishing and this was a good way to get him involved with the team. Facilitators typically stay neutral and don't become involved in the subject matter under discussion. What we found was that he and I could switch off facilitating to avoid subjects about which we had a concern.

Facilitators are invaluable when you have meetings with a large number of participants and have a desired set of results to achieve. What are the benefits of having facilitators conduct the meetings? Facilitators will:

◆ Help you focus on your desired results before the meeting and plan the meeting to achieve those results
◆ Make a meeting run smoother and more efficiently, therefore taking less time to obtain a given set of results
◆ Work until a consensus is reached and everyone is bought into the decision

How do you find a facilitator to help your team? First, human resources departments are often where company facilitators reside. Also, Total Quality Management programs and Business Process Improvement or reengineering programs usually have facilitators. If you don't have access to in-house facilitators and need to go outside, there are several possibilities.

◆ Consulting firms generally offer facilitators.
◆ Search on the Internet for facilitation companies or facilitation brokers.
◆ Send a message to the moderator of the Internet newsgroup misc.business.facilitators asking to post a message that you are looking for a facilitator and asking for replies by e-mail.

As expensive as meetings can be, accomplishing more in less time through having a facilitator can be money well spent.

How Does the Team Work?

Once we were able to get representatives from the appropriate areas, it was time for the team to get to work. In this section I'll talk about:

- Planning and agendas for team meetings
- Team meetings

Planning and Agendas

When we were almost ready to launch the team, it was time to do the planning and preparation for the kickoff meeting. As a facilitator, I learned that a lot of up-front planning was a key to a successful project and successful meetings. Since the facilitator was my former co-facilitator, it was easy for him to step in and plan the kickoff meeting. We talked about our goals for the team and what we wanted to accomplish in the kickoff meeting. He put together a preliminary agenda and we worked together to refine it. We did the same thing to plan agendas and subsequent meetings.

The team held its meetings to:

- Set its direction and the direction for the Internet and intranet
- Define its vision, mission, and objectives
- Communicate information about tools and techniques

Logistics

The kickoff meeting lasted an entire day, with about 35 attendees. When you're setting up a room for a team meeting, putting in a U-shape is best so that everyone can see each other. It makes for easier collaboration. Once you go above about 20 people, it's hard to set up a meeting room that is conducive to team participation. You end up with classroom-style seating, which doesn't work well because participants can't see each other. We took a large meeting room and set up the tables in a large U shape. It was pretty big, but at least people could still look at each other and get to know each other.

Refreshments

One thing I learned as a facilitator was to keep the team's energy level fairly even by carefully selecting the refreshments and snacks we would serve. With 40 to 55 people from all areas of the business, team meetings were very expensive and needed to be highly productive. In order to accomplish so much in a short time frame, we had to make team meetings highly focused and very intense. Though we didn't normally serve food at meetings, it was necessary to do so for the Internet Team meetings. Therefore, it was worthwhile to serve refreshments in the morning and at the afternoon break.

For morning breaks, in addition to the usual coffee and lots of water, it's best to have muffins, fresh fruit, and fruit juice rather than doughnuts and pastries. Muffins and fruit contain complex sugars that burn over a longer period of time and give a consistent energy level. Doughnuts and pastries contain simple sugars that burn quickly, giving a sugar high followed by a sugar low. You don't need your team's energy levels to be on a roller-coaster ride, so it's best to avoid foods full of simple sugars.

For afternoon snacks, it's best to have popcorn, pretzels, and fresh fruit, along with lots of water and fruit juices. If you choose to serve sodas, select them carefully.

To most people, it will seem really silly to concern ourselves about the selection of snacks for the team. I can say from experience that it's the small things such as this that can make a big difference in the team's ability to focus on its task. Doctors insist that sugar doesn't affect kids; however, most mothers will tell you otherwise. Kids can become wired, silly, or aggressive if they become overloaded with sugar. So can adults. You get a team of 40 or 50 adults on a sugar high and they can be just as silly and unruly as a bunch of kids at a birthday party after having cake and Kool-Aid. Forget accomplishing anything for a few hours—it just won't happen. You might as well play games until the sugar wears off.

Team Building and Bonding

One of the things often encountered by cross-functional teams is the difficulty in communication. When you mix people from information systems with people from other areas, they just can't communicate. They don't speak the same language. A skilled facilitator can help bridge that gap and can speed up the development of communication through team building and bonding exercises. Relationships take time to build and require that everyone be willing to work on building them.

An important role for the facilitator is to create this team bonding, which is a sense of unity and caring among team members. It takes time, but you can speed it up by having the team get to know each other personally and by working together. Our subteams helped us with this, as did some of the team creativity exercises.

There are several techniques you can use specifically to start and enhance the team-bonding process:

- *Experiential programs.* You can take your team off to an experiential program, such as Outward Bound or a *ropes course.* Ropes courses have team members do things like climb walls and walk tightropes. Experiential courses build trust and communication among team members, but you should be careful in using these courses. You need to know the team members and their feelings, because some people become very uncomfortable when thrust into the kinds of situations these courses involve. Those people may come away from these courses feeling more uncomfortable and alienated from the team. So choose these courses with care.

- *Trips.* My favorite is to take the team on a trip. My co-facilitator and I took our business process improvement team to visit a company known as one of the *best in class* for the process we were working on. We did this when the team was just getting started so that it was a good way for them to get to know each other. It's not that easy for 13 people to travel together, but with team members supporting and helping each other, it was very easy. The trip was great for building relationships. Team members did little things for each other, which grew into more and more support for each other. For example, some team members checked in the baggage while others parked the cars. When we arrived, some members retrieved the luggage while others picked up the rental vans. Over several days, there were lots of opportunities for personal conversations and to get to know each other better. I knew the team had bonded when I saw them splitting appetizers and desserts at dinner the last night. This team went on to truly care about and support each other through a very challenging project. Even though the team finished its project several years ago, we still try to get together from time to time to keep up with each other.

I encourage you to take your team on a trip if it's possible, even if it's just a day trip to someplace a couple of hours away. You can pile the team into a van or two and drive there. That will give team members a chance to visit and get to know each other more personally. You can visit another company, or even go to a seminar for some tool you want for your intranet. The important thing is to get the team out of the office and put them together in a way that they can relate to each other and share a common experience.

♦ *Social events.*   Another great technique is to get the team together for lunch, dinner, or just a get-acquainted event. It's especially good if you can do this away from the office, in a casual setting. Have everyone come dressed casually so they can *let their hair down* and just get to know each other. To keep up the momentum, you could set up a weekly or biweekly get-together lunch where people can just chat and keep up with what's going on with each other.

The Four Stages of Teams

Much of the literature on team building talks about the four stages of teams. Every team goes through all four stages. I repeat, every team goes through all four stages. There is no way to avoid a stage. The key is to help the team transition as quickly and smoothly as possible through these steps. They are:

1. *Forming.* This is the stage where the team is just getting together and figuring out what to do. Most people will be on their best behavior during this stage.

2. *Storming.* As the team members get to know each other, they start to feel comfortable disagreeing with one another. At times they may be very openly disagreeable with each other. This is a normal part of the development of a team. You shouldn't try to avoid this stage because it's a healthy stage for the team to go through.

3. *Norming.* As the team becomes very comfortable together, the team starts to develop routines, rituals, and norms of behaving. They have reached the point where they can work effectively together and have figured out who will do what. Team members take on specific roles and figure out how to best work together.

4. *Performing.* Once the team has figured everything out, they can start to work together cooperatively and effectively. By the time the team has reached this stage, things work smoothly and team members are starting to develop close personal relationships where they really care about each other.

The role of the facilitator is to help the team to move through these stages easily.

Creativity Techniques and Out-of-the-Box Thinking

I could write a whole chapter just on the subject of creativity techniques and out-of-the-box thinking, but I'll restrain myself since it isn't the main subject of this chapter.

Creativity techniques can assist you to:

◆ Help the team bond together
◆ Help people get out of their *box* and come up with unique and creative ideas and strategies

There are lots of techniques that you can use, some of which include:

◆ *Humor.*   Make sure you use lots of humor, fun, and games to get people laughing and enjoying themselves. The team will be more creative and productive if they're having fun.

◆ *Breaks.*   Make sure that you take frequent breaks so that people stay fresh and energized.

◆ *Engage the whole brain.*   You'll find that your team consists of *left-brained* people, who are logical and sequential thinkers, and *right-brained* people, who are more creative and holistic thinkers. To get everybody working together, you need to help the team start engaging and drawing upon both hemispheres of their brains. A couple of the many techniques that you can use are:

   1. *Draw pictures.*   Divide the team into groups of three or four people. Give them an assignment to think about what the future will look like and draw a picture to convey their ideas. Give them lots of colors of crayons or markers so they can be very creative. Remind them that the idea is what's important, not their artistic skills. When you bring the groups back together, have each group describe their vision for the other groups. A variation might be to have the other groups guess what the picture means. Drawing pictures and explaining them helps engage both hemispheres of the brain and jump-starts creativity.

   2. *Mind mapping.*   Mind mapping is a technique for capturing notes or brainstorming. You draw a picture in the center of the page representing the central idea or theme. As you get ideas related to that theme, you record them on spokes coming off the central concept. You add related thoughts coming off of those spokes. This helps to organize ideas or thoughts. By using combinations of words, pictures, and different colors, you jump-start the brain and become more creative. I have

found this to be a highly effective technique for team brainstorming and to stimulate out-of-the-box thinking because its basis is in how the brain actually works. Mind mapping is one of my personal favorites for using with teams.

If you would like more information about these techniques, I have listed some great resources in the Appendix.

Team Meetings

Next, I'll talk about the team's meetings, starting with the kickoff and moving through the first few meetings. I've included sample agendas for team meetings to give you an idea of how we structured the meetings and what kinds of things we did.

Internet Team Kickoff Meeting

Figure 10.1 shows a sample agenda for the Internet Team kickoff meeting. We started at 8:30 by welcoming everyone. The first thing we did was to start getting people to know each other. We went around the room introducing ourselves. We asked each participant to tell their name, department, and what brought them to the team. We also asked them to talk about their interest in the Internet and/or jWeb. If they were building content or applications, we asked them to tell us about their project. If their job involved the technical parts of the web, we asked them to talk about their responsibilities for the Internet and jWeb. When we finished the introductions, we started sending around a team roster for review and correction of contact information. We planned to send a roster to everyone the next day so they could recall who did what and know how to contact them with questions. These were the first steps in the communications process.

One piece of advice for you for during the introductions would be to make sure to give lots of recognition and kudos to those who have contributed to your current intranet and/or the external Web site. For example, recognize those who created and built the external Web site and the internal web, those who built the servers, and those who keep things running. Recognize anyone who has

8:30–9:00	Welcome and introductions
9:00–10:00	Demo: Internet and jWeb
10:00–10:15	Break
10:15–11:00	Demo: Internet Store and Gift Registry
11:00–11:30	Demo: New beta of Netscape and other tools
11:30–11:45	Discuss Internet and intranet plans
11:45–12:45	Lunch break
12:45–1:30	Team-building exercise with break-out groups

- ◆ Draw group picture of future with Internet and intranet

1:30–2:30	Facilitated session of brainstorming and discussion:

- ◆ Company's expectations and goals for web presence
- ◆ Positive and negative factors that could impact
- ◆ What team could do to improve or offset these factors

2:30–2:45	Break
2:45–3:45	Facilitated session of brainstorming and discussion (continued):

- ◆ What they expected the team to accomplish
- ◆ How team should work
- ◆ What they wanted to get from being member
- ◆ What vision, mission, and objectives should be

3:45–4:00	Make decisions:

- ◆ What to work on at next meeting
- ◆ When and how often team should meet—set dates and times

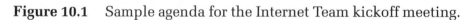

Figure 10.1   Sample agenda for the Internet Team kickoff meeting.

contributed to or built applications for the internal web. A little recognition among peers goes a long way toward making people feel special and appreciated for what they've done, especially when they've made an extraordinary effort.

After everyone introduced themselves, we showed our demo to level the field. Some had already seen the demo that we had just presented to the company's top executives, but others hadn't, so we wanted to make sure that everyone started out at the same place. We also went through all the new things that we were adding to jWeb.

After that, we took a break. You should schedule breaks every 1½ to 2 hours. Some people and companies seem to think it's macho or more productive to keep going and not take breaks. A good facilitator will schedule breaks at regular intervals and will call them whenever people's attention spans start to wane. Another good time for a break is if something controversial is being discussed and everyone is just going around in circles. Give people a few minutes to get away from the subject and you may find different perspectives emerge when you reconvene. At any rate, the typical attention span in a meeting is no longer than two hours. Make sure to stop to give people time to stretch and regroup.

After the break, it was time for a demo of the JCPenney Internet Store, which was going on the Internet within a few days. We followed that with a demo of the Gift Registry, which was going on the Internet at the same time. The people who built both applications were the ones to present them. That way, they could get recognition for the work they had done. They also were able to solicit feedback and answer questions.

Just as an aside, a really great use of an internal web is for putting out the applications that are almost ready to go on the external Web site. If you send out word about the application and ask for comments, you may solicit lots of good feedback. We used the team for soliciting that feedback also.

Next on the agenda was a demo of a new beta version of Netscape and other new tools, given by the manager of the web services group. This tool update became a regular feature at team meetings. Then we talked about the kinds of things we were building for the external and internal web sites.

After a lunch break, we started into a team-building exercise to help the team get to know each other better and to get everyone's brain in gear. An after-lunch creative exercise is great for helping people transition back into the meeting and become refocused on the task. The facilitator divided the team into small groups to draw a group picture of what they perceived the future to be like with the company having an external Web site and jWeb. Each group then showed and explained its drawing.

Then we moved into a facilitated session of brainstorming and discussion. We listed and discussed what the team thought the company's expectations and goals were for the web presence, what were the positive and negative factors that could impact that, and what the team could do to improve or offset these factors. After a break, we continued the facilitated session by listing and discussing what team members expected the team to accomplish, how they wanted the team to work, and what they personally wanted to get out of being a team member.

Several times during the meeting, there was a lot of discussion of organizational concerns. This is something you may encounter as well. What we were trying to do with the Internet team was alien to some people. The idea of being empowered to do things without securing permission concerned a couple of team members. Some of their major concerns were:

- Who were we to be setting the company's Internet direction? Shouldn't the executives set that direction? Is it OK for us to take the initiative and just do things? At the very least, shouldn't somebody approve what we're recommending?

- Will my boss let me have the time to do this? I already have a full-time job. We really just heard this from the few appointees to the team. Fortunately, the support they received from their bosses overcame these objections pretty quickly. When they saw that putting things on jWeb was a priority with the boss, everything was OK.

We assured the team they had the support of the champion and that there was support from the top for us to proceed and set the direction. Once everyone was comfortable that we could indeed create a vision and mission for the company's Internet and intranet efforts, the team was ready to continue.

The next step then was to discuss how to create a vision, a mission, and team objectives. The team decided that a small group should get together before the next meeting and draft a vision, mission, and objectives to bring for discussion. We asked for volunteers, and fortunately got six people, representing a good cross section of the company, to volunteer for this. We dubbed this group the Vision Workgroup.

Finally, we discussed how the team wanted to work, what the team wanted to work on at the next meeting, and how often the team should meet. We set dates for the next few meetings so everyone could get them on their calendars.

Vision Workgroup Meeting

At the kickoff meeting, we decided that a small workgroup would get together the next week to draft a vision, mission, and objectives to present at the next team meeting. We would base these items on the ideas developed in the kickoff meeting. I both facilitated and participated in this meeting. Typically, the facilitator should remain neutral and therefore can't participate. However, in this case it seemed to work fine because it was such a small group. To get everyone refocused on the ideas of the team, I hung on the wall the flipcharts from the kickoff meeting. We used them to develop the vision, mission, and objectives. As we finished the draft, I asked if anyone would be willing to present these items at the team meeting and lead the discussion. Two team members volunteered, which was an important part of giving them ownership of these items. Also, by having them present to their teammates, it gave the team ownership, as well.

Second Team Meeting

Figure 10.2 shows the sample agenda for the second team meeting, which came just two weeks after the kickoff. By the second meeting, the team had added many new members. I started the meeting by welcoming everyone and introduced the new members.

1:00–1:10	Welcome and introductions
1:10–1:30	Technical update, demo, and tools update
1:30–2:40	Vision, mission, and objectives

- ◆ Vision workgroup to present draft
- ◆ Facilitate consensus and acceptance

2:40–2:50	Break
2:50–3:00	Team-building/creative-brainstorming exercise—team home page
3:00–3:55	Work on plan to accomplish objectives
3:55–4:00	Announce logistics for next meeting and adjourn

Figure 10.2   Sample agenda for second team meeting.

We had announcements, a technical update from the webmaster, a demo of some new things on jWeb, and a tool update.

The Vision Workgroup presented their draft of the team's vision, mission, and objectives. The presenters and the facilitator brought the team to a consensus and acceptance of them. This was a highly challenging task because there were more than 40 members in attendance. There was a tendency to get into nit-picking over the specific words we used and how we should put them together. By the time we finished this task, it was definitely time for a break.

After the break, we resumed with a team-building creativity exercise. The premise was that we were creating a team home page. What should we put on it? There were all sorts of ideas, all very serious. When the serious ideas started slowing down, the facilitator encouraged creative ideas, and even silly ideas, to get people thinking. By the time we were through, everyone was laughing, having a good time, and really getting creative. We ended up with a great list of things we could actually do, plus people were thinking about the possibilities for the intranet.

The next step was to figure out how to accomplish the team's objectives. The team decided to set up small subteams, or task teams, to work on each specific objective. They determined what each subteam would cover, and people started volunteering for the subteams of their choice. Some even volunteered to lead their subteam. Some of these teams focused on the external Web site and others focused on the intranet. Subteams related to the intranet were:

- *Internet Team home page and communications.* The focus of this subteam was to:

    - Facilitate communication and sharing of information among Internet Team members
    - Share tips and techniques with others outside the team

- *Develop and communicate guidelines, standards, and policies.* The focus of this subteam was to:

    - Set the direction and guide development of the internal web
    - Set Internet policies
    - Train and support web publishers
    - Encourage publishing

- *Promote jWeb to employees.* The focus of this subteam was to:

    - Build enthusiasm for jWeb
    - Promote use of jWeb among employees

- *Promote the effective use of the Internet and jWeb.* The focus of this subteam was to:

    - Create training and support for users of the Internet and jWeb
    - Promote role modeling of the best ways to use the Internet and jWeb

♦ *Identify and spread tools and best practices.* The focus of this subteam was to:

- ♦ Evaluate and identify the best tools and techniques to use for web publishing
- ♦ Share this information with team members who were interested

The team decided that the subteams would meet over the next month and work on their assigned objectives. They would report their progress and plans to the entire team at the fourth team meeting.

At the end of the meeting, I discussed the logistics for the next meeting and then adjourned this one.

Third Team Meeting

Figure 10.3 shows the sample agenda for the third team meeting, which was two weeks after the previous one. Again there were new members to introduce to the team, and this time we had a guest speaker, our champion, the CIO. I didn't get the CIO scheduled until the third team meeting, which was really only a few weeks after the kickoff. I would have liked for him to speak at the kickoff except that he was out of town. He could have addressed and overcome the organizational concerns expressed at the kickoff. These concerns stemmed from the fact that, at the time, this was a very radical approach for us.

The CIO's words to the team were extremely inspiring, and he addressed all of their concerns. He encouraged us to set the direction the company would take with the Internet and to be as creative and innovative as we could. Since he was one of the top executives of the company, having support at his level was very encouraging to the team.

After the CIO left, everyone was on an adrenaline high. We did the announcements and recognized those who had done something special or unique since the last meeting. Then we had a review of the subteams and enlisted additional volunteers from the new members. We had an update on sales from the JCPenney Internet Store and testimonials that had come in via the Webmas-

1:00–1:10	Welcome and introduction of new members
1:10–1:30	Guest speaker: Chief Information Officer
1:30–1:40	Announcements and recognition
1:40–1:50	Discussion of subteams and enlist additional volunteers from new members
1:50–2:00	Update on Web sales and testimonials
2:00–2:10	Demo of new external home page design
2:10–2:25	Demo of new external Web features
2:25–2:35	Technical update
2:35–2:45	Break
2:45–3:00	Tools update and demo
3:00–3:50	Internet World and Web World reports
3:50–4:00	Announce logistics for next meeting and adjourn

Figure 10.3   Sample agenda for third team meeting.

ter. We also had a preview of the new external Web site home page design and another member gave us a preview of some new things going on the external Web site. The Webmaster gave us a technical update and showed recent statistics.

Following a break, we had a tools update and then those who had attended the recent Internet World and Web World presented to the team some of the things that they had learned. At the conclusion, we announced the logistics for the next meeting and adjourned.

Fourth Team Meeting

Figure 10.4 shows the sample agenda for the fourth team meeting. Again, we had more new members to introduce, and I also introduced our guest for the meeting, Jim Sterne. Jim is an internationally known guru on marketing on the World Wide Web, and he was there to do a seminar for us and our invited guests on the following day.

Next came the announcements and recognition of accomplishments, followed by the sales update, the Webmaster's technical update, and the tools update. Following that, we started into the

1:00–1:10	Welcome, introduce new members, introduce Jim Sterne
1:10–1:20	Announcements and recognition
1:20–1:30	Sales update on external Web site
1:30–1:40	Technical update
1:40–1:50	Tools update
1:50–2:40	Presentations by subteams—progress and plans
2:40–2:50	Break
2:50–3:55	Presentations by subteams—progress and plans (continued)
3:55–4:00	Announce logistics for next meeting and adjourn

Figure 10.4   Sample agenda for fourth team meeting.

presentations by the subteams as to what they had accomplished and what they were working on. That continued for the rest of the afternoon. At the conclusion, I announced the logistics for subsequent meetings and reminded everyone of the location of Jim Sterne's seminar, and then we adjourned.

What Are the Team's Objectives?

As I mentioned earlier, the team decided to create subteams to work on the specific objectives it created. There were five major objectives that we worked on:

1. Internet team home page and communications
2. Develop and communicate guidelines, standards, and policies
3. Promote jWeb to employees
4. Promote the effective use of the Internet and jWeb
5. Identify and spread tools and best practices

Internet Team Home Page and Communications

Communication was a critical issue since the team consisted of people from many different areas of the business. Techies who were members of the team had to take the time to truly listen to others and to learn to communicate without using technical terms and jargon. Everyone else had to learn to listen carefully and try to understand what the techies were saying. The team building was helping create the communication that we needed. This was a real challenge for everyone. All team members tried to communicate and to work together. Knowing this was an issue, the team decided to create a subteam specifically for continuing the communication among team members that we developed through the meetings.

Since the team met biweekly and there was so much to do between meetings, we really needed an effective way to communicate. We set up two ways to do this:

1. Team newsgroup
2. Team home page

Team Newsgroup

The newsgroup helped continue the work of the team between meetings. If someone had to be away and couldn't attend a meeting, the newsgroup contained the information to keep them up-to-date. We posted the minutes of team meetings, agendas for the next meeting, and items that we decided upon. We posted the team's vision, mission, and objectives, the team roster and contact information, and the lists of subteams and their members. Subteams would post their minutes and decisions to the newsgroup, as well.

To help the team members get to know each other better, we asked each member to post a bio and talk about their interests. The newsgroup was full of questions and discussions about all kinds of topics related to the team and building web content. Team members frequently posted ideas, tips, comments, requests, and reviews.

When we resolved technical issues, we posted that information to the newsgroup as well. When new tools were available, we posted that along with information about how to get them and how to use them. The Internet Team became a valuable resource for ideas as to how to use the intranet and how to solve intranet problems. People could use the newsgroup to bounce ideas off each other and this became, in effect, a community of practice.

Team Home Page

The newsgroup was just to get us started. When we brought up the team home page (Figure 10.5), we moved over many of the documents from the newsgroup for continuous access. These

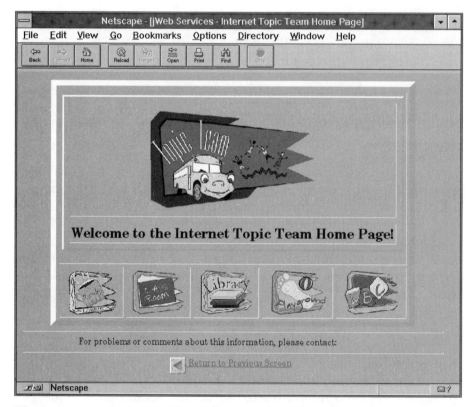

Figure 10.5   Internet Team home page. (*Used with permission. JCPenney Company, Inc., copyright 1996.*)

included the team roster, links to home pages, and information about the tools, techniques, and tips we had learned. That way, others also had access to this information. The team roster provided a list of experts for those who were new to web publishing to consult.

The brightly colored team home page is in blues, greens, reds, yellows, and pinks, with a fun, schoolhouse theme. The idea was to get people's attention and draw them in to find out about all the neat resources available to them at this location.

Develop and Communicate Guidelines, Standards, and Policies

This subteam had some of the biggest challenges of all the subteams. The person who created the initial jWeb led this subteam, joined by communicators, graphics artists, and others. This subteam had responsibility to:

- ◆ Set the direction and guide development of the internal web
- ◆ Set Internet policies
- ◆ Train and support web publishers
- ◆ Encourage publishing

Set Direction and Guide Development of the Internal Web

Some of the things they did to guide the development of jWeb were to:

- ◆ Create the jWeb home page and develop its structure and flow
- ◆ Determine whether we needed standards and approvals

Create the jWeb Home Page and Structure   The individual in IS who created the original jWeb also designed the new structure and flow of jWeb. She used lots of creativity and added in the input and feedback which came from the demos. Over time, Company Communications took over responsibility for both the external Web site and the intranet. Their graphics artists designed a new look for the home page, but the basic structure and flow remained.

Set Standards and the Approvals Process   Creating the initial look and structure was very easy compared to the challenges in this area. There were four major issues:

1. Should there be web standards?
2. What approvals and authorizations were necessary?
3. Should you allow personal home pages?
4. Who should ultimately own the intranet?

As in most other decisions related to the intranet, your choice depends largely on what is appropriate for your organization and its culture.

Should There Be Web Standards?   One of the subteam objectives was to determine if there should be standards and, if so, to set them. There are two extremes, standardized and regimented or loose and innovative. In other words, controlled or chaotic. This is a tough issue for your team.

1. *Standardized and controlled.*   Those who believe in standardization say that by having a consistently applied standard, everyone knows where to look for certain types of information on every page and navigation is consistent throughout the internal web. Approvals are necessary for every page published, not only to ensure consistency, but also to make sure that the content is appropriate and businesslike. The disadvantage is that if people have no room to experiment, the results can be truly boring. You won't get interesting and exciting things because you don't allow them.
2. *Loose and chaotic.*   Those who believe in not having standards say that this allows people to experiment and try new things. Those who favor this approach feel that you can see and learn what works well and what

doesn't. This can yield wonderful ideas that could never happen in a standardized environment. The end result may be things that help people do their jobs better. The disadvantage is that since content doesn't go through long approval cycles, things may get on the web that are not as businesslike as some would want. Since everybody has a different set of standards and different perceptions, some really ugly things can happen when you give everyone absolute freedom to create. Bad content and bad graphics will generally disappear as developers learn new ways of doing things. The truly ugly will generally succumb through peer pressure. The creativity and innovation spawned by lack of standards will more than make up for a few ugly pages.

Rather than developing rigid standards of how things had to look on our internal web, we decided to let people experiment, learn, and make mistakes. As many sites came up, their developers would put out a call on the Internet Team newsgroup for comments and ideas of how to do things better. This attitude of cooperation made the end results just that much better. Most employees know what's appropriate and I don't recall ever having someone put out something that wasn't appropriate. In certain areas of the company, management wanted to have a consistent look and dictated a consistent appearance among all groups within the department. It was certainly their place to do this if they desired, but it yielded some pretty boring sites.

What Approvals and Authorizations Were Necessary?   Another subteam objective was to determine what levels of approvals were required. They decided to let approvals reside in the individual departments that were putting up the content. The decision was really between the publisher and his or her manager. Some companies have formal procedures for approvals, but my gut feeling is that with most the decision tends to reside, as it did with us, at the level of the publisher and his or her manager. If you would have your manager approve a memo you send, then you will probably have that same manager approve your content. It may be worthwhile to have someone in employee communications to go to for guidance if there's something about which you're unsure.

Who controls permissions? If you maintain your content manually, and it resides on a server maintained by IT, there is probably someone who moves the pages out to the server for you. This person may grant you permission to move them to a certain subdirectory yourself. If you have the content residing on your own server, then it's up to you to decide. If you have lots of publishers in your department, then the system administrator for that server probably controls permissions for certain subdirectories. He or she may take responsibility for moving it all to the server for the department. If an automated system updates the content, then a systems administrator probably maintains permissions. Again, this is such an individual decision for each company that you will have to figure out what is right for your organization.

Should You Allow Personal Home Pages?   An issue related to standards is whether people will be allowed or encouraged to create their own home pages or whether you will discourage this. This decision usually parallels the decision for or against standards.

If you allow or encourage home pages, will you teach everyone how to do HTML? Can you do something to make it easy for them, such as creating a template or a tool to ease the process?

Some companies encourage everyone from the CEO on down to have a home page. You find more of these companies in high-tech industries, where techies predominate. The techies can learn HTML one day at lunch. With the advent of tools that make the task relatively easy, the capability for creating home pages becomes far more widespread. The value of having individual home pages is that, if you have a search tool, you can easily find people with the skills you need. If you're staffing a project and need certain skills, there is no easier way to locate them than through a quick internal web search. We aren't talking just about work skills. An executive I know needed to appoint people to several community positions and needed to do so very quickly. One required writing and speaking skills in a certain foreign language, and the other required experience as a community volunteer. If information about outside interests exists on home pages, you can quickly locate employees with the skills and interests you need.

Some companies discourage individual home pages. They feel that those with technical skills in HTML and graphics have an unfair advantage over others. In addition, they worry that people will waste too much energy trying to be fancy or outdo others. If this gets in the way of doing their job, it can impact productivity.

Who Should Ultimately Own the Intranet?   When we started, IS took responsibility for both the external Web site and the internal web. However, we knew we would turn over that responsibility when it was appropriate to some other area of the company. It seemed most appropriate that it belong to the folks who were responsible for setting the company image and speaking on behalf of the company. At the time, several different areas had those responsibilities. The people who spoke for the company were in External Communications. Just as we were starting to show our demo, External Communications was embarking on several special events that were perfect to put on the external Web site. We showed our demo to Cathy Mills, who was in charge of External Communications. Because of her excitement over what she saw, she had us start working with her folks to put these events on the external Web site. At about the same time, we started working with the graphics design folks in Company Communications to do a new design for our external home page. Within a few weeks, External Communications and Company Communications were brought together with Cathy Mills in charge. Shortly afterward, she took over responsibility for the JCPenney Web site. Since she's also responsible for communicating with associates, her folks have taken over responsibility for jWeb as well.

Generally, IT gets the intranet started, but will probably step aside when the appropriate manager in the business is ready to take responsibility for it. That is usually the manager who is responsible for fostering communication throughout the business. That manager is then responsible for the look, feel, and content of the internal web site, while IT controls the technical requirements of the site.

In some of the intranet-related discussion groups on the Internet, there have been discussions as to who should own the intranet. There have been comments that the owner was the corporate librarian, information technology, and in a few companies, communications. I think we'll start to see more and more intranets being owned by communications.

Cathy Mills says that what's happening is that everyone is understanding that it's not just techies who are the audience. It's the mass audience of everyone who works in your company. She says that as intranets develop and the information they contain needs to be in forms that people understand, they have begun to migrate to Communications for the interpretation of the words and the way that the graphics should be done. It's been a handoff in most cases. When you begin to see all the associate information applications for it, then it makes sense for it to reside in Communications where the parameters already exist. Only the medium has changed. Communications already knew what was proprietary, what you say, what you don't, and the words that you use. That part was already in place. They provide the communication with associates. However, the content throughout jWeb is the responsibility of the departments that put it there, and they maintain it. Many departments come to the Internet Publishing group in Communications, which is responsible for the external Web site and jWeb, to have them create their jWeb pages for them from their content.

For the most part, at other companies I spoke with, the group that put the content there maintains it, and the IT group typically owns the infrastructure.

Set Internet Policies

As I've mentioned before, there are fears and concerns over opening up access to the Internet. The team had to address this issue and make sure to develop appropriate policies. You will want to make sure that you create an Internet policy and publish it on the internal web for everyone to see. What you decide to include in it is a very individual decision. There are three basic issues related to Internet policies:

◆ Should you allow universal access to the Internet?
◆ Should you allow personal use of the Internet?

◆ How do you help people understand what is confidential?

Should You Allow Universal Access to the Internet? One of the most common issues that surfaced was whether or not we should give everyone access to the Internet. Many people believed that not everyone needed access to the Internet. What would happen to productivity if we gave people access? Managers worried over how would they keep their people from playing all day. This was not a new issue. People have always had ways to waste time. At least a person surfing the Net impacts only his or her own work and doesn't keep others from working. This really boils down to a management issue.

In our experience, when people first got access to the Internet, they went through the *gee-whiz* stage of surfing and had to check everything out. This might mean surfing during lunch, staying late, and coming in on weekends just to indulge themselves and experience it all. Productivity may dip during this period, but surfing is great for learning how to use and tap into the vast resources available on the Internet. After a few days or weeks, when the novelty wears off, users go to the Internet to find something specific rather than to surf. At this point, productivity should not only return to normal, but should start increasing due to the vast resources available to them to solve problems. If productivity doesn't return, then you do have a problem, but you probably already had that problem before the Internet came along—it just wasn't as noticeable.

The issue was whether to allow access and, if so, whether to control it. I'll talk about that in the next section.

Should You Allow Personal Use of the Internet? Will you allow personal use of the Internet? If so, how much will you allow? Do you allow your employees to use the telephone to make and receive personal phone calls during office hours? If so, does the same policy apply to using your company equipment to access the Internet? Some CIOs dismiss this as not being an issue. Their belief is that people gain experience through using the Internet, whether it's for personal or business use. It's a truly cheap way to allow people to train themselves in how to use the Internet and to stretch their knowledge. Some CIOs believe that any knowledge an employee gains, from whatever source, benefits not only the employee but also the company.

The most vexing issue to executives is what to do about access to certain sexually explicit sites. There are several approaches to this.

1. *Total laissez-faire.* We won't worry about that. Though some companies may have this attitude, I'm not aware of any specific ones. This may be more common at universities.

2. *Total control.* We will allow access only to certain sites from our computers. This is fairly common in businesses. They maintain a list of blocked sites and update this list constantly. They completely deny access to these sites.

3. *Middle of the road.* These companies trust their employees to use good judgment, but may block a few really explicit sites so no one accidentally stumbles across them and finds them offensive. They don't go hunting for sites to block. If an employee stumbles across an inappropriate site, then so be it, but management prefers to trust its employees to use its resources appropriately. They believe that if you can't trust your employees, then why did you hire them in the first place?

Another vexing issue relates to e-mail, and revolves around what employees say while using company e-mail addresses that contain the company name. Two approaches are common:

1. Some organizations take a hands-off approach by simply asking their employees to use their good judgment.

2. Other organizations have a formal policy requesting or requiring employees to include a disclaimer in their messages stating that they're not speaking for their employer and that their comments are their own.

These are issues that you must deal with, and the sooner the better. Assess your company's culture. Talk with those who are responsible for communicating your company's message and image. Be aware that what your policy says is less important than actually having one and making everyone aware of it.

How Do You Help People Understand What Is Confidential?

You need to make those who are publishing content aware of what's appropriate on the intranet and what's appropriate on the external Web site. It's important that internal information not find its way onto your external site. Therefore, you should educate your web publishers as to what is appropriate and what isn't. People can become somewhat confused when the internal and external webs look much alike. That could be a good reason for keeping the appearance of each distinctive.

This issue of confidentiality really doesn't apply just to the internal web. It also applies to e-mail. As part of your training for users you may wish to include what kinds of things shouldn't go outside the company via e-mail.

Train and Support Web Publishers

One of the keys to making jWeb successful was having lots of useful content. To get there, we needed to provide publishers with the tools to publish, train them in how to use the tools, and keep them updated on what was happening with tools and procedures. Having tools that are free or cheap helps get them deployed quickly and easily to publishers. There are many tools now available that can easily be acquired through corporate site licenses. Training people to use them is harder than acquiring the tools.

When we started, information on HTML consisted of little more than a few FAQs on the web and short chapters in a few books. When books on HTML started appearing, we bought every copy we could get our hands on and started giving them to those who were ready to start publishing. We put together a beginner's class to teach people how to author in HTML, how to use graphics, how to set up their web sites, and how to link their content into the corporate intranet.

The person who built the class and co-trained with an experienced trainer was the person who actually built the initial pieces of jWeb. She even put the training class on jWeb so it was available as a refresher for those who attended the class or to use as a tutorial for those who couldn't attend. She created a template that contained a tutor application—you could click on pieces of the template to get help with the syntax. We had people developing on the intranet in no time at all.

We put some members of the Internet Team and anyone ready to start publishing content through the first few classes. To train more publishers, we put the schedule of HTML classes on the intranet and offered them at no charge. With simply a click on a link, one could enroll in the class. As of today, they have trained hundreds of web publishers in beginning and advanced classes.

Encourage Publishing

To make it easy for publishers to get started, departments could put their own content on the IS server. It was only when they wanted or needed control that they needed to put up their own server.

Within a couple of days after the very first HTML publishing class, the first non-IS departmental home page appeared. At the next Internet Team meeting, we showed that site and made a big deal about it. The publisher received lots of attention and recognition, including having his site included in my demos along with mention of his name. All the hoopla paid off—within days, several more departmental sites appeared. We made a big deal about them, too, with the Internet Team and in demos, and the recognition paid off.

The first departmental sites contained mostly what you could call *vanity pages*. They had the departmental mission statement and a picture or message from the department head. Organization charts usually came next, along with links to sites on the Internet that were useful to the department. Then a departmental newsletter might appear. It would tell about exciting happenings in the department, updates on different areas of the department, information about promotions and new hires, work anniversary lists, birthday lists, or even recipes. At this point there were concerns about what was appropriate and what was frivolous. The Internet model says to let it be—the amount of bandwidth wasted is insignificant when measured against the creativity and cama-raderie created. The Traditional model won't tolerate this waste of resources. You have to decide which is right for you.

Once you have those pioneer publishers putting up web pages, you can start spreading the capabilities throughout your organization. As various departments start putting information on the internal web, you start to see the many different ways to use the information, and people start dreaming up ways that they need or want to use the medium. The initial publishers become the role models and experts you can enlist to develop the tips and techniques to help others.

Promote jWeb to Employees

Having a subteam focused on promoting jWeb was great because it could leverage the demos I was already doing. The subteam had lots of ideas and got busy right away to implement them.

Demos

Obviously, with my role in doing demos, I was largely the one promoting jWeb to associates, and I talked a great deal about that in Chapter 9. With the larger demos we were getting hundreds of attendees at a time. As the content grew, the desire to have access to it grew, also.

Pass It On

One of the ways to promote an intranet is through what you could call *chain-letter style,* or *pass it on.* If everybody you give a browser to shows just one friend, then you'll be continually spreading browsers and access. Very likely, people will show this thing to more than one friend and your intranet will grow even more rapidly. You can do this as an informal way of spreading access, or you can make it a formal program, as some companies have done.

Web Fair

The subteam staged a Web Fair, which is one of my favorite ways of promoting jWeb. As I mentioned in Chapter 9, the Web Fair was an all-day event focused around a surfing theme. People could drop by and see how various department web sites worked and surf the Internet while they were at it. There were training sessions, sign-ups for classes, vendor booths, drawings, and lots of fun activities. The attendance was incredible and made lots more associates aware of jWeb and caused them to clamor for access.

Promote the Effective Use of the Internet and jWeb

This subteam focused on showing users how to use jWeb most effectively. This focused on both individual and departmental uses.

Train and Support Users

Part of helping make the intranet an effective tool was training people on how to use it. Netscape is such an easy-to-use tool that you don't need much in the way of training. We included much of the training in the demo, since we showed people how to use Netscape, the Internet, and jWeb. This group focused on developing some tip sheets to get people started when they first received Netscape, and handed them out at the Web Fair. They also built the jWeb tutorial, which you could access from the home page. This provided most of the training that we needed.

Role Modeling

The Internet Team felt that it needed to set a good example in the use of the Internet and intranet, and find stories as examples of this to share with people. These stories would focus on how individuals and departments were using jWeb most effectively, and would appear in their section of the team's jWeb site.

Identify and Spread Tools and Best Practices

This team focused on identifying the tools that worked best for certain applications and identifying techniques to make the job easier for web publishers and developers. They published their findings and recommendations on their section of the team's jWeb site.

What Is the Impact of the Team?

The Internet Team was cross-functional, having representation from virtually every area of the company. We started by doing things to bond the team together, though that's somewhat hard to do with a team of 55 members. This cross-fertilization and cooperation provided a role model for the rest of the organization and proved instrumental in breaking down many of the walls that build up over time between departments and organizations.

Checklist: Create Widespread Enthusiasm and Capability

Figure 10.6 summarizes the steps involved in creating widespread enthusiasm and capability.

---

1. Why do you need an intranet team?

    ◆ What does the team do?

        ◆ Set the organization's direction for the intranet
        ◆ Guide the intranet in moving in that set direction
        ◆ Create the infrastructure
        ◆ Evaluate and select hardware and software
        ◆ Install and maintain servers
        ◆ Install intranet tools for people
        ◆ Create training for web publishers
        ◆ Design the structure of the internal web site
        ◆ Design the home page
        ◆ Develop content and design
        ◆ Create publishing guidelines
        ◆ Encourage web publishers to publish

- Approve content for the intranet
- Advertise and promote the intranet
- Encourage and support people in their use of the intranet
- Create applications
- Update publishers on new tools
- Keep it all moving forward

- Should you combine the Intranet Team with the Internet Team, or should they be separate?

  - Advantages of combining the teams

    - Avoid overlap
    - Leverage training on tools and sharing of tools and techniques

  - Disadvantages of combining the teams

    - Focusing on several different audiences causes fragmentation
    - Should you have the same standards and approvals for both?

- Composition of the team

  - Team leader
  - Web architects
  - Web services
  - Webmasters
  - Programmers and applications developers
  - Graphic artists and designers
  - Communicators
  - Web publishers

- ◆ Technical support
- ◆ Trainers
- ◆ Help desk and support
- ◆ Legal
- ◆ Facilitator

◆ Does the team really need a facilitator?

  ◆ Benefits of having facilitators conduct the meetings:

    ◆ Help focus on desired results and plan the meeting
    ◆ Make meetings run smoother and more efficiently
    ◆ Work until consensus is reached and everyone is bought in

  ◆ Where do you find a facilitator?

    ◆ HR departments, Total Quality Management programs, or Business Process Improvement or reengineering programs
    ◆ Consulting firms
    ◆ Search the Internet for facilitation companies or facilitation brokers
    ◆ Internet newsgroup misc.business. facilitators newsgroup

2. How does the team work?

  ◆ Planning and agendas

    ◆ Logistics—arrange the tables in a U shape so everyone can see each other

- Refreshments—use complex sugars to keep the team's energy level consistent
- Team building and bonding—ways

    - Experiential programs, such as Outward Bound or ropes courses
    - Trips
    - Social events

- Four stages of teams—teams must go through these stages

    - Forming
    - Storming
    - Norming
    - Performing

- Creativity techniques and out-of-the-box thinking—use

    - Humor, fun, and games
    - Frequent breaks
    - Engage the whole brain with techniques such as drawing pictures and mind mapping

- Team meetings—activities include

    - Welcome and introductions
    - Recognition for team members
    - Guest speakers
    - Demos of applications and tools to keep everyone up-to-date
    - Updates on Internet and intranet plans and results

- Team-building and creativity exercises
- Brainstorm and discuss expectations, vision, mission, goals and objectives, and how the team should work
- Subteams report progress and plans
- Reports from conferences and shows
- Set logistics for future meetings

3. What are the team's objectives?

- Communications

  - Team newsgroup
  - Team home page

- Develop and communicate guidelines, standards, and approvals

  - Set direction and guide development of the internal web

    - Create the intranet home page and structure
    - Set standards and the approvals process

      - Should there be web standards? Do you want your intranet standardized and controlled or loose and chaotic?
      - What approvals and authorizations are necessary? Who grants approvals and permissions?
      - Should you allow personal home pages?

- Who should own the intranet? Should it belong to Communications, IT, or another area?

◆ Set Internet policies and publish them

- Should you allow universal access to the Internet?
- Should you allow personal use of the Internet? Approaches include

  - Total laissez-faire
  - Total control
  - Middle of the road

- How do you help people understand what is confidential? Educate web publishers and users

◆ Train and support web publishers

- Make tools easy to acquire and cheap or free
- Create and teach classes
- Put publishing tutorials on the internal web

◆ Encourage publishing

- Let publishers put content on IT server
- Make a big deal about early publishing
- Make initial publishers the role models and experts for others

◆ Promote the intranet to employees

- Demos

- ◆ Pass it on
- ◆ Web Fair

- ◆ Promote the effective use of the Internet and intranet

  - ◆ Train and support users through tip sheets and tutorials
  - ◆ Role modeling and success stories

- ◆ Identify and spread tools and best practices

4. What is the impact of the team?

- ◆ Role model for the rest of the organization
- ◆ Break down walls between departments

Figure 10.6 Create widespread enthusiasm and capability—checklist.

chapter eleven

Make Your Intranet Pervasive

How Do You Make the Intranet the Universal User Interface?

Most of the companies I talked with see the intranet as their universal user interface for the future. That being the case, how do you make the intranet pervasive in your organization? How do you make it the place where everyone comes to look for information? How do you make it as comfortable to use as the telephone?

Design It for Users

The first way is to make your intranet user-friendly. Yes, it's become a cliché, but that's what you must do. Make the icons intuitive and the flow logical. Put information where people expect to find it. Make the navigation easy and logical.

Teach your web publishers many of the same rules of Web page design that apply to the Internet itself. On the Internet, bandwidth is a major issue because so many users have slow modems. Even those with fast connections may easily tire of waiting for slow graphics to load. If all of your intranet users are on fast T1 connections, speed of loading may not be much of an issue; however, if you have *road warriors* who will be dialing in at 28.8, or even 14.4, it will be an issue. Are all your locations on T1s, or are some hooked up at a slower speed? You want everyone to access your intranet without long, frustrating waits.

Know when it's OK to use large graphics and when it's not. If everyone is on a T1, large graphics may be fine. If they're dialing in, offer them a choice based on the speed of their connection. In addition, having no more than 256 colors in your graphics will help your pages load faster.

When web publishers use pictures, they should serve a purpose. Regardless of bandwidth, there are only three reasons for you to use multimedia:

1. *Decoration.* Decorative pictures and videos make your site look good. Keep these as small as possible without losing their effect.
2. *Navigation.* Navigational elements help the user get around your site.
3. *Information.* Informative components give the user information he or she could not get otherwise.

Is It User-Friendly?

One key to getting your intranet widely used is to make it very easy to use. Getting there may require several iterations of your design. One way to speed that up is to get users involved in testing the components and the interface prior to actually implementing it. There's a very interesting report on the WWW about how Sun Microsystems did this to create SunWeb, its internal web. Darrell Sano and Jakob Nielsen wrote this report, *SunWeb: User Interface Design for Sun Microsystem's Internal Web,* currently at http://www.sun.com/sun-on-net/uidesign/sunweb/. Be aware that it may move at any time, but you can use their search function to find it if necessary.

This report gives some good insight into how you can create and test your intranet as a user interface. Due to the short time frame available, this study was quick and informal. Much of the testing took place in just a single week and shows that, even on a tight schedule, you can make sure your home page design is intuitive and useful.

They performed four studies with three or four users in each one. The studies they performed were:

1. Card sorting to discover categories
2. Icon intuitiveness testing

3. Card distribution to icons
4. Thinking aloud walk-through of page mock-up

In the first one, card sorting, the purpose was to develop the
menu structure and determine what information would be within
each menu item. They started with a brainstormed list of 51 types
of information, each of which appeared on a note card. Each user
sorted the note cards into logical groupings and created a name
for each group. The researchers eyeballed the groupings and created a list of recommended groups as well as names for those
groups.

Next, they designed icons for each of the 15 groups of information. Design ideas came from a thesaurus, a pictorial dictionary,
and catalogs of international signs and symbols.

In the second study, icon intuitiveness, they brought in users to
perceive what the icons meant. Users easily recognized and inter-
preted some icons, while they found other icons confusing. Users
frequently misinterpreted a toolbox as a briefcase, so the designers
added a monkey wrench to the icon to emphasize the tool aspect.

The researchers sometimes had to rely on their judgment of
what to do with specific icons. With one icon, three of the four
users immediately recognized it, and they decided that they just
happened to get a user who didn't. They felt this shouldn't influence their decision. Another time, an engineer mistook a store-
front icon for a circuit board. It was important to consider their
population of users, and since they had a large population of engineers, this could be a frequent mistake. Since it could interfere
with the use of their system, they decided to change that one.
Some concepts, such as software, are just so abstract that it was
difficult for them to create a recognizable icon. They decided to
keep the one they had even though it was not easily recognizable.

The third study, card distribution to icons, took place after the
icon redesign. Working with enlarged printed icons arranged in
the planned home page layout, users sorted the note cards and
placed them on the appropriate icon.

In the last study, the thinking aloud page walk-through, users
worked with a layout of the home page and talked about what

they expected to find when they clicked on each icon. The researchers also asked for user opinions about the aesthetics of the icons and found that they hated two of them. Since it was important for users to like and feel comfortable with SunWeb, they redesigned those two icons.

The first two studies proved to be quite useful, whereas the last two were not as valuable. Importantly, this report shows that it's not very hard to go through simple user interface testing, and it can be very valuable.

Make It Easy to Navigate

Sano and Nielsen went one step further and talked about the actual design of the SunWeb home page and the structure of the internal web. The design and structure should involve good visual design techniques in order to make it pleasing to the eye and easy to use and navigate.

In the design of SunWeb, they used a consistent placement of elements to help users know where they were in the hierarchy and to make it easy for them to navigate. Every page of SunWeb contained a banner across the top with the SunWeb name on the left side and icons for navigation, search, overview (contents list), and help on the right side. On second-level pages, these banners also provided a link to the homepage and had the icons of the 15 categories to provide a quick way to return to the category home page. These icons made it easy for users to know where they were at all times.

They put the banner and icon *gif* files in a central library to encourage developers to use them. In addition, they made drawings available which showed the appropriate use of the banners for those who wished to maintain a consistent appearance throughout SunWeb. However, it's important to note that while the design standards existed and the components were available, these standards weren't mandatory.

The designers also used a consistent orientation and color palette throughout the banners and icons. Originally, each icon was an independent image. Later, they combined them into a simple image map to reduce loading time. Of course, text labels were available for those who didn't want to wait for the graphics to load.

Keep It Fresh and New

Once you've designed your internal web site for your users, tested its usability, and made it available for everyone to use, what do you do next?

That's really just the beginning. It's important not to let your internal web just languish and become stale. Just like external Web sites, you need to keep internal webs fresh and new so that people will continue to come back and use them. How do you do that? Here are some ways for you to consider.

- *What's new.*   The most obvious is the what's new section, which you should update frequently. Daily updating is not too often for those webs with lots of new content being added each day. You may want to build it as a running archive that adds the new things to the top of the list and notes the date of each addition. You could create a new page for each update and make the old ones easily accessible. That way, if people are away for a few days, they can easily catch up when they return.

- *Announcements and bulletins.*   You can keep your web updated with the announcements and bulletins that you already post on your bulletin boards. That way, people are likely to wander in to see what's new the same way that they wander by and check the bulletin boards. You can make it easy for them to know when you add new announcements if you add a blinking icon to alert them. As the home page becomes the universal entry point to all systems, users will likely be at the home page many times a day and will see those announcements quickly. If you add a PointCast I-Server to your intranet, you can even broadcast urgent messages to all desktops.

- *Newsletters.*   Put your newsletters on-line so people keep coming to find out the relevant news about the organization.

- *Make it useful.*   The most important reason people will keep coming back is because there's something there that they need and use. As simple as it is, the employee phone directory or locator usually comes first. It's one of the most useful applications you can put on the internal web. Phone directories are often out-of-date before you distribute them. Anytime you have content that is amorphous and constantly changing, putting it on the web can be valuable. Another early application is usually benefits. People don't care about benefits information until they need it, and then they want it quickly. You can scan in benefits booklets and forms, and people can pull them up and print them on demand. Important and relevant content is the most important reason people use an intranet.

◆ *New content.* Of course, you should keep adding new content as often as possible. At first, you may want to use documents in their native format and simply add and configure viewers into the browser. If you have highly structured documents, you can use a conversion tool, such as HTML Transit, to convert them to HTML. You can start loading new documents and other forms of information when you create them. You can put word-processing documents, spreadsheets, presentation slides and anything created with Adobe Acrobat on your internal web so everyone can access them.

◆ *Database information.* When you pull information dynamically from searches against databases, you can keep the web's data more up-to-date because you don't build HTML pages for each bit of data. Access to dynamic data makes the information more timely and relevant.

◆ *Graphics.* Interesting graphics are great for getting people's attention. Making the graphics nice and changing them from time to time can keep it fresh. Make sure you have sufficient bandwidth so that graphics load quickly. Otherwise, offer an option for those who wish to turn off the graphics. If you don't, your users will avoid your web.

- *What's interesting on the WWW.* If your employees can access the Internet, then you can provide them with a *What's New and Interesting on the WWW* page. It will alert your employees to interesting sites, such as those of your competitors and business partners. Have someone monitor new things coming onto the WWW and set them up quickly on this page. Your corporate librarian or your research organization could do this.

- *Publicize great internal pages.* Have a *great site of the week* (or day) to get people coming back to check out what's interesting on the internal web. It could be a business unit page or even a personal home page. It provides the incentive to your web publishers to keep things useful and interesting.

- *Interactivity.* Keep it fun and interesting. Check out Jim Sterne's book, listed in the appendix, for a whole chapter about this.

- *Sports and clubs.* If you have groups such as the softball team, golf team, running club, aerobics group, day-care parents' group, or whatever, let them put information on the web. They can even be eligible for site of the week. They will want to post schedules of events and report on interesting events and happenings. This offers some balance for employees.

- *Services.* Services such as the cafeteria, fitness center, and others can post information, such as cafeteria menus and fitness center class schedules, and even advertise their services. People will check these kinds of services frequently.

Review Your Bandwidth Needs Frequently

As you get more information on your intranet and more users, you'll need more capacity. You'll see many of the same things happening on your intranet that are happening on the Internet itself. There will be lots of graphics and other bandwidth-consuming applications. One CIO with a large intranet spoke of the problems of *gratuitous graphics and bulging bandwidth* loading up his LANs and WANs. Plan to monitor capacity constantly and schedule frequent reviews, and even upgrades, if necessary.

Sometimes you will find that there are other things that you can do about capacity issues. Just as we teach programmers to write efficient code, we should also teach web publishers how to create efficient web pages. They should always be mindful of the size of their graphics. In testing, they should look for graphics that seem to load too slowly. For instance, I heard a story about a company site that had a group of similar icons on virtually every page, and the pages seemed to load very slowly. Upon investigation, they noticed that the file size of one of the icons was five times as large as the others. They reprocessed the oversize icon and the file size became the same as the others. Now the page loads much more quickly. They still don't know exactly what happened, but they should have caught it in testing.

Add New Tools

The tools available for the Internet and intranets are constantly changing. A month on the Internet is about the same as a year anywhere else. Things related to your intranet will change daily. You should expect to have someone constantly watch the intranet tools and evaluate them to see which ones would be valuable to you. The beauty is that the tools for intranets seem to be so much less expensive than proprietary tools. Make sure to add new tools to help your publishers do a better job of publishing and your users to get more value from your intranet. Remember to teach them how to use them.

Continue to Coordinate the Team's Efforts

Whatever you do, make sure to keep the team going. They may not need to meet as frequently now as they did at first, but be sure to keep them together to share new ideas and tools. The team can continue to evaluate and disseminate new tools. The team should plan to review the status of the intranet on a regular basis and set new goals for the future. Just because you met your original goals doesn't mean you should stop. The greatest potential competitive advantage can come from brainstorming and implementing many of the things that you can do with your intranet beyond those that most companies do. Once everyone has an intranet, your advantage comes from how you use it. It's time to start thinking about workflow for streamlining your business processes and how you can use groupware for collaboration and communication.

What Are the Critical Success Factors?

When you start up your internal web, everyone will publish mainly vanity pages that contain mission statements and pictures and messages from the executives. Once your web publishers start moving from vanity pages to real and important content, you know your intranet is starting to make an impact. What are the things that you can do to ensure your intranet's success?

Provide Value to the Business

If your intranet doesn't provide value to your business, solve some of its problems, and meet some of its goals, then you might as well not be doing it. The internal web can be the answer for problems plaguing many user departments. In the dynamic business environment of today, customers have new needs which create new needs for business users. Almost every company today focuses on doing things faster, better, and cheaper. An internal web can help address some of these needs, and you don't have to be a programmer to create information for it. Therefore, departments can use their own people and their own resources to meet their own needs very quickly. If the intranet provides great value to the organization, it will be successful.

Communicate Throughout the Organization

Unless your organization is small, internal communication can be a challenge. It becomes especially difficult if you have people spread out around the world. Most ways of communicating globally are just too slow or too costly for today's business environment. Therefore, the intranet fills an important need in most widespread or global organizations.

You can fill another important communication need by using it to communicate among groups with similar interests and skills.

Provide Valuable and Relevant Content

Provide the information that everyone needs but isn't always easy to find or isn't always up-to-date. This includes the telephone directory, organization charts, employee handbooks, policy manuals, documentation, and technical contacts. Employees should expect to find the information they need by going to the web.

Provide Value to Your People

Provide things that are valuable to your people, such as access to employee benefits. Employees can use the intranet to query and update their own benefits.

Job postings and career development information also provide value to employees. This can include career-path information, what training is necessary for specific career paths, and when and how that training is available.

All of these can be accessible via kiosks for those who don't have computers. You can add leisure time activities for employees to help provide some balance in their lives.

Use It to Train and Develop Your People

Use the intranet to train and develop your people. This really has two parts.

1. Make sure to train your web publishers so they can do a good job of providing the right content in a well-designed application, and make sure to train your users in how to use the intranet and its tools.
2. Use the intranet to train and develop your world-class employees. Your training can be real time, always

up-to-date, and available when needed when delivered via the web. You even have the ability to deliver multimedia training. For training that works best in a classroom, employees can view the training schedule on the web and click on a hyperlink to schedule themselves for it. This information goes into a database that will send an e-mail reminder and course pre-reads prior to class. You can even use the web for administering pretesting, posttesting, and course evaluations.

Use It to Develop Your Products

You can use your intranet in product development to share drawings, request comments, discuss questions, and share expertise among those involved in product development. It will one day be used for computer-aided design tools to develop drawings and annotate them. Anything you can do to speed the product development cycle in your company will be valuable.

Use It for Things Related to Your Customers

Anything you can do with the intranet to do a better job of communicating with or serving your customers will also be valuable. You can create applications that help those who perform customer-service jobs to better serve the customers. You can share customer-service information so everyone knows what the customers want. You can put marketing information on the web for review prior to using with customers. Your web can keep everyone informed of advertising and promotions that are out in the marketplace.

Get Lots of People Involved So You Have a Diversity of Ideas

The more people with different backgrounds you have involved in your web, the more different ideas there will be. Use your promotion techniques to get people enthusiastic, then get people from every area involved in the development of the web. As you're building your intranet, make everybody involved feel important and that you value their contributions.

Let the Intranet Change the Culture

As every area gets involved and people get access to things they've never had access to before, people will start to understand more and start to feel empowered. As people start getting information and expect to go to the intranet to find it, the intranet will start to become ingrained in the culture. With users in control of what they publish, you'll start to see an information democracy. People may become more willing to share and communicate. Encourage this, as it's healthy.

How Do You Measure the Results?

Now that people are using the intranet and you're starting to see some results, it's time to assess what the impact has been. Let's look first at costs, and then at the benefits achieved. Please be aware that in this section I'll talk about the results of all the companies interviewed regardless of whether they used the Traditional model, the Internet model, or a hybrid approach of their own. Talking about them here shouldn't convey the impression that they used one specific model or the other.

Cost

Most companies that I spoke with weren't tracking the costs, haven't yet finished tallying the costs, or aren't able to divulge their numbers. Some companies consider the intranet to consist of both the network and the applications. Others treat it as the applications only, with the network being considered separately.

As we would expect, telecommunications companies consider the network a critical piece of their intranet. AT&T told about the cost to start its intranet, which was in the neighborhood of $50 million, with total costs over the past five years of about $100 million. This is for the entire network of a huge organization. As you can see from the size of this, that's why the networking piece requires elaborate planning, cost justifications, and appropriate approvals.

Other companies said that they already had their networks and that the incremental costs for the intranet were fairly small, especially when they used freeware. SAS used freeware, and one person started its intranet on his own time. Over time, this became a large part of his responsibility, so the cost for SAS has been about the salary of one person.

Most other companies didn't have numbers available. Rockwell said that they haven't tracked the costs for the total enterprise because they recognize the value of exploring the potential of Rweb and of moving through the learning curve at a logical pace.

Benefits

The benefits reported by companies were generally of two types:

1. Tangible—monetary
2. Intangible—nonmonetary

Tangible

Since most companies have either not tracked costs or could not provide cost information, they typically also didn't quantify benefits, with a couple of exceptions.

AT&T said that consolidating its many individual networks into a global unified network has saved the company about $30 million per year. These savings came primarily from the reduction of duplicate people, equipment, and network and tariff costs. Bell Atlantic estimated that it has saved several hundred thousand dollars through consolidation and reduced printing.

Those companies with offices worldwide found that intranets provided an inexpensive and fast way to share and disseminate information. It's reasonable to expect that they've seen significant cost savings as a result. Even if you don't have offices worldwide, an intranet will let you share information quickly and inexpensively among locations and will probably save you money.

SAS Institute has experienced cost savings due to shorter development cycles. With traditional LAN applications, programmers have to write different pieces for different clients. With applications that use a browser, the platform no longer matters.

Intangible

We always look for cost savings, but aren't always cognizant of the intangible benefits, those for which we can't generate hard numbers. The intangibles with intranets can be substantial.

Improved internal communications and easy access to knowledge and information were the most commonly cited benefits. Some of the intranet benefits various companies mentioned were:

- Provides for sharing information and knowledge
- Saves time
- Increases awareness and responsiveness
- Facilitates the timely delivery of information
- Increases communication
- Makes employees more effective
- Helps employees in other locations around the world feel like part of the team
- Makes information easy to get to and update
- Allows us to leverage a strategic asset: intellectual capital
- Changes the way we think about knowledge and information
- Opens up new business opportunities

Harry Meyer, of Rockwell, used a metaphor that I particularly like. He characterized Rweb as a *convenience store for knowledge and basic information.* We think of convenience stores as being quick, easy, and carrying a wide assortment of products, which is quite appropriate for an intranet. However, unlike convenience stores, the intranet is not more expensive than other ways of acquiring the information. That's a great combination!

Several companies summed it all up by saying they simply couldn't envision all of the possible benefits that they know they'll derive from having an intranet.

Justifying: Is Anybody Bothering with ROIs?

Usually, for information technology projects, we have to go through the detailed cost-justification process, complete with ROIs. It would appear that putting together an intranet fits nicely within the budgets of many organizations and that they're not going the traditional route. I really don't know how many companies are bothering with ROIs, but my guess is that there probably aren't many. Several members of the press have recently called intranets a *no-brainer*. It appears that many companies had already figured that out. They decided that the tangible and intangible benefits were so great that they really didn't need to go through the ROI exercise.

Checklist: Make Your Intranet Pervasive

Figure 11.1 summarizes the steps involved in making your intranet pervasive.

1. How do you make the intranet the universal user interface?

   ◆ Design it for users

      ◆ Make the icons intuitive
      ◆ Make the flow logical
      ◆ Know when it's OK to use large graphics, and when it's not
      ◆ Make it user-friendly by getting users involved in testing
      ◆ Make it easy to navigate

         ◆ Consistent placement of elements
         ◆ Consistent orientation and color palette

- Keep it fresh and new—ways

    - What's new
    - Announcements and bulletins
    - Newsletters
    - Make it useful
    - New content
    - Database information
    - Graphics
    - What's interesting on the WWW
    - Publicize great internal pages
    - Interactivity
    - Sports and clubs
    - Services

- Review your bandwidth needs frequently

    - Monitor capacity constantly
    - Schedule frequent reviews
    - Schedule upgrades
    - Teach web publishers how to create efficient web pages

- Add new tools
- Continue to coordinate the team's efforts

    - Keep the team going
    - Set new goals for the future
    - Start thinking about how to use workflow and groupware on your intranet

2. What are the critical success factors? Things you can do to ensure your intranet's success:

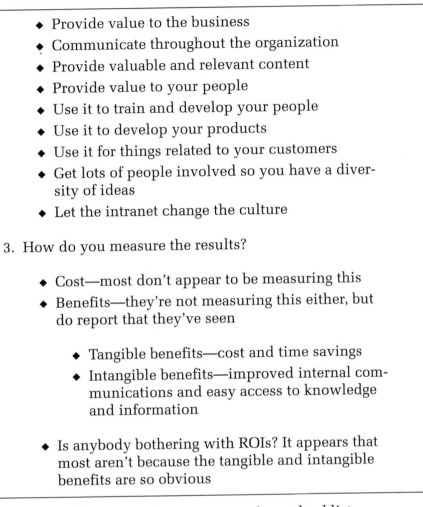

- Provide value to the business
- Communicate throughout the organization
- Provide valuable and relevant content
- Provide value to your people
- Use it to train and develop your people
- Use it to develop your products
- Use it for things related to your customers
- Get lots of people involved so you have a diversity of ideas
- Let the intranet change the culture

3. How do you measure the results?

- Cost—most don't appear to be measuring this
- Benefits—they're not measuring this either, but do report that they've seen

  - Tangible benefits—cost and time savings
  - Intangible benefits—improved internal communications and easy access to knowledge and information

- Is anybody bothering with ROIs? It appears that most aren't because the tangible and intangible benefits are so obvious

Figure 11.1 Make your intranet pervasive—checklist.

chapter twelve

What Lessons Have We Learned and Where Do We Go from Here?

What Lessons Have We Learned?

The 13 companies that I worked with were very generous in sharing their experiences so that you can have an easier time implementing your intranet. They talked about what worked well, and what they would do differently if they had it to do over again. Here are the 20 lessons learned that they shared with us:

1. Start it as a grassroots effort.
2. Have a champion and/or steering committee to push it forward.
3. Have business goals drive it.
4. Choose your technology early and carefully.
5. Get the network in place as soon as you can.
6. Plan capacity ahead of demand.
7. Determine who owns the intranet and how much the IT folks should be involved.
8. Involve all stakeholders and get them to work together.
9. Have someone in charge.
10. Decide if you want standards and, if so, then create them.

11. Start small and start quickly—you can always change it later.
12. Create the support structure early.
13. Focus on compelling content.
14. Modify the processes from paper-oriented to on-line.
15. Develop the skills you need.
16. Promote and advertise it.
17. It isn't easy to keep content up-to-date.
18. Beware of legacy applications.
19. Be prepared for concerns and fears.
20. Make sure the business knows what's possible for the intranet.

Start It as a Grassroots Effort

The way intranets frequently started was that one or two employees created the concept and got the attention of top management. Several respondents felt that allowing the intranet to grow chaotically, like the Internet, resulted in a critical mass of servers and applications being developed. This happened much more quickly than if a formal project had been in place. They felt that it was important to start and have some results to show very quickly.

Have a Champion and/or Steering Committee to Push It Forward

Typically, the grassroots effort got the attention of top management and garnered a champion and sometimes a steering committee. The champion can educate senior managers about the possibilities and ensure that they're aware and supportive. The champion can also remove obstacles and roadblocks. The steering committee often consisted of top managers from several areas of the business. They made sure to involve their areas in the intranet.

Have Business Goals Drive It

Business goals should drive your intranet. Focus first on your business problems. Create a business architecture to drive the intranet. The business benefits should drive the project initially and then continue to push what the future intranet can be.

Choose Your Technology Early and Carefully

It was important to find the right hardware and software to get it going quickly. One caution was to avoid bleeding-edge technologies, if possible. Tried-and-true products can produce very slick systems.

One suggestion was to have a single, common server to make it easy to maintain. Another was to start with a single server and let everyone put their content on it. When they're ready to bring up their own servers, provide a kit or package they can easily install themselves.

Other tool suggestions were to deploy a common, universal browser and to get a corporate license to make that even easier. Also, get a search engine as soon as you can.

Get the Network in Place as Soon as You Can

The network appeared to have been one of the biggest challenges at almost all of these companies. The hardest part of getting the client installed was enabling TCP/IP. Put a quality effort into getting TCP/IP to the desktop of all users. After that, the web browsers will go in with no difficulty. The advice to you is that if you don't have TCP/IP on the network, start now and get it done as soon as you can.

Plan Capacity Ahead of Demand

Very soon, you'll be facing network performance issues. Be aware of the load on the network and plan ahead of demand. Almost everyone said that the network demand grew far faster than they anticipated and that you should prepare for major growth. If they had it to do over, they would have done a better job of staying ahead of the demand curve on the network. Make sure to include capacity planning in the steps that you do early on in bringing up your intranet.

Determine Who Owns the Intranet and How Much the IT Folks Should Be Involved

This is a critical question, which each company approached differently. In most cases, the intranet originated in the IT area. IT typically got other areas of the business involved, and kept responsibility for the technical requirements and the infrastructure. In one company, IT maintained responsibility until the time was right for the appropriate area to take ownership. Several other companies said that the business must lead the effort, drive the strategies, take ownership, and decide which parts they want IT to manage and which parts they want to manage themselves.

In a highly technical company, such as TI, the end users can do most of it themselves, without help from the IT department. The users can even fund the R&D to get the intranet going. The IT department then becomes the provider of the network, and communicator and coordinator of the technologies. At some point, the users agree on a technology so that the IT department can provide the support for it. This makes it easier. However, if they were doing it over, they would have gotten the IT department involved sooner. They also would have provided more web server solutions for workgroups that didn't have the technical expertise to create their own servers.

The approach to ownership was a little different at Turner Broadcasting. Human Resources started the internal web, and the owner was the Director of Employee Services Development. He brought in the IT group at the appropriate time.

Involve All Stakeholders and Get Them to Work Together

Many of the companies said that involving all the appropriate stakeholders in a cross-functional team or network was a key to the successful implementation of their intranets. These teams typically involved the integration of all facets of the business.

They also said that it was a major challenge to get the groups to work together. Usually, that's because the skills needed to build an intranet involve a broad cross section of business skills and personalities. These can be as diverse as technologists, graphic designers, communicators, marketers, and product developers. Just think about how much fun it is to get all these different types communicating the same language and understanding each other.

In addition, people get very possessive about their part of the business and its importance relative to the greater scheme of things. It's not unusual for each area of the business to think that its area is the most important and should be on top of the hierarchy. Everyone has an opinion on how to structure the internal web. You can get the team all moving in the same direction with the same vision and goals, but it isn't easy.

Once the team gets moving together, the results can be amazing. Several companies even said that their intranet teams worked so well that they will use this as a model for other endeavors of this type.

Have Someone in Charge

One company said to make sure to involve many, but always have someone in charge. This may be the champion, or a representative of the champion, such as the Internet Team leader.

Decide if You Want Standards and, if So, Then Create Them

One thing that companies don't seem to agree on is whether you should have standards and guidelines. This lesson learned is subject to lots of debate and is a very individual decision for most companies.

Some said they should have established standards for content, look, and feel, as well as how to bring new servers into the web to fit properly in the information hierarchy. You should also treat the enterprise as a single information source. Others said they should have had guidelines in place to help people and keep them from wandering around looking for consulting and development skills. Another suggested that when you get into applications, you should have more development discipline to ensure that the application is solid and supportable.

Not all companies believed that standards were important. Others focused on doing whatever it took to get going quickly and to foster creativity.

Start Small and Start Quickly—You Can Always Change It Later

Here's the other side of the coin. Some companies say *just do it!* Start small and start quickly. Don't expect to get it right the first time. You can always change it later, but you need to show some results and value early. Don't keep waiting and trying to please everyone. Above all, foster creativity.

You can decide what's right for you.

Create the Support Structure Early

Almost every company said that since web technology is easy to deploy, the intranet exploded much faster than they anticipated. If they had it to do over again, they would put a support structure of help desks and technical support in place much earlier in the process.

Focus on Compelling Content

Another key with many companies was to focus primarily on the content and its use, as opposed to focusing extensively on the technology. The technology was only secondary.

One recommendation was to concentrate on compelling content in the beginning, rather than on fancy features. People want information that can benefit them in their jobs. Although fancy features are nice, they shouldn't be the top priority. Don't get too cute with the graphics, especially if you have remote users who come in over dial-up services. Also, avoid excessive hierarchy in your navigation, as it gets in the way.

To get lots of compelling content quickly, many companies placed things on the intranet in their native format, such as Word or Excel. One even used HTML *card catalogs* placed on top of the information to allow for better searching. You can also convert things in different formats into Adobe Acrobat PDF format to put them on the intranet.

Modify the Processes from Paper-Oriented to On-Line

Since most existing communication is very paper-oriented, you'll need to modify the existing processes. You should try to do that without adding a lot of extra work to the groups. Creating content for the intranet should be part of the process that creates it. It shouldn't be one group creating the content and then throwing it over the fence for another group to format for the intranet.

It will take time to clarify the differences in the creation of on-line documents versus paper documents. You have to consider many new things, such as colors, attention span, and how to access information. None of these were really as important in designing content for paper.

Develop the Skills You Need

Many of the skills needed for developing an intranet are still in short supply, so you'll need to train your people in HTML, Perl, CGI, and other skills.

Promote and Advertise It

Make sure to promote and advertise your intranet to make people aware of it and to get them using it. Turner Broadcasting went all out on a campaign to promote TESN, their intranet. Since networks and advertising are their business, they created an ad campaign and held launch meetings at the CNN Center in Atlanta.

It Isn't Easy to Keep Content Up-to-Date

Keeping the content up-to-date was one of the most cited challenges. One person said that getting an initial home page on the intranet is the easy part. Keeping it alive and full of current, relevant information is the challenge. Another said that many departments initially posted status and internal marketing information but have found that it is hard to keep current. If it isn't current, it falls into disuse. Another said to worry more about how to maintain the internal web and keep it current than what you initially put on the site.

Beware of Legacy Applications

As you start using your intranet to access legacy applications, you may find content management to be a challenge. One company said that its intranet pulls information from various legacy application databases and matches it with original content. They found that there were inconsistencies in the legacy data that required cleaning up at the source. This isn't a fun task and was probably quite time-consuming. As more companies start using legacy data on their intranets, we'll hear lots more about this problem.

Be Prepared for Concerns and Fears

Companies also encountered some unexpected concerns when they first started talking about intranets. For instance, at one company there was the concern that giving employees too much information would make it hard to deal with them. At several, there were concerns that the intranet wasn't secure and that people would spend all of their time surfing the Net. These just seem to be part of the normal course for any intranet project. There are always fears of the unknown or of change, even if it's *good* change.

Another big concern was viruses. Can an e-mail come in from outside the company and infect your systems? Can you accidentally infect your customers' systems with an e-mail? Want to see your lawyers freak out? This will do it! They're seeing all the potential exposure this could cause. Fortunately, there are now some solutions to this, such as MIMEsweeper which checks inbound and outbound mail for viruses.

Make Sure the Business Knows What's Possible for the Intranet

One last lesson learned was to take the time to make sure you help the business be aware of and understand all the wondrous possibilities for the intranet.

What's Next and Where Do We Go from Here?

Once you have your intranet in use throughout your organization, what do you do next? I asked every company about what it saw for the future of its intranet. Here are some of the things they expect to see:

- More and more applications on the internal web—virtually every company echoed this.
- The web will be the ubiquitous, universal user interface, just as the phone and fax are today.
- Data analysis applications will be front-ended by the web.
- Legacy systems will have web front ends.
- The intranet will be the primary vehicle for delivery of employee and company news.
- The intranet will become the platform of choice for applications development.
- More sophisticated search tools will become available.
- The intranet will become the main source of information in our company worldwide.
- More departmental information will be put on the intranet.
- All applications will be web-enabled or will be entered via the web.
- It will be the platform of choice for a cross-platform transaction-processing environment.
- The intranet will be the distribution and communications vehicle within the company.
- It will provide the ability for employees to customize the information they receive through the PointCast I-Server.
- More processes will be added to turn information into knowledge to increase the value the intranet delivers to each employee.
- Enable a significant degree of electronic bonding with our customers by allowing them to connect to our intranet.
- The web browser will become the user's *heads-up* display for timely access to business information.

If these companies are any indication, the next few years will be full of excitement as companies learn all the valuable things they can do with their intranets.

Some of the next steps we should consider are to use the intranet for:

- High-bandwidth applications, such as video and virtual reality
- Workflow
- Groupware

High-Bandwidth Applications Such as Video and Virtual Reality

Some companies are already using a lot of video and some virtual reality, but most are not. Few have the kind of bandwidth required for it. However, that will change. For example, SGI and Sun are well known for their use of video to deliver information to all employees. The use of video will become widespread over the next few years. Virtual reality will be next and will incorporate audio and video.

Workflow

Most companies that are implementing workflow today are doing so with proprietary solutions. However, many of the components are in place to make the intranet viable for workflow. Building intranet workflow today requires programming, and there are some examples of workflow in use today on internal webs. However, tools are being built that will allow almost anyone to create workflow applications on the web.

Groupware

Groupware is the sharing of information among people across a network of computers. With the emergence of groupware on internal webs, there's a lot of talk that proprietary groupware, such as Lotus Notes, is dead. This talk has accelerated since Netscape purchased Collabra and started incorporating the Collabra groupware product into their web client software. Since then, most proprietary groupware has become Web-enabled and many other companies are developing groupware products for the web, as well. The groupware market will be interesting for the next few years as companies start putting groupware on their intranets.

Groupware in use today on intranets includes internal newsgroups, chat rooms, shared whiteboards, shared documents, and videoconferencing. The companies participating in this book are using intranet workflow and groupware applications to:

- Coordinate scheduling
- Manage projects
- Maintain project documentation on requirements, design, status, and metrics
- Establish internal newsgroups for discussion
- Review documentation and incorporate comments
- Find and communicate with experts
- Select staff for planning new projects
- Conference and collaborate
- Communicate with all locations
- Hold real-time discussions via Internet Relay Chat (IRC)

Many of these companies are also using other groupware, such as Notes and Exchange. How are they using them simultaneously with intranets? Here are some examples:

- *We use Notes for small workgroups which require a higher degree of organization and interactivity than is available on the net.*
- *We use Notes for workgroups and selective Notes to web conversion.*
- *We utilize Notes for document-centric, workgroup-based, and end-user-developed applications. We tie Notes to the web and vice versa.*

♦ *We are adding processes to the intranet that work in concert with some of the MSExchange and Lotus Notes tools.*

♦ *Several projects are under way that will be sharing Lotus Notes and MSExchange information with the intranet.*

For those companies that already use Notes, there's little reason to change other than to enable Notes and the web to work together. To do this, you can now make a Notes server think it's a Web server.

The intranet still doesn't provide the infrastructure necessary for most groupware, such as security and data replication. However, replication may not be so critical with an internal web since you connect to the master copy of the database.

We'll see lots of activity in this area over the next few years as companies work to incorporate groupware into their intranets and vendors work to provide the products needed to do so.

Checklist: What Lessons Have We Learned and Where Do We Go from Here?

Figure 12.1 summarizes the lessons we have learned and where we go from here.

---

1. What lessons have we learned?

    ♦ Start it as a grassroots effort
    ♦ Have a champion and/or steering committee to push it forward
    ♦ Have business goals drive it
    ♦ Choose your technology early and carefully
    ♦ Get the network in place as soon as you can
    ♦ Plan capacity ahead of demand

- Determine who owns the intranet and how much the IT folks should be involved
- Involve all stakeholders and get them to work together
- Have someone in charge
- Decide if you want standards and, if so, then create them
- Start small and start quickly—you can always change it later
- Create the support structure early
- Focus on compelling content
- Modify the processes from paper-oriented to on-line
- Develop the skills you need
- Promote and advertise it
- It isn't easy to keep content up-to-date
- Beware of legacy applications
- Be prepared for concerns and fears
- Make sure the business knows what's possible for the intranet

2. What's next and where do we go from here?

- What companies see as the future of their intranets

  - More and more applications
  - The web will be the ubiquitous, universal user interface
  - Data analysis applications will be front-ended by the web
  - Legacy systems will have web front ends

- ◆ The intranet will be the primary vehicle for delivery of employee and company news
- ◆ The intranet will become the platform of choice for applications development
- ◆ More sophisticated search tools
- ◆ The intranet will become the main source of information in our company worldwide
- ◆ More departmental information
- ◆ All applications will be web-enabled or will be entered via the web
- ◆ It will be the platform of choice for a cross-platform transaction-processing environment
- ◆ The intranet will be the distribution and communications vehicle within the company
- ◆ It will provide the ability for employees to customize the information they receive through the PointCast I-Server
- ◆ More processes will be added to turn information into knowledge to increase the value the intranet delivers to each employee
- ◆ Enable a significant degree of electronic bonding with our customers by allowing them to connect to our intranet
- ◆ The web browser will become the user's heads-up display for timely access to business information

- ◆ Next steps for you to consider

    - ◆ High-bandwidth applications, such as video and virtual reality
    - ◆ Workflow
    - ◆ Groupware

Figure 12.1   What lessons have we learned and where do we go from here—checklist.

Summary

The final step in this book was to evaluate where and how intranet-based workflow and groupware could benefit your organization and then start working to implement them. I could talk at length about this subject, but it's time for me to wrap up this book and start on the next one. Stay tuned for my next book, *Intranet As Groupware,* in which I'll focus on ingraining intranet-based workflow and groupware throughout your business processes to improve your organization's competitiveness.

I hope you've had as much fun reading this book as I've had writing it. Thanks for reading it. I wish you the best of luck with your intranet. Please let me know how it turns out and any lessons you learn along the way that you would like to share with others. You can reach me at mhills@knowledgies.com. Also, be sure to check out the John Wiley Web site at http://www.wiley.com/compbooks/, where you'll find electronic versions of the checklists in this book.

Finally, I'd again like to thank all the many folks at Amgen, AT&T, Bell Atlantic, Booz Allen & Hamilton, EDS, JCPenney, Rockwell International, SAS Institute, SGI, Texas Instruments, Turner Broadcasting, United Parcel Service, and one anonymous company—you know who you are—for your contributions to this book. Without you, it wouldn't have been possible. Thanks again.

Appendix

Intranet Resources

Netiquette—Chapter 1

- ◆ *The Net: User Guidelines and Netiquette* at http://www.fau.edu/rinaldi/net/index.htm.

Demands on Businesses Today—Chapter 2

- ◆ Gary Hamel and C. K. Prahalad, *Competing for the Future,* Harvard Business School Press, 1994.
- ◆ Don Peppers and Martha Rogers, *The One to One Future—Building Relationships One Customer at a Time,* Currency/Doubleday, August 1993.
- ◆ Don Tapscott, *The Digital Economy: Promise and Peril in the Age of Networked Intelligence,* McGraw-Hill, 1996.

Learning Organizations—Chapter 3

- ◆ Peter M. Senge, *The Fifth Discipline: The Art and Practice of the Learning Organization,* Doubleday/Currency, 1990.

Uses of Intranets—Chapter 4

- ◆ *How Sun saves money, improves service using Internet technologies* at http://www.Sun.com:80/960101/feature1/index.html/.

Companies That Contributed to This Book—Chapter 5

- Amgen Incorporated at http://www.bio.com/companies/amgen.html.
- AT&T Corp. at http://www.att.com.
- Bell Atlantic Corporation at http://www.bel-atl.com.
- Booz Allen & Hamilton Inc. at http://www.bah.com.
- EDS at http://www.eds.com.
- JCPenney Company, Inc. at http://www.jcpenney.com.
- Rockwell International Corporation at http://www.rockwell.com.
- SAS Institute Inc. at http://www.sas.com.
- Silicon Graphics, Inc. at http://www.sgi.com.
- Texas Instruments Incorporated at http://www.ti.com.
- Turner Broadcasting System, Inc. at http://www.turner.com.
- United Parcel Service of America, Inc. at http://www.ups.com.

Building Your Intranet—Chapter 7

Security

- Eugene Spafford's computer security hot list at http://www.cs.purdue.edu/homes/spaf/hotlists/csec.html. This list doubles as the official WWW hot list of the Computer Operations, Audit, and Security Technology (COAST) Laboratory at Purdue. This is a great starting point in your quest to learn about firewalls and Internet security.
- Marcus J. Ranum's Internet Firewalls FAQ at http://www.v-one.com/pubs/fw-faq/faq.htm.
- World Wide Web Security FAQ at http://www-genome.wi.mit.edu/WWW/faqs/www-security-faq.html.

- Encryption technology from RSA Data Security, at http://www.rsa.com.
- Yahoo's list of companies that specialize in computer security at http://www.yahoo.com/Business_and_ Economy/Companies/Computers/Security/Consulting/.
- Newsgroups:
  - Comp.security.announce—announcements about security (moderated)
  - Comp.security.firewalls—anything pertaining to network firewall security
  - Comp.security.misc—security issues of computers and networks
  - Comp.security.unix—discussion of Unix security

Selecting an Internet Service Provider

- *Selecting an Internet Provider* in UUNET Technologies' Internet Business Applications Guide at http://www. uu.net/busguide.htm.
- The List at http://thelist.com. This resource provides a variety of searches to help you locate ISPs. It gives you information such as the names, area codes served, phone and fax numbers and e-mail addresses, their URL, and services they provide and the fees for them.
- Commerce Net's Internet Service Provider Directory at http://www.commerce.net/directories/products/isp/isp. html/.
- Newsgroups about Internet access providers:
  - alt.internet.services
  - alt.internet.access.wanted

Acquiring an Internet Domain

- InterNIC Registration Services at http://rs.internic.net/ rs-internic.html/. This site provides instructions for registering U.S. domain names. They are temporarily registering Canadian domain names, also.

◆ Yahoo's list of various domain registration authorities throughout the world is at http://www.yahoo.com/ Computers_and_Internet/Domain_Registration/.

Selecting Hardware and Software—Servers, Browsers, Authoring Tools, and Other Considerations

◆ Intranet Soundings at http://www.brill.com/intranet/ijx/ is a moderated message exchange dedicated to intranets.

◆ Web Compare at http://www.webcompare.com/ lists servers and browsers and includes comparisons and charts of features.

◆ Stroud's CWSApps List at http://cws.wilmington.net/ cwsa.html.

◆ World Wide Web FAQ at http://www.boutell.com/faq/ for researching web servers and browsers, authoring web pages, images, scripts, and other Web resources.

◆ The Complete Intranet Resources at http://control.cga. sc.edu/intranet.htm.

◆ Network World Fusion at http://www.nwfusion.com/.

◆ WebMaster Magazine's Technology Notes at http: //www.cio.com/WebMaster/wm_tech_notes.html.

◆ PC Magazine at http://www.pcmag.com/ has:

  ◆ Intranet Tools Directory at http://www.pcmag.com/ IU/intranet/reviews/ir-dir.htm

  ◆ Product Index at http://www.pcmag.com/ IU/index.htm

◆ HyperText Markup Language (HTML) at NCSA at http://union.ncsa.uiuc.edu/HyperNews/get/www/html. html. This is a good resource for current information on tools and authoring.

- Newsgroups about:

  - Servers:

    - Comp.infosystems.www.servers.mac—Web servers for the Macintosh platform
    - Comp.infosystems.www.servers.misc—Web servers for other platforms
    - Comp.infosystems.www.servers.ms-windows—Web servers for MS Windows and NT
    - Comp.infosystems.www.servers.unix—Web servers for UNIX platforms

  - Browsers:

    - Comp.infosystems.www.browsers.mac—Web browsers for the Macintosh platform
    - Comp.infosystems.www.browsers.misc—Web browsers for other platforms
    - Comp.infosystems.www.browsers.ms-windows—Web browsers for MS Windows
    - Comp.infosystems.www.browsers.x—Web browsers for the X-Window system

  - Providing Web access:

    - Comp.infosystems.www.providers—discussion of WWW server software, including general server design, setup questions, server bug reports, security issues, HTML page design, and other concerns of information providers.

  - For specific products, check out vendor sites such as:

    - Netscape at http://www.netscape.com
    - Microsoft at http://www.microsoft.com
    - SGI at http://www.sgi.com

Designing and Authoring Documents—Chapter 9

- Guides to Writing Style for HTML Documents (NCSA) at http://union.ncsa.uiuc.edu/HyperNews/get/www/html/guides.html.
- William Horton, Lee Taylor, Arthur Ignacio, Nancy L. Hoft, *The Web Page Design Cookbook: All the Ingredients You Need to Create 5-Star Web Pages,* John Wiley & Sons, 1996.
- Jim Sterne, *World Wide Web Marketing: Integrating the Internet into Your Marketing Strategy,* John Wiley & Sons, 1995. Jim is an internationally known WWW marketing guru. In this book, he focuses on what to do and not do. Many of the things he says apply equally well to intranets, where not all users have high-speed links. Jim also talks at length about navigation within a Web site. You may find lots of guidance in his book.
- Newsgroups about authoring:
    - Comp.infosystems.www.authoring.cgi—writing CGI scripts for the Web
    - Comp.infosystems.www.authoring.html—writing HTML for the Web
    - Comp.infosystems.www.authoring.images—using images and imagemaps on the Web
    - Comp.infosystems.www.authoring.misc—miscellaneous Web authoring issues

WWW Sites in Sample Presentation—Chapter 9

- AT&T at http://www.att.com/.
- General Electric at http://www.ge.com/.
- IBM at http://www.ibm.com/.
- Burlington Coat Factory at http://www.coat.com/.
- Whole Foods at http://www.wholefoods.com/wf.html.
- Massachusetts Institute of Technology at http://web.mit.edu/.

- University of Oklahoma at http://www.uoknor.edu/.
- U.S. Bureau of the Census at http://www.census.gov/.
- Thomas, the home page of the U.S. Congress, at http://thomas.loc.gov/.
- Securities and Exchange Commission EDGAR Database at http://www.sec.gov/edgarhp.htm.
- FTD at http://www.ftd.com/.
- Shopping 2000 at http://www.shopping2000.com/.
- JCPenney at http://www.jcpenney.com/.

Resources for the Intranet Team—Chapter 10

Locate Facilitators

- Newsgroup misc.business.facilitators.

Creativity and Out-of-the-Box Thinking

- C. W. Metcalf, *Lighten Up: The Amazing Power of Grace Under Pressure,* Nightingale Conant Corporation. This audiotape is about humor.
- Michael J. Gelb, *Mind Mapping,* Nightingale Conant Corporation. This is an audiotape about mind mapping.
- Carolyn Nilson, *Games That Drive Change,* McGraw-Hill, Inc., 1995. This book has a chapter dedicated to games for communication. This is just one of a number of books about games for teams and trainers.

Usability Testing—Chapter 11

- Darrell Sano and Jakob Nielsen, *SunWeb: User Interface Design for Sun Microsystem's Internal Web,* at http://www.sun.com/sun-on-net/uidesign/sunweb/. This very interesting report is about how they created and tested the user interface for SunWeb.

Index

accounting and financial processes, 115–16
ActiveX, 230, 239
ADSL (asymmetrical digital subscriber line), 219
Amgen Incorporated, 121, 136, 179
Andreessen, Marc, 5–6, 14
announcements and bulletins, 351
anonymous company, 170–73
Armerding, Peter, 136
asset management, 116
asymmetric digital subscriber line (ADSL), 219
Asynchronous Transfer Mode (ATM), 219
ATM (Asynchronous Transfer Mode), 219
AT&T, 136–37
    cost savings, 57, 138, 359
    customer access, 25
    future intranet use, 139
    home page, 260–61
    intranet uses, 137–38
    Knowledge Management System, 26, 133
    lessons from intranet use, 138–39
    results of intranet use, 56, 138
    teams, 62
    web address, 136
audience, creation of, 201–2, 237–44
Austin, Richard, 139, 141
authoring tools, 231, 248, 384, 386

bandwidth, 112, 217–18, 347, 353–54, 374
Bednarcyk, Lauren, 157–58, 160
Bell Atlantic Corporation, 139–40
    cost savings, 140
    future intranet use, 141
    home page, 73–79
    intranet uses, 140
    lessons from intranet use, 140–41
    results of intranet use, 140
    web address, 139
benefits, intangible, 360
benefits, tangible, 359
Benefits BPI sample proposal, 184–93
Bond, Kevin, 157–60, 178
Booz Allen & Hamilton Inc., 32, 141–43
    future intranet use, 145
    intranet uses, 143–44
    Knowledge On Line, 34, 128, 142–45
    lessons from intranet use, 144–45
    results of intranet use, 59, 144
    web address, 141
brainstorming, 251, 276–77, 314–15
browsers
    choosing, 230, 238–40
    cost per user, 32
    ease of use, 32–33
    enhancement tools, 14–16
    function of, 13–14
    future of, 20–21
    growth of, 8

browsers (*Continued*)
   installation of, 30–31
   upgrades, 241
   web resource addresses, 384–85
building enthusiasm, 276–86
bulletins and announcements, 351
Bureaucratic model, 207–8
Burlington Coat Factory, 260, 265, 386
business process improvement (BPI)
      projects, sample proposal, 184–93

cable modem, 219
capacity development, 120
card catalogs, 370
card sorting, 348–49
Carlson, Todd, 28, 145, 147, 151
CERN (European Laboratory for Parti-
   cle Physics), 5
chain-letter style, 337
chat, 19, 104–5, 151
Checklists
   Build Your Intranet, 233–36
   Create Widespread Enthusiasm and
     Capability, 339–45
   Create Your Audience, 242–44
   Make Your Intranet Pervasive,
     361–63
   Promote Your Intranet, 297–302
   Ways to Sell the Intranet to Your
     Organization, 209–16
   What Lessons Have We Learned
     and Where Do We Go From
     Here, 376–78
client. *See* browsers
client/server, 42–44
clubs, 353
Collabra, 21, 375
communication, 40, 355–56
   interpersonal and group, 103–5
   organizational, 95–105
communications processes, 95–105
communicators, 306
concurrent development, 25
consultant
   assistance provided by, 198–99
   determining need for, 197–98
   how to select, 199–200

conversion tools, 36–37, 231–32, 249,
   352
corporate internal home page. *See*
   home page, corporate
cost savings, 359–60
creativity techniques, 313–15, 387
customer support processes, 131–33

database query tools, 232
DBS (direct broadcast satellite),
   219
dedicated leased lines, 218
demo building, 202–4, 246–55
demo goals, 245–46
demo, presenting the, 204–5
   addressing questions and concerns,
     286–93
   building enthusiasm, 276–86
   sample presentation, 258–76
   scheduling, 255–57
   tailoring to audience, 257–75
development, shared, 25
dial-up analog modem, 218
direct broadcast satellite (DBS),
   219
document database tools, 232
document conversion tools. *See* conversion tools
Dodge, Marc, 169
domain name, 225, 383–84
domain name server, 227

EDGAR Database, 264, 278, 387
EDS
   Any[5], 28, 61
   background information, 145–47
   Career Library, 112
   EDS*WEB, 145–47, 153–54
   E*TIPS job posting system, 111
   future intranet use, 153–54
   home page, 88–91
   intranet uses, 31, 56, 147–51
   lessons from intranet use,
     151–53
   newsletter, 96–97
   organization chart, 90–92
   PointCast server, 98

Process Sourcerer, 90–91
product catalog, 123
results of intranet use, 57, 59, 61,
      151
software development, 117
Technical Consulting Continuum,
      113
web address, 145
Wildfire, 145–46
electronic data interchange (EDI),
      124–26
e-mail
   confidentiality, 335
   communication, 40
   functions of, 11
   need for ISP, 222–23
   mail lists, 16
   phone directory, 254, 352
   security, 47, 221–22
   SMTP server, 228
   use of company, 334–35
encryption, 220–22, 228, 383
engineering, 121–22
enthusiasm, building, 276–86
European Laboratory for Particle
      Physics (CERN), 5
Exchange (MSExchange), 375–76

facilitator, 307–8, 387
file transfer protocol (FTP), 19–20
financial reports, 115–16
firewalls, 37, 47, 98, 219–22
formal approach. See traditional
      model
forming, 313
four stages of teams, 312–13
frame relay, 219
FTD, 279–84, 387
FTP (file transfer protocol), 19–20

General Electric, 260, 262, 386
gopher, 20
graphics, 253, 347–48
grassroots approach, 177–78,
      194–207, 366
Graves, Michael, 161–63
groupware, 44–45, 54, 66, 374–75

home page, 5, 371
home page, corporate
   Acceptable Use Policies, 80–81
   company history and mission, 93
   contents of, 73
   directories, phone books and orga-
      nizational charts, 90–93
   feedback, 78
   index, 76
   Internet resources, 81–82
   organizational home pages, 95
   other tools, 90
   search tools, 75–76
   services, 93–94
   site map, 77
   starting points, 82–84
   support, 87
   tutorials and help, 87–88
   What's New, 89–90
home page, personal, 91–93, 112,
      330–31
home page, team, 326–27
home pages, examples of
   AT&T, 261
   Burlington Coat Factory, 265
   FTD, 279–84
   General Electric, 262
   IBM, 263–64
   JCPenney, 266–70, 288–93
   MIT, 271–73
   Shopping 2000, 285–87
   University of Oklahoma, 274–75
   U.S. Bureau of the Census, 276
   U.S. Congress, 277
   Whole Foods, 268–69
human resources processes
   career development, 112
   example of, 106–8
   job postings, 111–12
   other applications, 113–14
   payroll, 110–11
   policies and benefits, 108–10
   training, 112–13
HTML (Hypertext Markup Language)
   authoring tools, 231, 248, 384, 386
   conversion tools, 36–37, 231–32,
      249, 352

HTML (*Continued*)
  defined, 31
  document databases, 232, 253, 352
  learning, 202–3, 249
  use of, 31–32, 126, 157
  web resource addresses, 384, 386
hub, 10
Hypertext Markup Language. *See*
    HTML

IBM, 253, 260, 263–64, 386
IIS (Internet Information Server), 229
icon intuitiveness, 349
icons
  card distribution to, 349
  designing, 349–50
information systems processes,
    116–19
information technology, changing role
    of, 64–65
infrastructure
  determining needs, 219–20
  processes, 120
installation kits, 30–31
intangible benefits, 360
Integrated Services Digital Network
    (ISDN), 218
internal web, 11–16
  direction and development of,
      327–28
  keeping them fresh, 351–53
  training, 112–13
  See also intranet
Internet
  cost to access, 292–93
  domain name, 225, 383–84
  origin of, 5
  personal use of, 333–35
  rules of, 18–19
  setting policies, 80, 332–35
  See also intranet
Internet Information Server (IIS), 229
Internet model
  building your intranet, 200–201
  creating enthusiasm, 205–6
  creating your audience, 201–2
  determining need, 181, 195

determining readiness, 195
how to proceed, 195–200
lessons learned, 207
making it pervasive, 206–7
promoting your intranet, 202–5
Internet Relay Chat (IRC). *See* chat
Internet service provider (ISP),
    222–25, 383
interpersonal and group communica-
    tion, 103–5
intranet
  advantages and benefits of, 28–42,
      359–60
  advantages over client/server,
      42–44
  advantages over proprietary group-
      ware, 44–46
  applications of, 8–9, 109–10,
      355–58
  collaboration, 60–64
  concerns about, 286–93
  cost of, 358–59
  definition of, 3–4, 186–87
  disadvantages of, 46–49
  future of, 20–21, 139, 373–76
  growth of, 7–8, 367
  history of, 4–6
  intangible benefits of, 39–42
  measuring results of, 359–61
  need for, 49–50
  promotion of, 202–5, 294–302
  publishing and development, 31–32
  reasons to create, 23–28, 177–180
  responsibility for, 331–32
  results of implementation, 55–64
  selling the, 209–16
  uses of, 8–9, 23–28, 109, 135–173
  See also Internet; security; internal
      web
intranet team, 368–9
  as relates to Internet team, 305
  bonding, 310–12
  composition of, 305–7
  creativity techniques, 313–15
  facilitator, 307–8
  four stages of, 312–13
  impact of, 339

meetings, 315–24
objectives, 324–38
planning and agendas, 309–15
role of, 205–6, 304
intranetiquette, 18–19
inventory, 126
ISDN (Integrated Services Digital Network), 218
ISP (Internet service provider), 222–25, 383

JavaScript, 230, 239
JCPenney Company, Inc.
building the intranet, 177–78
communications, 99–102, 120
company history, 85–86, 93
home page, 84–88, 93, 98, 266–70
Internet Team, 177–78, 196, 246
intranet uses, 62
merchandise purchasing, 124
The Penney Idea, 85–86
See also jWeb
jWeb
communication, 60
development of, 254–55, 304–39
home page, 84–88, 93, 98, 271–75
promotion of, 293
team home page, 326–27
See also JCPenney Company, Inc.

Knowledge On Line (KOL), 34, 128, 142–45
knowledge, sharing, 41, 52–54, 119, 284–86
knowledge systems, xiv, 53–54
KOL (Knowledge On Line), 34, 128, 142–45

LAN (local area network), 10–11, 353–54, 359
Learning Organizations, 51–52
legacy applications, 372
List, The, 222–23, 383
Listserv, 16
local area network (LAN), 10–11, 353–54, 359
Lotus Notes, 44–46, 164, 374–76

mail lists, 16
maintenance, 232
Majordomo, 16
manufacturing, 127
marketing processes, 128–30
Massachusetts Institute of Technology (MIT), 262, 271–73, 386
MAU (Media Attachment Unit), 10
Media Attachment Unit (MAU), 10
message encryption, 220–22, 383
Metcalfe's Law, 242
Meyer, Harry, 154, 156
Mills, Cathy, 304, 331–32
MIMEsweeper, 372
mind mapping, 314–15, 387
MIT (Massachusetts Institute of Technology), 262, 271–73, 386
Mosaic, 5–6, 14, 157
MSExchange, 375–76
multimedia, 38–39, 267

National Science Foundation (NSF), 5
netiquette, 18–19, 381
Netscape
browser enhancements, 14–15
Collabra purchase, 21, 374–75
cost of, 240
development of, 14
Navigator browser, 21
training, 338
use of, 32, 271
web address, 385
See also browsers
network, 10–11, 367
newsgroups, 16–18, 104, 383, 386
Nielsen, Jakob, 348–50, 387
norming, 313
Notes, 44–46, 164, 374–76
NSF (National Science Foundation), 5

operational processes
electronic data interchange, 124–26
inventory, 126
manufacturing, 127
professional services development, 128
purchasing, 122–24

order fulfillment processes, 131
organizational communication, 95–103

pass-it-on method, 337
people processes. *See* human resources processes
performing, 313
personal use of Internet, 333–35
Phifer, Gene, 28, 163, 166
phone directory, 254, 352
PointCast, 56, 98–99, 150, 351
policies, Internet, 80, 332–35
Ponder, Ron, 136–37, 139
Process Sourcerer, 90–91
processes, 95–133
product development processes, 357
    engineering, 121–22
    research and development, 120–21
productivity, concerns over, 48, 288
proxy server, 228
publishers, 335–37

research and development, 120–21
Rockwell International Corporation, 154–55
    future intranet use, 157
    intranet use by, 155
    lessons from intranet use, 156–57
    Rweb, 154–56, 359–60
    web address, 154
Rweb, 154–56, 359–60

sales processes, 130–31
Sano, Darrell, 348–50, 387
SAS Institute Inc.
    future intranet use, 161
    intranet uses, 117–18, 158–60
    lessons from intranet use, 160–61
    organization charts, 91–92
    personal home pages, 92–93
    publishing, 56
    results of intranet use, 160
    SAS Wide Web (SWW), 157–60
    web address, 157
search tools, 230–231

security
    determining needs, 220–21
    EDS use of, 153
    firewalls, 37, 47, 98, 219–22
    intranet, 37, 289–90
    restricting access, 37
    risks, 47
    VPNs, 219–20
    web resources, 221–22
Security and Exchange Commission (SEC) EDGAR Database, 264, 278, 387
selling the intranet, 209–16
Senge, Peter, 51–52
servers
    cost of, 32
    defined, 13
    installation of, 30
    manufacturers of, 229
    selecting, 227
    types of, 227–28
    web resource addresses, 229–30
service provider, Internet, 222–25, 383
serving remote users, 218–19
SGI. *See* Silicon Graphics Inc.
shared development, 25
shared knowledge. *See* knowledge, sharing
Shopping 2000, 265, 285–87, 387
Silicon Graphics, Inc., 161
    Electronic Requisition System, 58
    future intranet use, 163
    lessons from intranet use, 162
    results of intranet use, 162
    Silicon Junction, 5, 59, 161–62
    web address, 161
Silicon Junction, 5, 59, 161–62, 178
Simple Mail Transfer Protocol (SMTP) server, 228
sites, examples of
    business, 260–62
    education, 262
    government, 263–64
    JCPenney, 266–70
    shopping, 264–66
    starting, 83–84
    jWeb, 271–75

SMTP (Simple Mail Transfer Protocol)
    server, 228
software
    downloads, 254–55
    initial installation, 240–241
    upgrades, 241
Spafford, Eugene, 221
standards, 369–70
    design, 350
    web, 327–29
starting sites (starting points), 83–84
storming, 313
Stricklin, Jimi, 166–69
Sun Microsystems, 102–3, 116,
    128–29, 348–50
Sun Web. See Sun Microsystems
support processes, 72, 105–20
SWW (SAS Wide Web), 157–60

tangible benefits, 359
TCP/IP (Transmission Control Proto-
    col/Internet Protocol), 11, 137,
    182–83, 217, 367
Telnet, 20
TESN (Turner Employee Services Net-
    work), 106–09, 114, 167–69,
    294–97
Texas Instruments Incorporated (TI),
    163–64
    Acceptable Use Policy, 80–81
    background information, 79
    future of intranet use, 166
    Information Systems & Services,
        116–17
    internal web, 78–84
    Internet Resources, 81–82
    internet uses, 164
    lessons from intranet use, 165–66
    results of intranet use, 59, 164
    starting sites, 82–83
    web address, 163
Thomas, 263–64, 277, 387
TI. See Texas Instruments
tools, adding new, 354
traditional model
    determining need, 181
    determining readiness, 184–84

developing a proposal, 184–92
implementing the project, 193
measuring results 193–94
presenting the proposal, 193
training, 356–57
Transmission Control Protocol/Inter-
    net Protocol. See TCP/IP
Turner Employee Services Network.
    See TESN
Turner Broadcasting System, Inc.,
    106, 166–67
    future intranet use, 169
    intranet uses, 167
    lessons from intranet use, 168
    results of intranet use, 167
    TESN, 106–9, 114, 167–69, 294–97
    web address, 166
tutorials, 87–88

UGN (Unified Global Network),
    136–37
upgrades, 241
University of Oklahoma, 262, 274–75,
    387
UPS (United Parcel Service of Amer-
    ica, Inc.)
    future of intranet use, 170
    intranet uses, 169
    lessons from intranet use, 170
    results of intranet use, 170
    web address
U.S. Bureau of the Census, 263, 276,
    387
U.S. Congress, 263–64, 277, 387
user training and support, 241–42

Vaccaro, Edward, 141–42
vanity pages, 336, 355
videoconferencing, 104
virtual private network (VPN), 219–20
Virtual Reality Modeling Language
    (VRML), 239
viruses, 291, 372
vision workgroup, 319
VPN (virtual private network), 219–20
VRML (Virtual Reality Modeling Lan-
    guage), 239

Web fair, 294, 337–38
Web HTTP server, 227–28
webmasters, 230, 306
web standards, 327–329, 369–70
what's new section, 89–90, 351,
    353

Whole Foods, 268–69, 386
Wildfire, 145–46
workflow, 374
workgroup, 319
World Wide Web (WWW), 5, 353,
    385–87